The Airway to Everywhere

The Airway
to Everywhere

A History of All American Aviation,

1937–1953

W. David Lewis
William F. Trimble

UNIVERSITY   OF   PITTSBURGH   PRESS

To Pat and Sharon

Published by the University of Pittsburgh Press, Pittsburgh, PA 15260
Copyright © 1988, University of Pittsburgh Press
All rights reserved
Feffer and Simons, Inc., London
Manufactured in the United States of America

Library of Congress Cataloging in Publication Data

Lewis, W. David (Walter David), 1931–
    The Airway to everywhere: a history of All American Aviation,
1937–1953 / W. David Lewis, William F. Trimble.
        p.   cm.
    Bibliography: p. 217.
    Includes index.
    ISBN 0-8229-3579-1
    1. All American Aviation (Firm)—History.   2. Airlines—United
States—History.   I. Trimble, William F., 1947– .   II. Title.
HE9803.A944L48   1988
387.7′065′73—dc19   87–25176
                                                            CIP

Contents

Acknowledgments

Originating in two separate projects, this study ultimately became a cooperative effort. W. David Lewis, planning to write a history of All American Aviation, began research on the topic in the summer of 1980 at the Hagley Museum and Library in Wilmington, Delaware, utilizing the collection of All American Engineering Company materials deposited there by Charles W. Wendt, a longtime executive who ultimately became president of the firm. Meanwhile, in Pittsburgh, William F. Trimble had access to materials on Lytle S. Adams, the inventor who founded All American Aviation, and was investigating the possibility of incorporating this information into a study of the origins of USAir. Fortunately, the two of us became aware of each other's interests and intentions and decided on a collaborative study, the implementation of which was greatly facilitated in 1985 when Trimble joined the faculty of Auburn University, where Lewis had been teaching for many years.

The successful completion of the project would not have been possible without the help of many persons whose assistance it is our pleasure to acknowledge. Charles W. Wendt for years wanted to have a professionally written study of All American and the unique airmail pickup system that it pioneered, and he spent hours discussing the history of the company with Lewis. This book is, in many ways, a tribute to his dedication and perseverance. The staffs of the Hagley Museum and Library and the Historical Society of Western Pennsylvania have been of inestimable help as the book progressed; we wish to thank particularly Mildred Bosco, Margaret K. Fisher, Charles Foote, Carol Hallman, Walter J. Heacock, Jacqueline Hinsley, Betty-Bright Low, Marjorie McNinch, Daniel T. Muir, Glenn Porter, and Richmond D. Williams for aid generously rendered at Hagley in the course of Lewis's work, and Ruth Salisbury Reid and Helen Wilson for assistance at the Historical Society of Western Pennsylvania to Trimble's work. Particular thanks are also due to Raymond Teichman at the Franklin D. Roosevelt Library.

Fellow historians generously contributed of their time in reading all or part of the manuscript while it was at various stages of completion and gave us the benefit of their constructive criticism. We are especially grateful to Roger E. Bilstein of the University of Houston—Clear Lake, William M. Leary of the University of Georgia, and Merritt Roe Smith of the Massachusetts Institute of Technology. Two successive department heads, Wayne Flynt and Gordon C. Bond, gave us unfailing encouragement, support, and advice. Any and all errors of fact or interpretation are, of course, ours.

Without the help of the skilled secretaries who gave unstintingly of their typing, word-processing, and administrative abilities, as various drafts of the manuscript proceeded toward completion, this work would never have been brought to fruition. We would like to acknowledge with gratitude the help of Ellen Maker, Flora Moss, and Susan Starr in this regard.

Many other persons assisted us in a variety of ways. We are grateful to those who were once involved with the airmail pickup and All American Aviation and who allowed us to interview them. In addition to Charles W. Wendt, we wish to thank Mildred E. Albertson, Ray Garcia, Victor J. Gasbarro, Gerald Lindemuth, Frank Petee, Jennings Randolph, Lloyd C. Santmyer, Walter Sartory, and William M. Wiley, Jr., for taking the time to talk with us about the company and its history. Calvin E. Martin of USAir and Flora Baumer and Robert L. Mullin of the OX-5 Aviation Pioneers organization in Pittsburgh were also of great help. Willis B. Adams provided valuable information on his father, Lytle S. Adams. In our own department at Auburn University, Wesley Phillips Newton's expertise was instrumental in helping us locate source materials relating to All American's pilot staff. Eden Harriss, Archie DiFante, and Howard Smeltzer helped locate and identify photographs for the book, and Nancy E. Lewis prepared art work for the book and one of the articles that stemmed from it.

We acknowledge with gratitude the various staff members of the University of Pittsburgh Press who smoothed the passage of the book through the various stages of production. Frederick A. Hetzel, director of the Press, was especially supportive of this project and kindly lent permission to publish two articles drawn from the book in *Technology and Culture* and the *Western Pennsylvania Historical Magazine.*

Finally, we are deeply indebted to our wives, Pat and Sharon, who shared many of the burdens and stresses of our work with love, support, and understanding. The dedication of this book to them is only one measure of our appreciation of all they have done.

The Airway to Everywhere

Prologue: The Airway to Everywhere

A significant aspect of the growth of American commercial aviation following World War II was the proliferation of feeder and commuter airlines connecting relatively small cities with larger metropolises and trunk route airlines, thus bringing the benefits of high-speed air transportation to many travelers.[1] All American Aviation, which later became known as Allegheny Airlines and ultimately acquired its present name of USAir, played a pioneering role in this type of service and, because its incorporation dates back to 1937, is regarded as the nation's first feeder airline. The company played that role so well that it eventually transcended it and became a major trunk line in its own right, establishing itself in the process as one of the few American air carriers to make consistently dependable profits in an age when most of its competitors were experiencing serious financial adversities under the impact of the Airline Deregulation Act of 1978.

Owing its existence to a series of inventions that permitted specially equipped aircraft to pick up and discharge mail and express cargo without landing, All American began operations in the late 1930s by providing airmail service to a string of relatively small towns and cities, many of which lacked airports, in Delaware, Pennsylvania, West Virginia, and Ohio. Calling itself "The Airway to Everywhere," it captured the spirit of the New Deal era by conveying an image of aerial democracy, and it is not surprising that such persons as Eleanor Roosevelt figured importantly in its early efforts to earn its wings and fly. Its corporate image was defined by its unique function and its esprit de corps. Its small but sturdy Stinson Reliants, with their distinctive gull-winged configuration and maroon and white color scheme, navigated a network of routes crossing the rugged Allegheny Mountains in all sorts of weather, swooping down to pick up and to drop containers of mail and then climbing rapidly to prepare for another descent into a nearby valley to repeat the process. Perhaps more than any other American commercial airline flying at that time, All American typified the human daring and resourcefulness of the earliest years of aviation, characterized by Charles Lindbergh, Howard Hughes, Wiley Post, and Amelia Earhart.

All American's nonstop airmail pickup system was consistent, also, with patterns of technological change that emerged in America by the beginning of the twentieth century. A common model posits invention as an act of individual creative genius. Often there are heroic overtones, as the inventor battles against established norms to demonstrate the superiority of his or her creation. Following the initial act of invention comes a period of development, during which the new technology undergoes a transformation into a functional state. Finally there is innovation. In this phase, the invention finds its first commercial application, which may or may not redound to the personal financial benefit of the inventor and his or her backers. This model is useful in many respects, but it also distorts and oversimplifies the picture of technological change. Far from being linear, technological change is convoluted and interactive, with complex feedback occurring during all three phases as the invention metamorphoses from nebulous concept to concrete reality. Further, as Thomas P. Hughes has aptly demonstrated in his recent study of the evolution of electric power systems in Europe and the United States, political and economic factors weigh heavily in shaping the direction and scope of modern technologies.[2]

These dynamics are evident in the airmail pickup, which arose as the inspiration of Dr. Lytle S. Adams, a self-styled inventor in the classic nineteenth-century mold. He viewed invention as a means of turning technology to the public good and making it available to the greatest number of people at nominal cost. At the same time, he was aware of the need for development. He spent years bringing the pickup to a fairly workable form, which meant securing alliances with others who could supply the necessary capital and engineering expertise. It was at this point in 1938 that a young gliding enthusiast named Richard C. du Pont and his personal wealth came more to dictate the course of All American and the pickup. Thereafter, the technology functioned as an innovation within a climate generally conducive to its growth and expansion, and it continued to undergo development in response to changing political and economic conditions. Within a few short years, the principals, Adams and du Pont, were gone, but there remained a cadre of advocates philosophically committed to the technology even after it became apparent that it would have to be superseded by more conventional airmail and passenger service.

All American's founders saw no reason why the pickup and its unique brand of aerial pioneering could not spread all over the United States and, indeed, the rest of the world. Du Pont publicly lamented that most American communities were cut off from the air transport enjoyed by large metropolitan centers situated on major trunk lines, and he worked hard to cover the country with what would have been a vast wcb of pickup routes similar to the ones his firm had established in the mountains of Pennsylvania and West Virginia. Looking back at a century in which the American economy had been decisively shaped by the railroad, he envisioned a future in which multiengined aircraft would pull long trains of gliders through the sky like so many passenger cars, cutting them loose at intervals so that travelers who had been snatched aloft from small airfields around the countryside could drift downward to make connections with conventional trunk line carriers at cities blessed with large airports. He saw nothing unduly daunting for the average passenger in the prospect of taking off from a small airport in a plane that would make repeated low-altitude pickups and deliveries at a number of locations until it finally delivered him to a major metropolitan airport. From the vantage point of the 1980s, his visions seem almost ludicrously unrealistic, but many of his contemporaries, under the spell of what historian Joseph Corn has called "the winged gospel" when America's "romance with aviation" was yet alive, saw nothing unbelievable in them.[3] For a time, even the relatively staid and conservative Civil Aeronautics Board took them seriously, though it never agreed to their implementation.

During World War II, All American's unique expertise led to the development of glider pickup and dispatching techniques on the battlefield and to a method of snatching individual military personnel or espionage agents aloft from tiny jungle clearings or other places where aircraft were unable to land or take off. The company also lost its charismatic young leader, when Richard du Pont was killed in a military glider accident in 1943. On the home front, All American's pickup service thrived on the airmail flowing to sons and daughters in faraway theaters of war from the small towns and villages it served.

After the war, however, reality quickly intruded upon All American's futuristic dreams; and du Pont's vision, like the proverbial road not taken, faded, while a more prosaic, though ultimately profitable, scenario took place. Postal revenues dwindled steadily, partly because the improvement of highways and the development of mobile post offices operating on these roads made All American's services less necessary, and partly because federal authorities, for safety considerations, would not permit the firm to make overnight deliveries of mail. As it became obvious that passenger operations would be necessary to earn satisfactory profits, company officials persisted for some time in hoping that these could somehow be combined with the firm's pickup and delivery operations. This possibility, however, became increasingly unrealistic, and important managerial changes loomed as Charles W. Wendt, treasurer of the corporation and former financial advisor to Richard du Pont, went looking for a new permanent chief executive to succeed Hal Bazley, a veteran pickup enthusiast who had replaced the fallen leader as president.

Confronted by mounting indications that the CAB would not permit combined pickup and passenger operations and that federal authorities would not indefinitely sanction what amounted to a mail subsidy, Robert M. Love, the person upon whom Wendt's choice fell, concluded that he had no choice but to steer the company toward a more conventional future. Following a series of CAB decisions that closed the door on further expansion of the pickup service but opened the way for All American to take over a potentially lucrative network of feeder lines throughout the Middle Atlantic area, All American abandoned pickup operations in 1949 and, with a fleet of DC-3s replacing its older Stinsons and Beechcrafts, became a regular carrier of passengers, cargo, and mail. It was not an easy transition; company employees were proud of their identification with an operation unique in the history of American commercial aviation. Thanks in part, however, to the constructive role played by Bazley, who had the respect and affection of All American's rank and file and who remained as vice president for operations after Love took over, the firm successfully weathered this difficult period.

The significance of the transition went deeper than personnel problems, however; it demonstrated the limits of technology in the face of economic realities, even when a technology is cherished by a loyal work force that identifies with it and ardently desires to keep it in use. Lytle Adams was a prolific inventor whose brain teemed with novel ideas but who, despite dedicated and persistent effort, had never been able to develop his aerial pickup and delivery system to a point at which it would work repeatedly and dependably. Richard du Pont recognized clearly the necessity of such performance levels if All American were to become a profitable enterprise. Shortly after becoming involved in Adams's plans and taking over a controlling financial interest in their exploitation, he spearheaded a major effort at his ancestral estate in Granogue, Delaware, to redesign the system. The effort succeeded, but at the cost of alienating Adams, who ultimately accepted a cash settlement and severed connections with the firm. In time, All American's pickup and delivery techniques permitted a complicated and potentially dangerous service to be performed with almost foolproof consistency. But mere technological effectiveness was not enough to save the system when All American encountered a changed set of economic and social circumstances. Ultimately the company had to give up something that had made it unique among American airlines, no matter how well it accomplished its basic purpose.

Yet not all was lost. With the World War II experience in mind, company officials knew that a technique unacceptable for civilian purposes may serve military ones quite acceptably. In a recent study, historian Merritt Roe Smith and a team of coauthors have massively documented the impact of military needs upon civilian technological development.[4] In All American's case, however, the relation was reversed, for the company's engineering division, with its special expertise, continued to play a significant and profitable role in devising air and sea rescue equipment, catapults for assisting takeoffs from short runways, arrester gear, and other equipment for the armed forces. Ultimately, when the airline division changed its name to Allegheny, the engineering component became a separate corporation in its own right and continues to function successfully as part of a larger conglomerate. Both in it and in the larger enterprise that now bears the name of USAir, the spirit of the earlier venture once known as All American Aviation lives on, bearing testimony to the hardiness of both human and technological traditions. For a considerable number of reasons, therefore, the story of this pioneering enterprise is well worth telling.

1 • The Apostle of Pickup

All American Aviation grew out of the work of a stocky, gray-haired inventor named Lytle S. Adams. Born in Paint Lick, Garrard County, Kentucky, on January 31, 1883, Lytle Schuyler Adams claimed direct lineal descendance from the famous Massachusetts clan that spawned two presidents and numerous other prominent Americans. He attended public school in nearby Mount Vernon and went on to the University of Kentucky and St. Louis University, where he completed his doctoral degree in dental surgery in 1905. His practice took him first to Parsons, Kansas, and then to southern California, where he earned enough from real estate transactions and selling oil-bearing properties to buy a ranch outside San Diego. There his restless genius gave birth to such inventions as a rotary planting machine and a spiral plow. After obtaining a patent on the latter, he manufactured it in East St. Louis, Illinois, during World War I.[1]

Where and when Adams became interested in aviation is a matter of some speculation. It may have been during his years in Kansas, but Adams himself had stronger memories of California. Soon after he arrived on the West Coast in 1909 he became friends with Glenn L. Martin, the noted aircraft designer, and watched Martin build his first successful airplane, a large Curtiss-type, in Santa Ana.[2] Regardless of the source of Adams's involvement in aviation, by the 1920s, he, like many others, had had his appetite whetted by the airplane and its seemingly boundless potential.

Upon moving to Seattle in 1923 and temporarily resuming his dental practice,[3] Adams became preoccupied with an idea that he thought would enhance one of the airplane's major advantages over other forms of transportation—speed. He recognized, as did others, that an airplane's time on the ground loading or discharging fuel, freight, and passengers was essentially wasted, and that the airplane as a transportation system was most efficient when it was in continuous flight. If, he surmised, an airplane could refuel and exchange cargo without landing, its inherent superiority over other modes of travel would be considerably augmented. Moreover, the ability of the airplane to pick up and deliver cargo without landing would involve added benefits: numerous costly airports would not be needed, and air service could be extended to smaller, out-of-the-way communities that would otherwise be bypassed for economic and operational reasons.

The democratization of air travel—that is, making it more accessible to the people—had a particular appeal to Adams. He said in 1939 that he had "always dreamed of the time" when aviation could be made "a real success for the majority of our people."[4] To this extent, Adams's concepts of an air pickup device fit traditional American patterns of innovation. As noted by John Kouwenhoven, Hugo Meier, and other historians of American technology, Yankee inventors had established a long record of contriving ingenious devices to promote the convenience and material well-being of the masses.[5] Viewed in this light, Adams's ideas were characteristic of what Kouwenhoven called the "vernacular" tradition. In a more immediate sense, Adams understood that a widespread practical application of the air pickup, especially for mail and express, could attract both public and private financing. Transforming these ideas, however, into a system that was both efficient and profitable would occupy a decade and a half of Adams's life.

Adams was not the first exponent of air pickup. The concept had its precedents in the nineteenth century with the nonstop pickup and delivery of mailbags from speeding trains. Godfrey L. Cabot, a Boston scientist and engineer, took the idea and sought ways to apply it to aircraft. While serving in the navy during World War I, he invented a system consisting of two vertical walls converging in a V-shape, at the narrow end of which a weighted cable trailing from an airplane passing overhead would engage the object to be picked up. On October 2, 1918, Cabot successfully tested the device in Boston Harbor, picking up a 155-pound package. Three years later, Cabot used the invention to pick up a can of gasoline, thus demonstrating the feasibility of in-flight refueling. Patents for the invention, filed in November 1918 and February 1919, received approval in 1920 and 1924.[6]

Apparently independent of Cabot, Adams began work on his own air pickup device in Seattle in 1924. Protected under a series of patents applied for and received between 1928 and 1933, Adams's pickup system was strikingly similar to Cabot's. A seventy-five-foot-long wire cable with a steel ball attached to its lower end was drawn by an airplane into a special receiving apparatus on the ground. This consisted of a metal pan or trap, wide at one end and enclosed by vertical walls that gradually tapered upward and came together in a small slot at the narrow end. Flying at an extremely low altitude, the plane would drop the cable into the wide end of the trap and its forward motion would carry the steel ball upward and inward toward the slot. As this happened, the ball, acting as a grapple, slipped inside a thimblelike coupling at the apex of the slot, carrying it into the air along with whatever was attached to it, such as a package or mailbag. Almost simultaneously, a frangible connection at the end of the ball opposite the cable attachment would break upon impact, thereby depositing the incoming cargo at the narrow end of the trap.[7]

As his work progressed, it became evident to Adams that some sort of shock-absorbing mechanism was needed to overcome the kinetic forces resulting from the sudden engagement of the ball with the coupling on the ground. The impact could be, and was in fact, damaging to the structure of the aircraft. His first remedy was simply to connect the cable to the plane with an elastic cord; later, he supplemented this with a spring incorporated into an apparatus for reeling in the cable and cargo. When these methods were shown to be inadequate in cushioning the shock, Adams designed an adjustable, spring-actuated catapult to throw the package forward at a speed approximating that of the pickup aircraft.[8]

Relying on his own capital and working in whatever hours he could spare from his dental practice in Seattle, Adams built and tested hundreds of scale models before moving on to experiments with a larger mechanism. At this point in the development of the pickup, he obtained the timely support of William E. Boeing, the Seattle aircraft builder. Boeing's engineers helped design and construct a full-scale device that was mounted on a turntable so that it could be rotated into the wind. At Gorst Field, where Boeing had his factory, two pilots, Clayton

("Scotty") Scott and L. Van Rawlings, flew a series of pickups in August 1928. A Travel Air biplane repeatedly picked up and delivered a thirty-five-pound mailbag, achieving a 98 percent success rate, according to Adams's calculations. These experiments were encouraging enough for Adams to close out his practice, thereafter devoting all his time to perfecting the pickup system and casting about for the financial backing necessary to bring it to fruition.[9]

In September 1928, Adams journeyed to New York, where he expected to establish contacts within the business community and stimulate interest in his invention. The country was still in the flush of the Lindbergh boom, and capital was pouring into a wide range of aviation ventures. The first to see possibilities in the air pickup device was Gordon A. Smith. A fairly well-to-do author with experience in aviation from the naval reserve flying corps during the war, Smith moved easily among various New York elites and lent respectability to Adams and his work. The pair approached Charles L. Lawrance, president of the Wright Aeronautical Corporation, with a proposal to use the pickup for expanding mail service to rural communities. Less optimistic than Adams or Smith about the application of the pickup to airmail, Lawrance, nevertheless, thought Adams's device was "exceedingly interesting" and invited him to demonstrate it to Charles Lindbergh, then a trustee for the Daniel Guggenheim Fund for the Promotion of Aeronautics. He and Lindbergh had previously discussed long-duration flights involving aerial replenishment, and the Adams invention appeared immediately adaptable as a solution to that problem.[10]

Lindbergh and the Guggenheim connection allowed Adams to get an audience with the postmaster general, Harry S. New. Perhaps due to Lindbergh's influence, New was less intrigued about using the pickup for expanding mail service than he was about employing the device for endurance flying. New ordered his department to fit a Travel Air cabin monplane with Adams's pickup rig. Christened the "Postmaster" in Washington on December 18, the plane, piloted by Rawlings and three others, picked up food and fuel during test flights at Roosevelt Field on Long Island in late December 1928 and early January 1929. For unexplained reasons, the trio did not make a major endurance attempt.[11]

To arouse public and financial interest in his invention, Adams drove himself almost ceaselessly in 1929. Among his efforts was the promotion of the device at aviation shows. Adams and Smith exhibited an elaborate working model of the pickup system in the Grand Central Palace during the New York Aviation Show, February 6–13. Substantial crowds gathered around the display as a model plane "flew" down a wire over the trap to pick up a small mailbag. From New York, Adams went on to Buffalo for a show at the Regiment Armory in the last week of March.[12] Though time consuming and costly, these demonstrations were necessary to acquaint aviation people and the general public with Adams and his pickup device.

Concurrent with Adams's public relations work in early 1929 was the formation of two companies to develop and market his invention. The first of these, entirely owned by Adams, was the Airways Patent Holding Corporation, which took over all of Adams's patents and distributed licensing rights to the pickup system. For North America, these rights went to Adams Air

To promote his invention, Adams hit the aviation show circuit in early 1929. This model plane and pickup device were exhibited at the New York and Buffalo shows in February and March. (ACP)

Express, Inc., a New York firm set up in February whose purpose was to publicize and distribute the pickup system. The total capitalization of the company initially was 130 thousand shares of stock, divided into 30 thousand of class A and 100 thousand of class B. No par value was set for either class, but an offering was to be made of 23 thousand units of stock, each unit consisting of a share of class A and a share of class B, and priced at thirty-five dollars. For the licensing rights, Adams received 44 thousand units of the express company's paper, making him the largest single shareholder.[13]

Adams Air Express initially directed its publicity at chambers of commerce in small towns—particularly those in the Midwest—that might be interested in an express or airmail service. In its literature, the company emphasized the limited extent of the present commercial air transport network, urged the need to "do something better" to keep ahead of potential civic rivals, and pointed out how the Adams pickup and delivery system offered a relatively inexpensive means of connecting with nationwide air routes. On appointment, Adams would provide information on installation fees, rentals, maintenance, aircraft scheduling, and anticipated revenues of an air express service. After the establishment of such an operation, the company would help arrange a government airmail contract.[14] These proposals were, of course, pure salesmanship based on unrealistic expectations of community interest and Post Office Department action, but they did offer purpose and direction to the new company and clearly set out Adams's long-range personal objectives.

At the same time, Adams was alert to any opportunities to demonstrate practical uses for his pickup device. One of these was a method of shortening the time required to deliver transatlantic mail. In the early spring of 1929, Adams and Frank Mallen, an associate in the air express firm, studied the existing ocean mail connections and offered recommendations for their improvement. Mail from an incoming liner, they reasoned, often took more than twenty-four hours to reach Newark, which served as the eastern terminus for the transcontinental airmail system. If, however, the mail could be picked up while the inbound liner was still at sea and flown to Newark, at least a day would be saved. An even greater economy of time would be made possible by the aerial delivery of mail to outbound steamers, since they usually left port only two days a week and mail often accumulated up to five days awaiting the next departure. This idea caught the attention of Paul W. Chapman, president of the United States Lines and an aviation enthusiast. At the end of March, while Adams was in Buffalo publicizing his invention, Chapman agreed to install the pickup system on the liner *Leviathan* and determined to equip a big Burnelli monoplane he had recently bought for the initial at-sea tests with the pickup device. The Post Office Department sanctioned the demonstration as part of its encouragement of experimental airmail applications.[15]

When the *Leviathan* pulled away from the pier at New York on May 25 bound for Southampton, her silhouette was considerably altered. Straddling her aft deckhouse was a forty-foot-high steel framework, atop which was a turntable mounting for the pickup trap. The plan was for Chapman's Burnelli to meet the ship six hundred miles out from New York on her return from England. Adams, on board the *Leviathan* to supervise the installation of the device and oversee the pickup experiment, had high hopes for its success. As he wrote to Thomas A. Morgan of the Sperry Gyroscope Company and an Adams Air Express director, "I am very anxious that this first pick up should be a successful one. While I do not feel that it would mean our defeat I do feel that to make the pick up at the first trial would be a tremendous send off for our company." Adams must have experienced a keen sense of disappointment when he learned that the Burnelli had been severely damaged in a ground accident at Keyport, New Jersey, on June 6. The next day, a Loening Air Yacht, hurriedly fitted with the pickup rig, took off to rendezvous with the *Leviathan* off Nantucket. To Adams's further dismay, stormy weather and a defective radio prevented the Loening from finding the liner, and no pickup took place.[16]

It was an inauspicious combination of circumstances that caused the at-sea pickup experiment to fail, but as the *Leviathan* made ready for the next eastbound crossing, Adams was prepared to try again. Aboard the ship when she sailed at 3:30 P.M., June 12, was the second assistant postmaster general, W. Irving Glover, who wanted to see firsthand the Adams system in operation. Three hours later, with the *Leviathan* sixty miles at sea, Rawlings and George R. Pond, in a Fairchild cabin plane, deposited a mailbag in the trap, only to have the pickup mechanism malfunction. Rawlings and Pond made twelve more passes at the trap while nearly two thousand passengers cheered them on. Finally, on the thirteenth attempt, the fliers' luck changed and they were able to guide the cable and steel ball through the trap, soaring away to Newark with their first ship-to-shore mail.[17]

This accomplishment was both encouraging and discouraging to those who advocated the widespread adoption of the Adams air pickup. Though it had worked, it was also obvious that there were serious obstacles to a fully operational ship-to-shore mail transfer system, not the least of which were locating vessels in bad weather, poor visibility, and carrying out pickups from heaving decks. Adams did manage to drop four sacks of mail to the *Leviathan* about fifty miles out from Boston on July 23, but the pickup tests were not repeated. Nevertheless, Glover reportedly was favorably impressed by the *Leviathan* demonstration, and postal officials looked at it as general confirmation of the feasibility of the pickup as a means of extending airmail routes.[18]

Among those in attendance at the New York Aviation Show in February had been Clifford Ball, operator of C.A.M. (Contract Air Mail) Route 11 between Pittsburgh and Cleveland via Youngstown, Ohio. Ball started in aviation in 1925 as the co-owner of a fixed-base operation just south of Pittsburgh. In March 1926, under the provisions of the 1925 Kelly Air Mail Act, he won the Pittsburgh–Cleveland contract, which, after operations began a year later, turned out to be one of the few profitable early routes. In the Adams system, Ball saw a method of augmenting the volume of mail on his route without having to add time-consuming stops, which, considering the short distance between the two cities, would have seriously cut into his line's already slim advantage over surface mail. A meeting with Adams led to an understanding whereby Ball would provide partial funding and seek Post Office approval to try out the pickup on C.A.M. Route 11.[19]

Planning and preparation for the air pickup on the Pittsburgh–Cleveland route consumed most of the spring and summer of 1929. Ball and Adams met with E. B. Wadsworth, superintendent of the airmail service, in Washington toward the end of April and came away with his pledge to support the installation of the pickup system at Youngstown, and perhaps also at Beaver Falls and New Castle, Pennsylvania. Following negotiations with the appropriate officials in Youngstown, it was agreed to erect the turntable and pickup trap at that city's Lansdowne Field. Some delays resulted while the *Leviathan* device was disassembled and shipped to Youngstown, where it did not arrive until early August. By the end of the month, though, the system was in place, and two of Ball's Fairchild FC-2s were equipped for the pickup experiments.[20]

With the completion of preliminary trials, regular pickups began at Youngstown on August 30 and lasted for about a month. On the first day, a sizable group, including the mayor, Post Office representatives, and airline officials, watched as pilot Trowbridge Sebree missed the trap on his first attempt but made a perfect exchange on his second. In contrast, Harry Sievers, flying the second Fairchild, could not manage a pickup and was forced to land to take on the mail. Adams, undaunted by the mixed results that day, was reportedly "all smiles," and promised that things would go smoother after "ironing out the kinks." Yet potentially serious problems arose during the Youngstown demonstrations that were never fully resolved. On one flight, for example, the pilot attempted a pickup after the incoming mail sack had accidentally broken from the cable; the steel ball glanced off the trap with such force that it bounced up and over the plane, struck the propeller, and caused some worrisome moments in the cockpit before an emergency landing could be effected. A similar incident nearly ended in tragedy when the rebounding cable jammed in the pickup plane's elevators, forcing the aircraft to nose over into a sudden dive. Only the quick reactions of the pilot freed the controls and prevented a crash. Cable breakage, usually caused when the ball caught under the overhanging lip of the trap and did not move smoothly forward to engage the thimble at the end of the slot, was another common fault of the system. Nor had the shock problems been completely eliminated. At the end of the tests, Ball found the airframe of one of the Fairchilds so weakened by the severe loads that the plane had to be rebuilt. As the tests drew to a close, Adams agreed to reengineer the cable attachment to mitigate the rebound problems and to work out a better design for the trap.[21]

Back in New York, Adams improved the ground apparatus by lengthening it and providing a lip to smooth the passage of the ball and cable through the mechanism. Another series of experiments took place with the pickup system at Hoover Field in Washington, which only two weeks before the Youngstown demonstrations had become the southern terminus for Clifford Ball's line. Some of the difficulties at Youngstown, Adams insisted, had been due to the relatively high speed of the Fairchilds, and he talked Ball into using a slower New Standard biplane. The first pickups were made on March 4, 1930, with Trow Sebree doing most of the flying. Among the dignitaries present were Glover; Clarence M. Young, assistant secretary of commerce for aeronautics; and Senator Royal S. Copeland of New York, an advocate of bringing the airmail to small towns. The Hoover Field tests were a qualified success. Adams's modifications to the trap virtually eliminated cable breakage, while a close-tolerance sleeve around the elastic shock cord dampened the dangerous rebound phenomenon. Over a seven-day period, the pickup rate was a creditable 75 percent.[22]

The next step was an extended trial of the pickup system on the Pittsburgh–Cleveland route. Glover wrote to Adams on April 1 expressing general satisfaction with the Hoover Field results and suggesting a few minor alterations to the ground equipment. He went on to authorize a six-month service test on Ball's line but stressed that his department did not intend to underwrite any costs. These would have to be paid for by Adams or Ball or be derived from the communities chosen as pickup points on application to the Post Office Department. Ball went to work immediately. Through Congressman Jesse H. Swick of Beaver Falls, he persuaded chambers of commerce in that city and New Castle to submit applications. Niles and Warren, Ohio, thought to be other likely candidates for the pickup, declined to participate.[23]

Adams and Ball worked feverishly through the early summer of 1930 to get ready for the service demonstration, scheduled to begin in early August. Adams spent most of his time supervising the erection of pickup traps at the Beaver Falls municipal airport and at Bradford Field in New Castle. In the interval, Ball in-

Adams with postal officials standing in the ground apparatus at Hoover Field in March 1930. A series of experiments there significantly improved the reliability of the pickup system. (ACP)

stalled reels and cables on two Fairchild FC-2s and chose two of his most experienced pilots, Sebree and Lowell B. Scroggins, to fly the pickup routes. Pilots George Smith and Dixon Markey were Ball's choices to handle the mail sacks and to operate the onboard equipment. Ground arrangements also had to be made with the Post Office, not only for the transferral and sorting of mail but also for individuals to load the traps and turn them into the wind for the approaching planes—a critical procedure. On the afternoon of August 4, a crowd in the hundreds watched Sebree, flying in from Cleveland, battle hot, gusty winds to make the first pickup at Beaver Falls. Scroggins, who had dropped a mailbag at New Castle on his flight to Pittsburgh, made pickups at Beaver Falls and New Castle on his return to Cleveland later that day.[24]

Despite the success of the inaugural pickups, Ball requested the Post Office Department to relieve him of the service after less than two months of operations. Accordingly, on September 24, Washington officials announced the end of the pickup trials. Ball's reasons for abandoning the system appeared in a detailed report to the department on October 6. Standing out among nagging equipment problems and a clash of personalities between Ball and Adams was the simple fact that the pickup did not generate enough mail volume to justify its considerable expense. Ball had been assured that Beaver Falls and New Castle each would supply at least five pounds of mail daily, when in fact their average was less than ten letters apiece. Ground installations cost thirty-five hundred dollars each, supposedly to have been paid for by the two communities. Unfortunately, aviation committees of the chambers of commerce in Beaver Falls and New Castle raised a total of only nine hundred dollars, forcing Ball to make up the difference from his own funds. Adams, although reputedly on a twenty-five-hundred-dollar monthly retainer from the express company, according to Ball either could not or would not help share the costs. By late September, Ball himself was desperately trying to stave off a takeover of his airline by wealthy Pittsburgh interests and had neither the time nor the inclination to pursue Adams's invention further. The sale of Ball's company, since named Pennsylvania Air Lines, to Pittsburgh Aviation Industries Corporation on October 24 effectively terminated the Adams-Ball association.[25]

Adams and Clifford Ball, operator of C.A.M. Route 11 between Pittsburgh and Cleveland, agreed to try out the pickup on Ball's airmail line in 1929. The Post Office Department authorized a demonstration of the system, and flights began on August 4, 1930, with pickup points at New Castle and Beaver Falls. This photo shows Clifford Ball and the pickup device in one of his Fairchild FC-2 cabin monoplanes. (Willis B. Adams)

The acquisition of Pennsylvania Air Lines by Pittsburgh Aviation Industries Corporation was part of a major realignment of the country's air transport network in 1930 that seriously undermined Adams's credibility and whatever support his pickup system had enjoyed among commercial operators and postal officials in Washington. Walter Folger Brown, the postmaster general, had as one of his policy objectives streamlining the nationwide air map by eliminating small, undercapitalized independents like Clifford Ball, whose short airmail route was incompatible with Brown's grand reorganization scheme. To accomplish his ends, Brown freely exploited the McNary-Watres Act, a 1930 amendment to the Kelly Air Mail Act, that gave him wide latitude in selecting new airmail contractors and extending the routes of older ones. Brown gave special attention to airline owners with sufficient resources to operate multimotored equipment and who had demonstrated an interest in flying passengers as well as mail. If Ball was excluded from the postmaster general's plans, it followed that Adams would be, too. His idea of bringing the airmail to small towns and remote communities ran directly contrary to Brown's philosophy of encouraging the development of passenger service between major metropolitan centers. At one point, an anonymous staff assistant for the Post Office Department, when queried about the cancellation of the Beaver Falls and New Castle service trials, commented, "We're absolutely done with pick-ups. They've been a failure."[26] Under such circumstances, it is not surprising that the Adams air pickup went into temporary eclipse.

Adams, however, was undeterred by these adverse developments and clung tenaciously to his dream of expanding air service into the nation's hinterland. December 1931 found him screening a film of the pickup system before the aviation committee of the Chicago Association of Commerce. The committee subsequently agreed to conduct a survey, at Adams's expense, of businesses and chambers of commerce in the Chicago area that might have an interest in the pickup device. The response was highly favorable. Most encouraging was a request by the Milwaukee Association of Commerce to meet with Adams in April and May 1932 to discuss practical applications for the pickup, including a test of the equipment at a forthcoming air show and the establishment of a possible demonstration line between Milwaukee and Detroit. The Chicago association's endorsement of the pickup as "the ultimate solution of air transport development" for smaller communities was another hopeful sign.[27]

Although gratifying, none of this rhetoric translated into pecuniary assistance, and in the meantime Adams's financial position deteriorated. His constant travels (in June 1932 he toured southern Illinois, Missouri, and Arkansas), the costs incident to hotel accommodations, and fees incurred by the various chamber of commerce surveys depleted the slender resources of Adams Air Express. One of his attorneys notified him in May that the company had lost its New York charter for failure to pay franchise taxes since 1929 and that immediate reimbursement in cash was necessary to enable the firm to continue in business.[28] Throughout the bleakest two years of the depression, Adams found himself alone, without allies, and unable to raise the capital needed for even a small-scale demonstration of his pickup system.

Not until 1934 did Adams find his way out of this dilemma. In that year, largely as a result of a sensational congressional investigation by Senator Hugo Black of alleged collusion in the letting of airmail contracts under Walter F. Brown, the administration of Franklin D. Roosevelt called for reform. Revised legislation in June allowed both newcomers and the more established independents to bid successfully on airmail routes. Adams was delighted, telling Thomas E. Braniff, president of Oklahoma City's Braniff Airways, that "I have fought the battles of the independent operators since the McNary-Watres bill was proposed. I would be very favorable to forming a strong alliance with them." Though he cemented no alliances, Adams did interest two companies—Braniff, low bidder on the Chicago to Dallas route, and Pittsburgh's Central Air Lines, the new holder of the Cleveland–Pittsburgh–Washington contract—in another test of the air pickup. Braniff ordered staff assistance and helped secure official sanction from the Post Office Department, while Central agreed to loan Trow Sebree, Adams's most experienced pickup pilot. The demonstrations were scheduled for the Century of Progress International Exposition in Chicago.[29]

Sebree, flying a Stinson, made the first pickup on September

19; starting the next day, Adams provided thrice-daily mail service between the fair and Chicago's municipal airport. The trap, erected on a float in one of the lagoons, was advantageously located where most visitors could get an unobstructed view of the pickup flights. While there were no untoward incidents during the demonstration, Tom Braniff became alarmed by the apparent dangers of flying low over a congested area with constantly variable winds. On October 1, he wrote Adams that he had "come to the conclusion that there is an unusual risk incident to this operation and we would like to be relieved from it." Only Adams's considerable persuasive powers and a trip to Chicago by Braniff for a firsthand look at the pickup trials prevented their premature termination. By the end of the fair on October 31, Braniff was something of a convert, expressing to Adams "congratulations upon success attained and best wishes."[30]

To Adams's dismay, the Chicago trials did not lead to any commitments by either Braniff or the Post Office Department for more prolonged tests of the air pickup. Braniff was understandably reluctant to invest in the device until Adams could give some indication that the government favored full-scale operations. Briefly, the Chicago Association of Commerce urged the adoption of a shuttle service between downtown and the airport using a pickup apparatus on the Post Office roof, but Harlee Branch, the second assistant postmaster general, put an end to the proposal in early December with a direct statement that "the Department . . . at present has not found it advisable to inaugurate any such service." Adams pleaded with Braniff that the only obstacle to putting the pickup into operation was more capital, but Braniff was adamant in his opposition to any further involvement in the venture by his company.[31]

These latest obstacles to Adams's aspirations helped to precipitate a reevaluation of the entire pickup system in 1935. The complex ground mechanism had never been entirely satisfactory, as the earlier service tests with Clifford Ball had shown. Moreover, each installation was expensive—often ranging from thirty-five hundred dollars to as much as six thousand dollars, by Adams's own estimates. Support for Adams's work at this critical juncture came from Richard Archbold, a well-to-do naturalist and aviation enthusiast who in 1933–1934 had led an expedition to New Guinea. At Thomasville, Georgia, where Archbold's family owned an old plantation, Adams devoted his attention in the spring of 1935 to modifying the pickup apparatus. He wanted to simplify the trap so that it could be transported into remote areas and used by Archbold for aerial resupply and for carrying out specimens for further study. At first, Adams's modifications took the form of a trench with a wooden V at one end, working on the same principles as his earlier ground apparatus. Adams soon found that this was still unsatisfactory, and he began experimenting with a less complicated device that produced much better results. It consisted of two upright poles between which was suspended a loop of manila rope connected to the object to be picked up. Replacing the steel ball at the end of the cable trailing from the plane was a grapple to engage the suspended portion of the loop. Initially, Adams retained the catapult from his earlier mechanism as a means of reducing the sudden loads imposed by the pickup, but tests revealed that the loop itself acted as a shock absorber, and Adams was able to do away with the catapult altogether. In addition to the virtues of simplicity and lower cost, the new device permitted the plane to carry out pickups at significantly higher speeds.[32]

The new pickup device, for which Adams received a patent in 1937, was not without antecedents. In 1927, American marines in Nicaragua had made pickups using two fourteen-foot poles placed seventy-five feet apart with a rope loop loosely strung between them. Attached to the loop was a leather pouch for messages. A marine DH-4 trailing a fifty-foot weighted line then flew between the poles and snared the rope, hauling it and the message pouch aloft. Godfrey Cabot had developed a roughly similar system that A. W. Card and H. G. Bushmeyer tested in 1929 and 1930. Cabot combined a line strung between two short vertical poles with a catapult. As a hook beneath the plane contacted the tautly stretched line, it simultaneously picked up the object and triggered the catapult release. The system was compact, mobile, and relatively inexpensive to install and operate, but Cabot had no luck in getting Post Office approval for anything more than brief experiments.[33] Although the similarity of Adams's pickup mechanism to earlier ones is remarkable, there is nothing in the record to indicate that Adams intentionally copied anyone else's ideas. It seems that Cabot did little, if anything, in the mid-1930s to improve his pickup device, while Adams moved swiftly to perfect his own. In the end, the Adams system proved to be demonstrably more efficient than previous devices, even if there were undeniable parallels.

Upon completion of the Thomasville experiments, Adams returned to the north and took up residence in Irwin, Pennsylvania, east of Pittsburgh. He had, apparently, bought property in Irwin around the time of his association with Clifford Ball, but because of his frequent travels had spent little time there. By 1935, Adams had a small hangar and field at Irwin, and he evidently considered the location convenient for a new round of inquiries regarding backing for the pickup. The first positive response came from Wheeling, West Virginia, where William P. Wilson, president of the Ohio Valley Industrial Corporation and former chairman of the board of Fokker Aircraft, had been following Adams's work for a number of years. Through Wilson, Adams gained a key advocate in Jennings Randolph, a New Deal congressman from West Virginia's Second District, whose parochial interests had been aroused by the relative lack of attention scheduled airlines had given to his state. A meeting ensued in Washington during which Adams impressed Randolph as "a man of creativity." After a demonstration of the pickup device at Morgantown later that year, Randolph's interest was doubly aroused: "suddenly," he said, "the implications of the thing caught my imagination."[34] Over the years, he became the most persistent and vocal friend of the pickup on Capitol Hill.

This kind of congressional support proved crucial in the long run, but it did little to help Adams alleviate his pressing financial needs in late 1935. On December 31, desperately hoping to "gain the ear of the President himself," Adams made a direct overture to Eleanor Roosevelt. Appealing to the First Lady's democratic instincts, he argued that the pickup "provides an economical means by which *every* community, regardless of size, can enjoy luxuries and conveniences now only available to the dwelers [sic] of large centers of population." Eleanor Roosevelt passed Adams's correspondence on to her brother, G. Hall Roosevelt, who had unsuccessfully promoted a scheme to pick up and deliver mail at center-city post offices by airship. He counseled her that Adams's ideas were unlikely to impress

postal or airline officials. Adams learned a few days later that
Eleanor Roosevelt had been interested in his idea but considered it impractical to initiate under the present air transport
system.[35]

The Roosevelts' negative response forced Adams to look
elsewhere for financial backing. He found what he needed with
Arthur P. Davis, president of the Arma Engineering Corporation
of Brooklyn, New York. Davis believed the pickup had practical
applications and through a substantial loan helped Adams fund a
new company, All American Aviation, Inc., chartered as a Delaware corporation on March 5, 1937. All American's purposes
were broadly defined; among other things, it was to "operate
and conduct aerial passenger, freight, express, and mail lines
. . . and to engage generally in the business of commercial aviation and the operation of aircraft for pleasure, industrial and
other purposes." For the time being, though, Adams and Davis
decided that its main function would be to hold patents and
issue licenses for the pickup system. In return for his support,
Davis received a one-half share in the patent Adams obtained for
the pickup apparatus.[36]

Simultaneously, Adams and Davis established a separate
company, Tri-State Aviation Corporation, to act as the operating arm of their enterprise. Located at the Irwin field, Tri-State
was to take over where Adams Air Express had left off in carrying
out pickup experiments and developing an airmail and express
network. At the invitation of Congressman Randolph, Adams
and Davis transferred flying operations in 1937 to a new municipal airport at Morgantown, West Virginia, where pilot Norman
Rintoul and mechanic Victor Yesulaites helped with additional
testing of the pickup system. One of the first customers to make
use of Tri-State's express service when flying operations started
on September 9 was Kaufmann's Department Store in
Pittsburgh. The attendant publicity led other stores and mail
order houses, such as Montgomery Ward and Company, to take
advantage of air shipments. By 1938, Tri-State had three Bellan-
cas and one Stinson flying routes out of Morgantown to
Pittsburgh, Charleston, West Virginia, and Baltimore, with a
chain of stops and pickup points in between.[37]

Tri-State's business expanded unevenly in 1938. Flying on a
daily basis when weather permitted, the company's planes

hauled up to eighty-four thousand pounds of express per month and sometimes as many as fifteen hundred packages in a single day. A major proportion of this volume passed through twenty-one pickup points in western Pennsylvania and West Virginia. All cargo flew on a strictly contract basis, with no attempt made to provide regular scheduling. This allowed the firm to operate its planes at maximum capacity and offer prices competitive with ground transportation rates. Tri-State also carried passengers, apparently between selected airports, but usually there were no more than eighty per month. While Adams insisted that such an air express service could be run profitably without a government subsidy, it seems certain the company lost money. A detailed 1939 study based on Tri-State's experience included a strong argument in favor of short-haul airmail and anticipated nearly a third of revenues being derived from airmail payments by the federal government.[38]

Airmail, obviously, was crucial to the company's long-term survival, and Adams knew it. One of the many demonstrations of the pickup flown in 1937–1938 took place on June 3, 1937, at College Park, Maryland. Norman J. ("Hap") O'Bryan, a Tri-State pilot from Greensburg, Pennsylvania, showed twelve members of the House Post Office and Post Roads Committee how effective the pickup was. He flew in low over the ground apparatus, deposited a container filled with six quarts of Scotch whiskey, and grabbed a sack of mail before zooming away. Whether the Scotch greased the legislative wheels is uncertain, but less than a week later, on June 9, Congressman Harry L. Haines, a Democrat from Pennsylvania, introduced H.R. 7448 to authorize the postmaster general to entertain proposals for center-city autogiro mail service and for experimental airmail service to rural areas. The House passed the bill on August 2 and sent it to the Senate, but the session ended before the upper body could bring it to a vote. Not until March 31, 1938, did the Senate pass an amended version of the bill, which then had to be reconsidered by the House. Finally, the House acted on April 6, sending the measure to the White House for President Franklin D. Roosevelt's signature on April 15.[39]

The Experimental Air Mail Act of 1938 called upon the Post Office Department to advertise for bids for autogiro service and for what the legislators assumed would be some form of airmail pickup and delivery in rural areas. While the law set rates for such services, it did not authorize any expenditures by the Post Office. For some weeks, postal officials refused to do anything, despite the pleas of such individuals as Jennings Randolph. At one point, when Randolph tried to get an audience with Harlee Branch, the assistant postmaster general, he overheard Branch saying to his secretary, "Oh yes, I know. That's Randolph out there again with that damned airmail pickup service." Nevertheless, Randolph pushed through an amendment to the act on June 8 that gave discretionary power to the Post Office to use up to $100 thousand of its current airmail appropriation for the experimental service. The way was now clear for the postmaster general to solicit bids for the airmail pickup.[40]

Tri-State was flying, and it now had definite prospects for receiving an experimental airmail contract. But, in spite of the infusion of capital from Arthur Davis, the company was far from a viable enterprise. Adams, therefore, continued to pursue every opportunity he could to generate additional money. Even though he had failed to engage their support two years before, Adams tried once again to interest the Roosevelts in the pickup system. He explained to Eleanor Roosevelt in early 1938 that Tri-State could play a key developmental role in depressed rural areas like West Virginia by giving isolated mountain folk access to finished goods and a means of getting agricultural products to eastern markets. Adams struck just the right chord with Mrs. Roosevelt, for she had taken an active role in promoting the welfare of the people of the Mountain State and had collaborated with Congressman Randolph on self-help and homesteading projects in his district. In March, Adams wrote a long letter to the president expressing the same themes he had brought to the attention of Mrs. Roosevelt. He said that aviation had "barely touched" the lives of the "majority of the people" and illustrated how his company had aided West Virginia "to develop itself" by furnishing air service to more than a hundred towns. Roosevelt read Adams's letter and at least looked at a detailed memorandum Aams had enclosed on short-haul airlines and pending civil aeronautics legislation.[41] Although Adams might not have known it at the time, he had achieved a breakthrough for his company and the pickup.

Adams's opportunity came in June. Eleanor Roosevelt had

agreed to host a luncheon for a group representing the National Editorial Association at a homestead in Arthurdale, West Virginia, just south of Morgantown, but she was reluctant to be away from Hyde Park for any extended period. Consequently, Adams offered to fly her to Morgantown and back in one of Tri-State's ships. She accepted. On June 25, Adams and Norm Rintoul flew to Hyde Park, where they spent the evening with Mrs. Roosevelt, her family, and friends. The next morning, Adams breakfasted with Mrs. Roosevelt and Earl R. Miller, a New York state trooper whose original assignment to guard the president's wife had evolved into an intimate friendship. Adams elaborated on the details of his aerial pickup system during the meal and on the flight to Morgantown and Arthurdale. Miller was enthusiastic about Adams and his work and promised him that he would query other members of the Roosevelt family about financial assistance.[42]

Adams really had little reason for optimism that the Hyde Park connection would lead to much; after all, years of experiments, surveys, trials, demonstrations, and even successful operations had not yielded either sustained government support or the private capital needed to place the pickup on a secure footing. Yet present that weekend at Hyde Park was Franklin D. Roosevelt, Jr., and his bride of barely a year, the former Ethel du Pont, of Greenville, a wealthy residential suburb just north of Wilmington, Delaware. She had a cousin, Richard C. du Pont, who was an experienced glider pilot and who might be willing to invest in the Adams air pickup.[43] It turned out that du Pont was indeed interested. His involvement with Adams would determine the future development of the inventor's pickup system and, for the first time, place it on a sound financial footing.

2 • Takeoff in Delaware

Although it appears obvious that the involvement of Lytle S. Adams and his struggling aerial pickup project with Richard Chichester du Pont can be traced to Adams's fortuitous meeting with Ethel du Pont at Hyde Park in June 1938, it is not clear precisely when the two men first met. However obscure the exact time and place, it was a fateful encounter. For Adams, perennially full of ideas and enthusiasm but chronically short of funds, it secured the financial backing he had so desperately sought for fifteen years as he nurtured his pickup scheme through a succession of meager accomplishments and incessant frustrations. Du Pont's support, however, came at a high price, for Adams lost effective control of his brainchild and within a few short years would no longer have any formal connection with it. For du Pont, who had already won an impressive list of achievements as an aviation pioneer, the meeting launched an extremely creative phase of a brilliant career that would end in a tragic air accident over California in September 1943.

It was for All American Aviation itself, however, that the encounter was especially crucial, for the firm would not only outlive the two men but ultimately spawn two highly significant enterprises. One of these, All American Engineering Company, would make important technological contributions to aerial pickup and launching systems; to the development of energy-absorbing methods involving arrester gear, braking, barriers, and netting; and to air rescue techniques, all with a wide variety of civilian and military applications. The other enterprise for which the way was being prepared was destined to become a much better known corporation, now one of America's most profitable commercial air carriers. Going through a succession of name changes, it would be known as, in turn, All American Airways, Allegheny Airlines, and USAir.

In the tall, clean-cut personage of Richard du Pont, Adams had met a man with both the financial resources and the leadership skills needed to transform what was still largely a vision into a functioning business enterprise. Du Pont was born at Wilmington, Delaware, on January 2, 1911, into a family whose wealth derived from a technologically oriented enterprise. It is not surprising, therefore, that he became a model airplane enthusiast at an early age and was later taught how to fly a powered aircraft by his older brother, Alexis Felix du Pont, Jr., a licensed pilot who flew for a time with the Ludington Line between New York and Washington. Although Richard ultimately secured a pilot's license for motored planes in 1930, his chief passion was not for powered flight but for gliding, in which he was to achieve international fame. At the age of seventeen, while vacationing on Cape Cod, he acquired a homemade glider and learned how to fly it. After entering the University of Virginia, he organized a club devoted to this sport. Captivated by gliding, he left Charlottesville at Christmastime in 1932 without graduating and shortly thereafter went to California to study aeronautical engineering at the Curtiss-Wright Technical Institute in Glendale. Here he met Hawley Bowlus, an instructor in mechanics and expert in glider technology under whose tutelage he became adept at designing, building, and operating these fragile and graceful craft. Of special significance to his later accomplishments was his growing mastery of the art of thermal soaring, in which maximum advantage is taken of upward air currents in order to maintain altitude. Returning east in 1933, he began taking part in the annual National Gliding and Soaring Meets in Elmira, New York, and quickly became one of the most outstanding glider pilots in the world. Over the next several years he set American and international records for both distance and altitude and won five consecutive national soaring championships. Through his involvement in the sport he met Helena Allaire Crozier, a fellow gliding enthusiast, and married her in 1934.[1]

Seeking ways of expanding his involvement in aeronautics, du Point joined Bowlus in establishing a glider manufacturing company in California. Although this was short lived, it no doubt whetted his appetite for further business ventures in aviation. Thus he was primed to respond enthusiastically to the challenge presented to him when he met Lytle S. Adams in the summer of 1938. It is easy to see how the idea of aircraft swooping down from the sky to snatch mailbags out of midair and darting swiftly away without landing aroused his interest and led quickly to his involvement in what promised to be an exciting new enterprise.

Before committing himself, however, du Pont went to Morgantown with a group of advisors to witness the pickup system in operation. What he saw was hardly reassuring. Charles W. Wendt, then a young accountant and investment analyst who served as du Pont's chief financial advisor, made the trip and later recalled that three pickups were attempted. Of these, only one was successful, and even it did not go smoothly. Some of du Pont's friends and relatives were highly skeptical about the whole idea and counseled him against proceeding any further, arguing that Adams's patents "weren't worth much." According to Wendt, however, du Pont returned from Morgantown with his faith in Adams's technical abilities shaken but still convinced that whatever problems plagued the system could be worked out.[2]

The first step in the joining of forces between Adams and du Pont was to rescue Adams from the financial exigencies resulting from his previous efforts in pursuing his pickup project. On August 16, 1938, du Pont advanced Adams forty-five thousand dollars for this purpose, repayable within two years at an annual interest rate of 1¾ percent. As collateral, Adams assigned to du Pont three of his patents, comprising the ones most critical to the success of the pickup method he had developed. A related agreement between the two men gave du Pont the option within the two-year loan period of acquiring 40 percent of Tri-State Aviation's class A nonvoting stock and a controlling 51 percent of its class B voting stock in exchange for cancelling the August 16 note and paying Adams an additional forty-five thousand dollars.[3]

Du Pont's loan arrangement with Adams was precipitated by an action of the United States Post Office Department, which on August 15, 1938, advertised for bids on two new airmail routes, both converging on Pittsburgh, which would utilize the type of pickup system Adams had pioneered. This announcement, made pursuant to the act of April 15, 1938, authorizing the postmaster general to create experimental airmail services on a trial basis, led quickly to the activation of All American Aviation, which Adams had set up partly with such a contingency in mind. The stage was thus set for breathing life into a business entity that hitherto had only a shadowy existence.

This vitalizing function was performed on September 12, 1938, when Adams and du Pont executed an agreement that, in addition to ratifying the previously mentioned provisions of the August 16 loan arrangement, set forth the financial conditions under which All American Aviation would carry out its future operations. This document stipulated that All American's au-

Without the financial and organizational contributions of Richard C. du Pont, All American Aviation, founded in 1937, would not have become a functional entity. Du Pont, of the wealthy Delaware family, was a young glider pilot who met Lytle Adams in the summer of 1938 and provided the capital to get All American off the ground. Du Pont became president of the firm. (76.410.51, Hagley Museum and Library)

thorized capitalization of 250 thousand shares, each with a par value of one dollar, would be amended to provide for 250 thousand shares of class A nonvoting stock with a par value of one dollar and a hundred shares of class B voting stock with no par value, thereby paralleling Tri-State's structure. In return for assigning to All American both his present patents and any future patents he might obtain pertaining to "the picking up and delivery of mail by airplanes in flight," as well as turning over to the newly activated firm all of his existing pickup and delivery equipment, estimated to be worth approximately five thousand dollars, Adams would receive 120 thousand shares of class A and 49 shares of class B stock. On his part, du Pont agreed to pay into All American's treasury eighty-five thousand dollars in exchange for 80 thousand shares of class A stock and 51 shares of class B, thereby giving him voting control of the firm. It was further provided that Adams would be employed by All American as technical advisor with a monthly salary of $450 if the company secured airmail contracts for both of the routes advertised by the Post Office Department or $350 per month if it secured a contract for only one. Adams also agreed to act as the company's agent in submitting the bids for the routes in question.[4]

At a special meeting of All American's board of directors held at the Du Pont Building in Wilmington the same day, the various provisions of the agreement were ratified and the composition of the board was modified to reflect the new realities under which the firm was now operating. As was to be expected, Richard C. du Pont was chosen president and Adams became vice president. To the post of secretary-treasurer was elected Charles W. Wendt, who was destined to play a long and extremely important series of roles with both All American Aviation and one of its successor corporations, All American Engineering. At the September 12 meeting Wendt also became a director in place of Arthur P. Davis, who temporarily stepped down. Shortly thereafter, however, Davis acquired twenty-four shares of class B stock from Adams and was reinstated as a director on November 16, 1938, on which date Alexis Felix du Pont, Jr., was also elected to the board. These changes left no doubt that the du Pont interests, possessing three board memberships out of five, were in control of All American Aviation.[5]

Despite the fact that the Experimental Air Mail Act of 1938 had been passed due to the lobbying of Adams and his supporters, the Post Office Department was in no hurry to respond to the bids submitted by Adams on behalf of All American, and not until December 13, 1938, were contracts for two experimental routes formally offered to the firm. At that time, the company received authority for one year from commencement of service to pick up and deliver mail in flight on what had been officially designated as routes 1001 and 1002 at a rate of thirty-two cents per airplane mile for the former and forty-three cents per airplane mile for the latter. Route 1001 was to extend from

Du Pont's right-hand man and chief financial officer of All American was Charles W. Wendt. His managerial skill was highly valued, and he stayed with the firm and its successor All American Engineering for many years before his retirement in the 1970s. (76.410.48, Hagley Museum and Library)

Philadelphia to Pittsburgh by way of twenty-four intermediate points dotting 465 miles of mostly rugged terrain: West Chester, Coatesville, Lancaster, Columbia, York, Hanover, Gettysburg, Chambersburg, Mount Union, Huntingdon, Altoona, Tyrone, Clearfield, DuBois, Ridgway, Kane, Warren, Corry, Titusville, Oil City, Franklin, Grove City, Butler, and New Kensington. Route 1002, providing service to twenty-eight locations scattered throughout 413 miles of Appalachian Mountain territory, would begin at Pittsburgh and swing eastward to Irwin, Jeannette, Greensburg, and Latrobe, from which point it would follow a southwesterly course to the Pennsylvania communities of Mount Pleasant, Connellsville, and Uniontown. Crossing the West Virginia line, it would connect twenty-one points in that state and Ohio: Morgantown, Fairmont, Clarksburg, West Union, St. Mary's, Marietta, Parkersburg, Pomeroy, Point Pleasant, Gallipolis, Huntington, Barboursville, Milton, Hurricane, Nitro, Dunbar, Charleston, Spencer, Grantsville, Glenville, Weston, and back to Clarksburg for the return trip to Pittsburgh.[6]

The mere recitation of these names indicates the degree to which the sprawling network promised to fulfill the vision of aerial democracy that Adams and such political leaders as Jennings Randolph had so energetically promoted. With the exception of the two nodal points of Philadelphia and Pittsburgh, fully half the communities to be served by All American had populations of less than 10 thousand; Glenville, West Virginia, numbered only 799 souls. Because of the mountainous topography, a number of the towns, particularly in West Virginia, were unfit for airports. To a high degree, the birth and subsequent development of All American Aviation embodied the spirit and idealism of the New Deal in action.

By December 27, 1938, Richard du Pont and other company officials had signed the contracts for the two routes and had executed the necessary surety bond required by Post Office Department procedures, committing themselves and the firm to carry and deliver airmail "in a safe and secure manner, free from wet or injury," and to fulfill a variety of other conditions stipulated by the government. A list of assets and liabilities submitted to federal officials in connection with the new contracts revealed clearly that the firm, despite the du Pont wealth that undergirded it, scarcely ranked among the nation's largest commercial aviation companies. On the credit side it showed $80,000 in cash; three Stinson airplanes with an aggregate value of $21,868.05; miscellaneous equipment worth an estimated $5,000; and other assets, including Adams's patents, of no assigned value, for a grand total of $106,868.05. Liabilities included $90,000 worth of stock outstanding and $16,868.05 payable to the Stinson Aircraft Corporation; evidently $5,000 of the cash invested by Richard du Pont at the time the company was activated had been expended as a down payment for the three planes.[7]

Obviously, many preparations had to be made before the firm could inaugurate the services to which it was now pledged, beginning with the employment of personnel to carry its commitments into effect. On January 1, 1939, James Ray, Sr., a Texan who had won his spurs as a test pilot and executive for Pitcairn Aviation and who played an important role in the development of autogiros as vice president of the Autogiro Company of America, was named operations manager. A stickler for detail with an autocratic temperament, his technical expertise was soon put to use in a major overhaul of Adams's pickup system, much to the displeasure of its inventor. In March, Harry R. Stringer was named director of public relations. A former Washington newspaperman, he had handled similar duties for the United States Maritime Commission before joining All American. Among his other responsibilities, he was to work jointly with Adams in conducting consultations and negotiations with businessmen, municipal leaders, and postal officials in the various communities to be served by the company, looking toward the formal commencement of operations in May. Du Pont had originally assigned these functions to Adams alone, but was disappointed with the progress the latter was making and had begun to suspect that Adams was claiming reimbursement for expenses that were actually incurred in operating Tri-State Aviation. Stringer, it was hoped, might salvage the local arrangements, but the growing alienation between du Pont and Adams would only continue to worsen.[8]

A particularly critical need of the enterprise during this formative period with regard to personnel recruitment was for pilots who could execute the intricate maneuvers demanded by the pickup system. Because of the skills required, the company established a rule that no pilot would be hired who did not have at least ten years of flying experience and four thousand hours in the air. The choice for chief pilot fell logically upon Norman Rintoul, who had been assisting Adams since the beginning of Tri-State Aviation's pickup operations at the Morgantown Airport in West Virginia, and who was as familiar as any man alive with both the procedures involved and the geographic conditions under which they would have to be carried out. Along with Adams and mechanic Johnny Graham, he was one of All American's first three paid employees.[9]

During the early months of 1939 the firm hired five other pilots: Holger Hoiriis, Thomas T. Kincheloe, Gerald E. McGovern, Jimmy Piersol, and Camille D. ("Cammy") Vinet. These men were a capable and colorful lot. Kincheloe, who had begun flying in 1930 in Dallas, Texas, subsequently spent some time barnstorming in the Carolinas and then managed a flying service at Santa Cruz del Norte, Cuba. Leaving Cuba during the turbulent revolutionary conditions prevailing there in 1933, he worked as a charter pilot in such cities as Detroit and Richmond before joining All American. McGovern, from Cape May, New Jersey, had been a pilot for the United States Coast Guard. Piersol, who had learned to fly in Minnesota and had done some barnstorming in the 1920s, was also a newspaperman who had served as aviation editor of the *Detroit News* and the *New York Times*; he had also invented camera installations for news photoplanes that could be either operated by the pilot or actuated by remote control. Vinet had been a pilot for a number of aviation enterprises, including Pitcairn, Johnstown Air Service, Atlantic Airways, and the Harrisburg Autogiro Company; from 1935 to the time he joined All American in 1939, he had been director of aeronautics for the commonwealth of Pennsylvania.[10]

The most fascinating of these veteran airmen, however, was Holger Hoiriis, a Danish immigrant who had given up a possible career in agricultural science to come to the United States, where he took flying lessons at Curtiss Field on Long Island and went into barnstorming. While taking passengers aloft for joyrides at a Catskill Mountain resort in 1930, he met a wealthy photographer, Otto Hillig, who was himself a German immigrant. Sensing from their conversation that Hillig had both abundant means and a lust for adventure, Hoiriis suggested that his new friend might like to sponsor a flight from New York to Copenhagen and come along as a passenger. Hillig agreed, and the two men negotiated successfully with the well-known Delaware aircraft manufacturer and designer, Giuseppe Mario Bellanca, to build a high-wing monoplane for the venture. Christened the "Liberty" after Hillig's hometown in the Catskills, and decorated with the crossed flags of the United States and Denmark, the gleaming red and white ship took off from Teterboro Airport near Hackensack, New Jersey, on June 18, 1931, with Hoiriis and Hillig aboard and reached Copenhagen eight days later after stops in New Brunswick, Newfoundland, and Germany. Receiving a tumultuous welcome in the Danish capital, they were both knighted by King Christian X; then, putting their aircraft on a freighter bound for Maine, they returned to the United States aboard the liner *Mauretania* to be given an enthusiastic reception in New York. Known from this time onward as Sir Holger Hoiriis, the young Dane subsequently became a flight instructor and test pilot for Air Services, Inc., and the Bellanca Aircraft Corporation before joining forces with All American in 1939.[11]

Two other pilots, Raymond Elder and Lloyd Julson, signed on with the company as reserves during these early months. Another key requirement was for "clerks," soon to be called flight mechanics, who, in addition to sorting the mail collected along the company's two routes, handled the complicated apparatus that picked up and delivered mailbags at the various stations. Johnny Graham was hired for one of these positions; another was taken by Victor Yesulaites, who had assisted Adams and Rintoul in Morgantown and was still officially on the payroll of Tri-State Aviation. His status of being "on loan" from Tri-State to All American, coupled with work he was to perform for the latter firm in helping to refine the pickup system, would add fuel to bitter controversies that erupted between Adams and Richard du Pont before the year was out. Three other flight mechanic jobs soon went to Dalton R. Osborn of Wilmington, Delaware; Roy J. Allman of Etna, Pennsylvania; and Glen Rymer of Weston, West Virginia.[12]

The company's new pilots and flight mechanics would need

all the skill and experience they could muster to perform difficult pickup techniques while flying over a rugged territory, much of which lay within the notorious Allegheny Mountain "Hell Stretch." Although the term was largely journalistic hyperbole, the region was mountainous and prone to sudden weather changes and dense fogs that made for hazardous flying. For such a challenge, the fliers also needed extremely dependable aircraft, and the company was fortunate to find such a model in the Stinson SR-10 Reliant, the latest version of a series introduced in 1933. Equipped with speed arresters that permitted a steep glide and enabled its nose to be held at an unusually high angle during descent, the emergent SR model was much admired for its excellent landing characteristics. During the mid-1930s it was modified from a straight-wing configuration to a gull-wing design, which gave it a highly distinctive appearance, and its center of gravity was pushed backward with appropriate engineering modifications to prevent flat spinning. Its remarkable stick-free stability and lateral control made it a

One of All American's Stinson SR-10C Reliants. This plane, with its exceptional ruggedness and the reliability of its 260-horsepower Lycoming engine, was an ideal aircraft for the airmail pickup mission. The knife blades mounted on the landing gear were installed to sever the transfer line if the aircraft descended too low in making a pickup. (87-2469, Smithsonian Institution)

highly "forgiving" craft, and it proved very popular among bush pilots flying in the Arctic, including the Reverend Paul Schulte, Canada's famed "Flying Priest."

Despite some untimely crashes in Norway and northern Ontario in 1937 and 1938 that resulted in improvements to its wing-bracing system, the plane was noted for its structural durability, a definite plus for All American considering the repeated stresses and strains that were to be imposed upon it under the demands of the pickup system. In addition, its tight turning radius, in combination with the other features already noted, gave it the excellent maneuverability that would stand it in good stead while heading into and climbing out of the narrow, mountain-ringed valleys along the company's routes. Equipped with a nine-cylinder radial Lycoming engine with a 260-horsepower rating and capable of a cruising speed of approximately 155 miles per hour, the SR-10 would prove itself many times over a wise choice on All American's part. Stinson delivered the first of these sturdy planes to the firm late in 1938, and it was soon joined by four others as preparations for service continued.[13]

Before the aircraft could be put into operation, however, refinements and modifications needed to be made in Adams's pickup equipment and methods. As an approach to solving these problems, Richard du Pont assigned James Ray, Norman Rintoul, Victor Yesulaites, and other All American employees to redesign the pickup system in cooperation with representatives of the Kirkham Engineering and Manufacturing Company of Farmingdale, Long Island, of which du Pont was a director. Adams was not invited to take part in this activity and played no role in it. The project was carried out early in 1939 at the du Pont estate of Granogue in northern Delaware and served to intensify an already strained relationship between du Pont and Adams. In a related move to strengthen the company's patent position, the firm's board of directors decided at its February 3, 1939, meeting to offer 750 shares of All American stock to Godfrey L. Cabot, who was later that same day elected a director at the company's annual meeting. This arrangement involved the acquisition of Cabot's patent rights in aerial pickup technology, antedating Adams's own, along with other equipment, including two catapults designed by Cabot.[14]

The Irenee du Pont estate at Granogue, Delaware, as it appeared in 1931. Extensive tests of the airmail pickup system at Granogue in early 1939 yielded important changes that significantly upgraded the efficiency of the pickup apparatus. (70.200.6142, Hagley Museum and Library)

The experiments at Granogue yielded a series of changes in Adams's pickup system that he bitterly resented. In the technique he had worked out by this time, an aircraft deployed a single cable, carrying both the grappling device to pick up the outgoing mailbag and the bag containing the incoming mail, which was attached to the end of the cable by a frangible connection. The aerodynamic results could be unfortunate if the airflows encountered by the incoming mailbag caused it to oscillate, impeding the accuracy with which the grapple engaged the pickup loop. Should the grapple miss the loop entirely and hit one of the poles, it might break, requiring the cable to be retracted into the plane for the attachment of a new one and a second pickup attempt; alternatively, the grapple might bounce off a pole or the ground and shoot upward toward the plane, damaging the fuselage or the wings. In another undesirable scenario, the repeated gyrations of the incoming mailbag might induce metal fatigue in the cable, causing it to snap; should this happen, the grapple could be sent hurtling through the air at great speed, risking serious injury or damage to any person or object happening to be in the way. Accordingly, it was decided at Granogue that pickup and delivery would have to become two distinct operations, involving the simultaneous deployment of a pickup cable and a delivery rope.

Another change involved the pickup loop itself, which in Adams's system was made of a fifty-foot length of three-inch hemp graduated into a rubber shock cord connected to the outgoing mailbag. Victor Yesulaites designed a simple contrivance that rendered unnecessary this heavy and bulky arrangement, which had been intended to cushion the sudden impact of the grappling device with the load it would carry off the ground. The new device, based upon an ancient Chinese puzzle and known as a polygram or slide fitting, consisted of two blocks of wood that faced each other between two metal plates and would stay open in the absence of pressure but tighten once pressure was applied. It was attached to the transfer rope in such a way that the impact of the grapple would throw it off center and gradually force the blocks together like a pair of jaws, providing a few split seconds in which the sliding rope could become firmly engaged and thus giving the mailbag an interval to catch up to the speed of the aircraft. In yet another improvement, knots called monkey fists were tied in the transfer rope to ensure a

A collection of pickup equipment, including winches, cables, grapples, hooks, and reinforced mailbags used at various times in the evolution of the pickup. To the left in the photo are the knots or monkey fists that helped secure the transfer line to the grapple. (87-2472, Smithsonian Institution)

tight connection with the grapple, which was itself made heavier in an effort to prevent it from swinging backward too far in the descent toward the ground station and becoming ensnarled with the delivery rope carrying the incoming mailbag. Meanwhile, a release mechanism, operated by the pilot, was designed for installation in the plane so that the bag could be dropped on the ground a few seconds before the grappling cable made contact with the transfer rope to which the outgoing sack was attached.[15]

In a detailed letter to Richard du Pont on February 3, 1939, Adams strongly criticized these changes, beginning with the separate pickup cable and delivery rope. Under his previous system, he claimed, the weight of the incoming bag attached to the rear of the grappling hook stabilized the entire pickup and delivery process; in addition, rough weather might cause the now separated cable and rope to become entangled with one another. A swivel arrangement he had devised to attach the mailbag to a single pickup and delivery cable was sufficient, in his estimation, to guard against any ill effects that might result from oscillations of the bag, and its elimination in the new system was, as far as he was concerned, the main cause for the kinking of the pickup cable against which the experimenters at Granogue were trying to guard. Overweighting the grappling hook was also, in his view, a serious mistake that would cause it to be too far ahead when the pickup cable came into contact with the transfer rope, and throw the entire system out of balance. After taking a dig at "irresponsible helpers" who had wantonly discarded his original ideas "before they have been properly tried out," Adams closed his letter by declaring,

> I believe if the same money had been expended in perfecting our own ideas we would now be in a far better position. I strongly recommend that this development be put under the strict supervision of some one who has had experience and that no changes of the slightest nature be made, without his approval, in the principals [sic] of the system and the employees working on the development should be put under his direction.[16]

Obviously, Adams had himself in mind for such a role. Nor is it difficult to understand the intensity of his feelings. After all, he was the chief pioneer and prophet of aerial pickup technology. For nearly two decades, at great emotional and financial cost, he had developed his projects through a succession of frustrations and vicissitudes that would have broken the will of a less determined man. Under the terms of his agreements with du Pont, he had been formally designated technical advisor, with a salary to match, in a firm that was based upon his inventions and patents. He was also vice president of the company and one of its directors. It was therefore only natural for him to resent being bypassed in the company's effort to revamp the system he had created.

On the other hand, it is not difficult to appreciate the considerations that led du Pont to pursue the course of action followed at Granogue. Wendt's reminiscences make it clear that, from the time du Pont first observed Adams's pickup system in operation in Morgantown, he had serious doubts about the inventor's ability to solve the problems that prevented it from yielding the consistency that would be required in regular, day-to-day operations under the company's contract with the Post Office Department. So far as du Pont was concerned, Adams's status as technical advisor did not require that he be consulted unless this was deemed to be in the firm's best interest, and there was good reason to believe that he was too emotionally involved in the existing system to cooperate effectively with others in its renovation. It was particularly unlikely that Adams could work harmoniously with the new operations chief, James Ray, who regarded certain features of the existing system as dangerous and whose technical judgment du Pont respected much more than that of Adams. Wendt himself was increasingly frustrated by the difficulties of preparing bids and cost analyses on the basis of procedures and equipment that he knew were incapable of meeting the standards expected by federal postal officials, requiring him to make what he later described as "tongue in cheek" projections. In short, faithful performance of the company's responsibilities and the ability to earn dependable profits required a system that would work successfully close to 100 percent of the time, and this, in the estimation of du Pont and his closest advisors, required not the talents of a visionary promoter and inventor but the practical, down-to-earth efforts of technicians and engineers. And so a mutual distrust and alienation deepened between Adams and the rest of the company, leading eventually to a final breakdown of relationships.[17]

Meanwhile, however, du Pont continued to value Adams's abilities as a promoter and his political contacts in Washington. The company continued to employ him actively, along with Stringer, in preparations for the formal commencement of airmail service only a few months away. Part of this process involved negotiations with local businessmen and municipal leaders along the firm's two routes to defray the cost of the necessary ground equipment and messenger service. The fee requested was $450, with $150 going toward the provision of ground equipment and $300 for the community's share of the expense associated with securing messengers who would travel by car to the pickup site, make the necessary physical preparations for a pickup and delivery, and take the incoming mail back to the local post office. One community, Altoona, Pennsylvania, declined to contribute on the grounds that such payment was strictly voluntary, the company's contract with the Post Office Department plainly specifying that All American was to provide "airport and field facilities at authorized stop points." Leaders and residents in Morgantown, West Virginia, were also incensed at being asked to help defray the expense of a system their city had already done so much to promote. By early May 1939, on the eve of the formal inauguration of service, the company had received payment for ground equipment from only three communities, but was expecting "that after operating a month or two the rest of the localities will follow suit."[18]

Meanwhile, All American had staged a number of demonstration pickups and deliveries at selected points along its routes, both to whip up local enthusiasm and to give the company's pilots and flight mechanics valuable training. The first such event was held at Coatesville, Pennsylvania, on March 6, 1939. In a detailed account of what happened, the Coatesville Record proudly explained that the city had received this special honor by virtue of being the first community to notify All American that it would cooperate in establishing the new service. More than twenty-five hundred persons, including magazine, newspaper, and press association writers; airplane, rope, and steel manufacturers; mail handlers; and the "just plain curious," witnessed the event. Richard du Pont, Lytle Adams, and James

Ray, Sr., arrived early on the day of the demonstration aboard one of the firm's gleaming new Stinsons, with Norman Rintoul at the controls and Victor Yesulaites poised to operate the pickup equipment to be deployed from the interior of the plane. After setting up the ground apparatus, they made two practice pickups that went perfectly and then waited until four o'clock in the afternoon for the public performance.

Unfortunately, the first attempt did not go well, as Rintoul and Yesulaites "let down the incoming mail bag too late to avoid Guldin & Millard's auto graveyard and the grappling hook fouled the dropped line with the result that both bags were carried away." Two more tries, however, went perfectly, and the company officials were described as being "very much pleased with the demonstration and the interest shown by the public." Whatever satisfaction Adams may have felt because of the entangled pickup and delivery lines was not made public; he merely commented that the future of the system was unlimited and that "mail has been successfully picked up and deposited on ships at sea and on the tops of buildings." Meanwhile, the *Record* assured its readers that before formal service was started, a strip would be cleared through the auto scrapyard "so that fouling will not occur again."[19]

Between early March and the formal beginning of service in May, other demonstrations took place at selected points along the company's route system. A collection of newspaper clippings that Public Relations Director Harry Stringer later incorporated with many others into a valuable "Headline History" of the firm's progress revealed the excitement that the new pickup process aroused. Typical was an account in an Oil City, Pennsylvania, paper whose headline proclaimed, "3000 View Thrilling Demonstration of Air-Mail Pick Up Equipment at Memorial Park Saturday Afternoon: Plane Makes Three Successful Pick-Ups in High Wind Before Huge Crowd," and a story in a Warren, Pennsylvania, paper headlined "Airmail Pickup and Delivery System Demonstration Draws Thousands to Warren Airport." Similar demonstrations were conducted at such Pennsylvania towns as Franklin, Corry, and New Kensington.[20]

The successful performance of three pickups and deliveries under the adverse weather conditions described by the Oil City newspaper indicates that All American, due at least in part to the experiments conducted at Granogue, was indeed making progress in learning how to execute this difficult and demanding operation, which required expert coordination of men and equipment. On the floor of the Stinson's baggage compartment was a pick-up hole, approximately eighteen inches in diameter, through which mailbags could be lowered and admitted. Immediately forward of this hole on the port side of the ship, securely attached to the floor and the wall of the fuselage, was a hand-cranked winch and an accompanying shock-absorbing mechanism in which oil sprayed from a piston acted as a damper to cushion the piston's entry into an air chamber as contact was made between the grapple and the transfer line on the ground. As the plane approached the ground station in a gentle downward glide at approximately ninety miles per hour, the flight mechanic paid out from the winch a fifty-foot steel cable with an eight-pound, four-fingered grapple at its lower end, and also deployed the delivery rope with the incoming mailbag attached. A one-pound brass ball was attached at a point on the pickup cable about three feet from the drum of the winch; this had to be fitted by the flight mechanic into a slot in the shock-absorbing mechanism at the precise moment the grapple came into contact with the transfer line. If the device were prematurely engaged, the action of air currents impinging upon the hook and cable would set off the air-oil apparatus and the work of the shock absorber would be wasted, with potentially damaging consequences, when the moment of impact came.

On the ground were two steel poles, each thirty-three feet long, embedded in concrete, with the lower five feet below the surface and the remaining twenty-eight feet extending into the air. Atop each of the poles, which were spaced fifty-four feet apart, was a triangular marker made of sheet iron with its right-angle sides two and four feet in length respectively. To promote visibility, the poles were painted white and the iron markers bright yellow or international orange. Attached to the poles and triangles by means of pulleys, cleats, and spring clips was the transfer rope and a patented fiber and canvas mail container with a steel ring fastened in its nose; this complex assemblage also featured four knots in the rope itself, two large monkey fists at the ends of the rope, and Yesulaites's slide fitting device.

As the plane glided toward the ground station, its pickup and delivery lines dangled in the air, their drag-weight ratios giving them differing spatial curves. Descending to an altitude of between fifty and seventy feet, the pilot first released the delivery rope, causing the incoming mailbag to fall to the ground. The plane then passed between the two poles and, as the grappling hook engaged the transfer line, the clerk slipped the brass ball into the slot in the shock absorber. As the spring clips gave way and the slide fitting gradually tightened its jaws around the transfer line, the grappling hook became tightly engaged with one of the knots or monkey fists, and the line rose into the air, carrying the outgoing mailbag with it. Thanks to the combined

An All American Stinson making a pickup in 1939 or early 1940. The pickup system at the time used two cables, one to effect the pickup and the other to hold and drop the incoming mailbag a split second before the second cable and grapple engaged the transfer line strung between the two steel poles. In the scene shown here, the drop has already occurred. (ACP)

action of the shock absorber aloft and the slide fitting on the ground, the impact of pickup was described as being "scarcely noticeable to the occupants of the plane."

In the event that the grapple or delivery cable was accidentally fouled by an obstacle on the ground, a safety link was devised that would break. As the pilot slowly climbed out at a steep angle, the flight mechanic hand cranked the winch to reel in the pickup cable, transfer line, and the attached mailbag. The slower the climb, the easier it was for the mechanic to accomplish this part of the task. Once the bag was safely inside the plane, the mechanic stowed it and attached another delivery rope with the mailbag bound for the next station in the proper position for deployment. Normally, the plane's passenger seats had been removed and wooden bins and other equipment installed to facilitate the sorting of mail by the mechanic when he was not otherwise occupied. Meanwhile, down on the ground, a messenger would pick up the mailbag that had been dropped and take it to the local post office.[21]

Such was the system with which All American Aviation began service in May 1939. Company officials, knowing that the volume of mail to be carried on the first flights would be unusually heavy due to philatelic cachets posted by stamp collectors, and that the pace of activity would also be slowed by inaugural ceremonies along the routes, arranged a schedule staggered in such a manner that selected communities would begin to receive service on or before May 14; others would be served by June 1; and every point on the two routes would be served by June 15. In actuality, it would take until July 2 until full service was achieved.[22]

The long-awaited commencement of service took place on Friday, May 12, 1939, on Route 1002 from Pittsburgh to selected points in Pennsylvania and West Virginia. So great was the volume of mail and other ceremonial materials that three planes took off for Latrobe, Pennsylvania. The first was to pick up a bag containing scrolls, commemorative plaques, and airmail stamps to be kept by the company and distributed to prominent government officials; the other two were to pick up mail, including an expected large number of first-day philatelic cachets. As was perhaps to be expected, things did not go smoothly; the first pickup, made by Chief Pilot Norman Rintoul, went perfectly, but the second and third planes had to make three passes before they executed their tasks successfully. In the case of the second plane, strong winds blew the grappling hook inches away from the transfer line on the first try, and the plane's excessive speed on the second resulted in breakage of the metal ring holding the bag to the line.[23]

Nevertheless, things had gone relatively well at Latrobe considering the newness of the operation. After another pickup at Uniontown, the planes proceeded to Morgantown, where the day's principal inaugural ceremony was to be held, climaxing festivities already in progress there. The city was so honored because, as a local newspaper put it, "Early experiments with the Air Pick-Up had been conducted at the Morgantown Airport and local citizens and the state's national legislators in Congress had been extremely influential in obtaining the passage of the legislation creating the Air-Mail Pick-Up service." Accordingly, the mayor of the municipality proclaimed a half-holiday beginning with a special luncheon and continuing with five hours of special events including a review of about one thousand Reserve Officers Training Corps cadets on the campus of West Virginia University.

Among the dignitaries on hand were Representative Jennings Randolph, whose support had been so crucial to Adams and the founding of Tri-State Aviation; United States senators Neely of West Virginia, McKellar of Tennessee, and Mead of New York, staunch advocates of the pickup idea; Governor Homer A. Holt of West Virginia; Harold Kramer and J. N. Alderson of the Works Progress Administration, which had helped build the city's new $1.5 million airport; Dr. Charles E. Lawall, acting president of West Virginia University; Colonel W. Sumpter Smith of the Civil Aeronautics Authority's Safety Board; Clinton Hester, Administrator of the CAA; Charles Graddick, superintendent of the airmail division of the Post Office Department; Colonel Edgar S. Gorrell, president of the Air Transport Association; and the noted aviation journalist, Wayne Parrish. Representing All American Aviation were Richard du Pont and Lytle Adams. Approximately seven thousand persons flocked to the airport to witness the pickups, which took place at about five o'clock in the afternoon, accompanied by appropriate speeches and the presentation of rabbits' legs to five of All American's pilots by coeds of the university as symbols of good luck.[24]

Service on Route 1001 got under way two days later, on May 14, as planes were loaded with sacks of mail at the postal depot in Camden, New Jersey, directly across the Delaware River from Philadelphia, by the postmaster of the Pennsylvania metropolis, Joseph F. Gallagher. For reasons that are not clear, the process took much longer than anticipated, and the aircraft were two hours behind schedule when the takeoff took place. Fog and a highly unseasonable snowstorm further complicated operations as the planes headed for Coatesville, where a big crowd waited until two o'clock in the afternoon for the first pickup to be made, after which the Stinsons proceeded to Gettysburg and Clearfield. Further complications ensued at the latter point when the pickup line of the first plane was lowered too abruptly and the grappling hook failed to make contact with the transfer line, requiring another try; the second aircraft also experienced difficulty when, upon contact between the grapple and the transfer line, the metal ring holding the outgoing mailbag in place snapped off and had to be replaced before a successful second pass took place. The planes then proceeded to Du Bois, where they landed for refueling and checking and were greeted by a crowd estimated at four thousand people, after which they continued on to Pittsburgh by way of Corry, Warren, and Grove City. Seven thousand people gathered at the pickup site in Grove City to witness the event. Other inaugural flights, attended by appropriate ceremonies and large crowds, took place at various communities on All American's two routes throughout May, June, and early July.[25]

By the early summer of 1939, therefore, All American Aviation was in business and the dreams of Lytle S. Adams had at last been realized. A dubious United States Post Office Department had been persuaded to launch the pickup service on an experimental basis; thanks to the connection that had been established with the du Ponts, adequate financing had been obtained; an administrative hierarchy had been created; and a staff of capable pilots and flight mechanics had been matched with a small fleet of highly dependable aircraft. Meanwhile, a series of refinements had been made to the pickup method itself, which, however controversial, had solved enough of the problems involved to permit the successful inauguration of service with a minimum of difficulty, considering the relative newness of the techniques. From its headquarters in downtown Wilmington and its chief maintenance and repair base at the Du Pont Airport along the Lancaster Pike northwest of the city, officers and employees of the company could take satisfaction in the firm's accomplishments since Adams and du Pont had joined forces in the summer of 1938. Just ahead, however, loomed a year of operations, which, though marked by a number of solid successes, would bring more than its share of disappointments and crises. Despite all the excitement and enthusiasm that marked its first official flights, the struggling young enterprise was going to need all the skill and determination it could muster merely to survive.

3 • Visions and Vexations

As All American's recently acquired Stinsons took off on their inaugural flights in the spring of 1939, the world was poised on the brink of a cataclysm. Within the next twelve months Hitler's legions overwhelmed Poland, Denmark, and Norway; on May 12, 1940, the first anniversary of the inauguration of operations over the firm's two pickup routes, the Netherlands and Belgium were being overrun by Nazi troops and the French city of Sedan fell to the force of German arms for the third time in less than a century. Meanwhile, at home, President Franklin D. Roosevelt slowly nudged a reluctant electorate toward supporting increased material assistance to the Allied cause, while aviation hero Charles Lindbergh warned his fellow countrymen not to become involved in the spreading conflict and stressed the dangers of locking horns with the apparently invincible German war machine.

Against this somber backdrop, All American Aviation went through an arduous year highlighted by a successful record of operations achieved in the face of abnormally severe weather conditions and by efforts to secure governmental approval for a vastly expanded network of pickup routes. In the process, the company gave a public demonstration of its methods and equipment to large crowds in Washington, D.C., during a national postmasters' convention and later conducted successful experiments in the pickup and delivery of mail at night. Unfortunately, the financial returns that accrued were disproportionate to the energy expended, and government officials, far from expanding the pickup service, failed to put the existing routes on a permanent footing. The result was a suspension of service on May 13, 1940, pending the outcome of a vigorous fight by company leaders and congressional allies to save the firm from extinction. Meanwhile, relations between Lytle Adams and Richard du Pont continued to deteriorate, casting further doubt on the company's future.

By any standard, All American's first twelve months of operations produced a record of accomplishments in which the company could take legitimate pride. Its planes completed 438,145 miles of scheduled flying and made more than twenty-three thousand pickups, an average of seventy-eight per day. In the process, All American handled seventy-five thousand pounds of mail and sixty-five hundred pounds of air express, without accident to personnel, aircraft, or cargo and with a successful completion rate of 91.6 percent. This was a remarkable record considering the weather and topographical conditions faced by All American's pilots and flight mechanics as they made their daily rounds. Many of the communities into which they descended for pickups and deliveries were scattered on mountainsides or nestled in river valleys. Fog often shrouded the pickup sites and industrial emissions surrounded such places as Pittsburgh, Wheeling, Weirton, and Charleston. Even on good days it was not easy to find the pickup stations, which were sometimes located in cemeteries, on golf courses, or in tiny clearings in heavy forests. Skimming over the countryside at treetop level, pilots had to become adept, as their predecessors had done in the earliest years of the national airmail service, at identifying barns, haystacks, crossroads, or other landmarks. Frustrated by the dangers and hardships involved, some, Jimmy Piersol among them, gave up and resigned. "Either you liked this kind of flying or you hated it," was the way one writer later put it. "Either you joined in combatting the problems facing you, or you changed jobs."[1]

The unusually cold and snowy winter of 1939–1940, followed by heavy spring flooding, further complicated the situation. In one respect, All American could take some satisfaction in the fact that the relatively small size of its planes and the nature of its pickup methods permitted it to operate under conditions that occasionally rendered larger airlines helpless. At one point in mid-February when the worst snowfall on record hit Pittsburgh, shutting down the city's airport to normal traffic, company employees created a sloping fifteen-hundred-foot runway by laying railroad ties on packed snow, permitting Norman Rintoul to fly airmail to the outside world for the first time in three days. While the heavier planes of the major trunk lines were immobilized, All American's lighter Stinsons continued to use the field "practically without stint," although the company did have to sign a release exempting the county from liability in case of accident. During spring floods in the Ohio Valley, the firm was able to serve such communities as St. Mary's, Parkersburg, Point Pleasant, Gallipolis, Marietta, and Pomeroy despite levels of inundation that prevented normal modes of ground transportation from functioning. Rowboats were used to carry mailbags to water-covered pickup stations, where they were slung between partially submerged poles and borne aloft without difficulty by All American's Stinsons. Dropping incoming bags was more of a problem under such circumstances, but in one instance, when the Gallipolis airport was under two feet of water, one of the company's planes circled the town and managed to drop a mail pouch in the yard of the local post office.[2]

Despite the firm's record of accomplishment, however, its financial rewards were extremely disappointing. An early statement, issued to members of the board of directors in August 1939 and covering the first six weeks of operations, set the tone for future developments by revealing a loss for this period alone of $6,127.01. Expenses connected with the beginning of service were bound to be high; nevertheless, the picture did not improve. A balance sheet issued by the company in June 1940, covering the first full year of operations ending in mid-May, showed a net loss of $53,588.27. Clearly, pickup operations had not yielded a bonanza for All American Aviation.[3]

The reasons for this discouraging situation were inherent in the very nature of All American's operations and were complicated by the lack of federal support. Limited by the size of its planes and the basic technology it employed, the company offered only a restricted type of service to a group of communities that, however numerous, were widely dispersed and, for the most part, extremely small. The Post Office Department was compensating the firm with flat mileage rates that were obviously insufficient to cover basic expenses. At the very least, it was crucial for the company to persuade postal officials to agree to more realistic rates capable of ensuring a reasonable return on its investment, and efforts along these lines would be made repeatedly in the future. For two reasons, however, the chances for making really substantial profits by pursuing this line of attack were not good. First, as events would demonstrate, the

Post Office Department was at best lukewarm about the pickup system; over the years, All American stayed in existence only because of the support of loyal and determined members of the Congress headed by Jennings Randolph. Second, ever since the passage of the McNary-Watres Act in 1930, federal policy toward commercial aviation had been to attempt to wean airlines from an excessive dependence upon airmail subsidies and to encourage them to derive as much revenue as possible from passenger operations. This made it even more unlikely that postal officials would look favorably upon what amounted to a perpetual subsidy to All American in the form of escalating rates.

One possible way of breaking out of this bind was for All American to combine the pickup system with passenger operations. But given that even conventional airlines were finding it necessary to employ elaborate advertising campaigns in an effort to convince the public that air travel was not dangerous, it may appear strange that Richard du Pont could have seriously believed that travelers would endure a mode of flying involving frequent descents into fog-shrouded valleys in out-of-the-way places to pick up and discharge mail at extremely low altitudes—even in the unlikely event that the Civil Aeronautics Board would authorize such an experiment. Nevertheless, All American Aviation would pursue this project doggedly for nearly a decade, the strenuousness of its efforts reflecting the strength of its desire to escape the earnings limitations of the pickup. While some of the communities served were small or topographically incapable of having airports, others were both larger and more favorably situated; presumably these could serve as nodal points, at which passengers could be collected in periodic landings and funneled to such cities as Pittsburgh and Philadelphia, where they could make connections with larger trunk lines.

There was a second way for the company to increase its profits: given enough planes, personnel, and ground stations, All American's equipment and methods were capable of supplying airmail service to virtually every place in the United States, however small. Indeed, as the firm's later efforts to establish subsidiaries in such countries as Brazil would demonstrate, its techniques had worldwide applicability. If the Post Office Department could be persuaded to authorize even minimally satis-factory mileage rates, large profits could be realized on the basis of sheer volume of operations, the classic strategy of a mass production economy.

Nor would it be necessary for All American itself to operate all of the additional routes; if it could secure a sufficiently strong patent position, it could thrive by permitting other enterprises to utilize its techniques on a royalty basis and by manufacturing the apparatus needed. In an important memorandum to the firm's board of directors in August 1939, Richard du Pont out-lined such a strategy, stating his belief "that the best policy for All American Aviation, Inc. to follow would be to continue business as a manufacturing, sales, licensing, and development organization, and to continue as an operating company only in so far as it can be made to prove profitable to the company and continues to be an asset in its development work." Such an approach, he argued, would give All American "greater freedom and fewer restrictions" than any other. As he noted, "In order to pursue a policy of this kind, I believe it necessary, first, that we maintain a good patent situation and, second, that we have a sound and progressive engineering department."[4]

During the same month, du Pont submitted to the Civil Aeronautics Authority and the Post Office Department an am-bitious plan for the establishment of a "comprehensive air feeder system" that, "without an extravagant expenditure of public funds," would enable every community in the United States, regardless of its size or location, to enjoy the benefits of regularly scheduled commercial air service. Only about one-fourth of the country's population, he stated, was now served by established air routes; excluding the 54 places served by All American, only 210 of the 4,000 American communities with more than five thousand people had airline connections. "Everyone is paying for air mail service," he argued, "and now that a practical means of providing it to all is available, depriving them of its full advantage is manifestly unfair."

Du Pont's proposal embodied a combination of passenger and aerial pickup operations. Networks of feeder lines would radiate outward from major trunk line centers for a distance of about 250 miles. Actual landings would be made along the feeder lines only for passengers who had made reservations; otherwise, airmail pickups and deliveries would be made with equipment such as that used on All American's present routes, but using larger, multiengined aircraft instead of the company's Stinsons. A two-engine plane with a two-man crew and capable of carrying from five to seven passengers, with a cruising speed of between 150 and 180 miles per hour, seemed to du Pont "admirably suited to this type of service." Without conceding that pickup operations could not be conducted at night—in point of fact, All American would prove the practicability of this idea before the end of the year—du Pont envisioned that the services he was proposing would be carried out primarily during daylight hours. In the morning, planes would depart from a central terminal to deliver mail and express that had accumulated overnight; in the late afternoon or early evening they would fly back over the same route to collect the daily intake from post offices along the way. "Over a feeder network of this kind that was properly coordinated with the trunk lines," he asserted, "mail and express could go to any point in the United States from any other point in less than twenty-four hours."

Anticipating objections to combining pickup and passenger operations, du Pont acknowledged that there might be "certain psychological resistance on the part of some people to flying this way," but he was confident that this would "disappear as performance demonstrates that it is just as safe and comfortable as ordinary transport flying." All American, he said, had already conducted experimental flights in which small multiengined planes had carried passengers under conditions in which pickups and deliveries had been simulated; in these cases, "none spoke of feeling any mental or physical discomfort in making the frequent approaches to the pick-up stations." So far as safety was concerned, he asserted, "the pick-up operation is safer than making a landing because the plane never closely approaches its stalling speed and is consequently always under excellent control. No contact with the ground is involved and the climb can be made without imposing the heavy strain on the motors which occurs in a regular take-off." In any event, he believed the advantages offered to travelers by the new service would go far toward overcoming their resistance. As an illustration, he pointed out that a person living in the small community of West Union, West Virginia, could go to the nearby Clarksburg airport and be in Stockton, California, in twenty-one hours by making a connection in Pittsburgh with the transcontinental sleeper service offered by a major air carrier.[5]

Mounting a publicity campaign in behalf of his ideas, du Pont hosted a luncheon in the national capital for staff members of various wire services, newspapermen representing important syndicates, and radio personalities, including such noted commentators as Fulton Lewis, Jr. According to an article in *American Aviation*, the young executive made a very good impression: "clean-cut, intelligent, obviously sincere, he had a message to tell. Why not tell it to the men who write the nation's news from Washington, the men who cover appropriation hearings, the men who ask questions of Congressmen and government officials?" It is scarcely surprising that du Pont had drawn favorable attention from a journal whose publisher, Wayne Parrish, was one of the country's leading aviation enthusiasts, but Parrish was not alone in applauding the proposed new system. Within a short time, editorials endorsing it appeared in such newspapers as the *Hartford* (Connecticut) *Times*, the *Boston Traveler*, the *St. Paul* (Minnesota) *Dispatch*, the *St. Louis Star Times*, and the *Bridgeport* (Connecticut) *Telegram*. Al Williams, a Scripps-Howard staff writer, supported the cause with a nationally syndicated column entitled "Cities Need 'Feeder Lines.' " Perhaps most encouraging to du Pont was a laudatory editorial that appeared in the *New York Times*. "Mr. du Pont's suggestion is a bold approach to a real problem," it commented. "It certainly is worthy of most careful consideration by the agencies concerned with civil aeronautics."[6] Of equal significance, however, were expressions of interest voiced by newspapers in cities of a size that would make them logical focal points on the feeder routes: Kalamazoo, Michigan; Springfield and Worcester, Massachusetts; Elmira and Rome, New York; Ashland, Ohio; Hickory, North Carolina; Rockford, Illinois; and Tyler, Texas.[7]

A meeting of the National Association of Postmasters at Washington in mid-October 1939 gave All American a chance to demonstrate its pickup system before members of several crucial clienteles: the postmasters themselves, officials of the Post Office Department, key leaders in both houses of Congress, members of the Washington press corps, and important federal administrators in the various bureaus and agencies composing

Roosevelt's New Deal entourage. The capital city's Mall offered an ideal place to conduct what turned out to be an impressive show. In a roped-off area adjacent to the new National Gallery of Art, a typical All American pickup station was erected. On October 12, one of the company's Stinsons, with chief pilot Norman Rintoul in the cockpit and Victor Yesulaites serving as the flight mechanic, made repeated successful pickups. A newspaper article describing the event referred to the "huge crowds" that witnessed it and the way in which, "heading toward them at 90 miles an hour, the plane lowered a hook-like device to which was attached a mail pouch." Flying toward the ground station at an altitude well below one hundred feet, with the Capitol building providing a backdrop, "the plane in the twinkling of an eye left behind the loaded mail pouch and picked up another, pursuing its flight." As the aircraft climbed into the sky over the Washington Monument and the outgoing mailbag slowly disappeared into its belly, a ground crew began preparations for another pickup. The "demonstration was repeated time and again." The members of Congress present had earlier heard Jennings Randolph, on the floor of the House of Representatives, laud the firm and its recently established service. And the postmasters attending the convention could view a special exhibit that the company had put on display for their benefit.[8]

Another benchmark in the progress of the enterprise occurred later in the same month when, after a series of experimental flights, the company made the first public demonstration of its ability to conduct pickups and deliveries at night. Wilmington's Bellanca Field was the scene of this event, which took place on October 29, 1939, with Holger Hoiriis as the pilot and William Burkhart as the flight mechanic. The outgoing mailbag was deployed between two forty-foot masts, the tops of which were neon-lighted, and cheers resounded as three pickups and deliveries were made. Among those in attendance were C. M. Knoble, assistant superintendent of air mail service in the Post Office Department; Richard S. Boutelle, director of the CAA's Bureau of Safety Regulation; Edward Yuravich, chief of the air carrier inspection section of the CAA; J. E. Whitbeck and Edward K. Mills of the CAA's legal division; the ever-supportive Jennings Randolph; and All American officials, including Adams and du Pont. Various details concerning the development of an adequate lighting system for the pickup station, which under normal conditions could be seen at night from a distance of six miles, were explained to the assembled visitors, who were also told about the advantages this type of service would offer to businessmen in small communities. Through its use, letters mailed at the end of the day could arrive at destinations in distant cities by the following noon.

Because of their location at the extreme western end of the route from Philadelphia to Pittsburgh, three communities—Grove City, Natrona, and Butler—were selected by the company to be the first to receive night service under a one-month experimental authorization granted by the Post Office Department. On November 15, 1939, the first official night airmail pickup in history occurred at the Natrona Heights airport, with Hoiriis and Burkhart again composing the crew of the plane that carried out the mission. Hundreds of spectators came to the field to witness the spectacle as Hoiriis guided the ship directly over the ground station and the mailbag was whisked into the air. In addition to the red neon lights that outlined the triangular markers at the top of the two masts supporting the delivery line, a twelve-foot horizontal neon bar of the same color was mounted on a frame ten feet above the ground under the suspended bag. Accompanying the pickup plane was another aircraft carrying Richard du Pont and James G. Ray, who took part in the ceremonies. Postal officials were sufficiently impressed by the results of the early night pickups to grant a brief extension permitting the experiment to last six weeks but declined for the time being to make it permanent, even though Charles P. Graddick, superintendent of the air mail division, expressed satisfaction with its results at ceremonies on December 22, marking the final flight in the series.[9]

The conservative attitude of postal officials regarding the expansion of All American's activities did not prevent du Pont from continuing to press for the adoption of his proposed feeder system. The annual convention of the National Aeronautic Association at New Orleans in January 1940 gave him a convenient forum for a stinging attack upon the manner in which the growth of the nation's commercial air network since 1934 had failed to benefit a vast number of cities. A desire to capitalize upon the speed of the airplane, he charged, had resulted in a "fixed format" of operations that had prevented an increase in the number of destinations served proportionate to the growth in the number of miles covered, which mainly reflected the creation of "additional schedules over the same routes." In 1934, he pointed out, the nation's airlines had flown slightly more than twenty-nine million miles, serving 178 cities; by 1939 they were flying fifty-two million miles, representing an increase of 80 percent, but had added service to only 32 new cities. Thus, he maintained, "speed, which is aviation's greatest asset, has become the worst handicap to the general expansion of air transportation." The tendency was toward larger and more powerful planes making "fewer stops and longer jumps," while a favored few metropolitan centers monopolized the rewards of the system.

Du Pont specifically criticized recent trends in the development of the airmail service, asserting that the increase that had taken place in 1939 was the smallest since 1935 and pointing out that a large volume of airmail—341 million pieces in 1939 alone—was actually transported by rail. Part of the problem, he argued, was that many cities could not afford adequate airport facilities. There was, however, one bright spot in this generally unsatisfactory situation: the recent experimental establishment of All American Aviation's pickup system, which "has brought direct air service within the reach of every city and hamlet in the country." Because of the nature of the technology it employed, considerations involving size and location, or even the total lack of an airport, were no longer relevant: "A community may be small and produce little traffic, but with the air pick-up system it is nearly as easy to serve it as to fly over it."

Du Pont pointed with pride to his firm's first eight months of operations, during which more than fourteen thousand pickups had been made, over 325 thousand miles had been flown, and a performance level of nearly 95 percent had been achieved. He called this record "really astonishing, considering that the routes lie over terrain where some of the worst flying conditions in the country are encountered." Asserting that the company's record had demonstrated the existence of "an almost limitless field for expansion," he concluded his presentation by summarizing the merits of his proposed feeder network:

The possibilities of a feeder system on a natonal scale have opened a new door to the future of aviation. Its development will take air transport out of its strait jacket, enabling millions of our people who are now deprived of direct air service to have its advantages. It will provide a new market for the aircraft industry; new outlets for capital. It will create a new and large field of employment. It will put every city and town in the country within overnight reach of each other, which will provide a big stimulus to business and industry generally. It will make available to all the benefits that are now reserved to the few.[10]

Like all other activities that he and his company had been pursuing within the past several months, du Pont's rhetoric was focused at least in part upon a forthcoming series of hearings to be conducted by the Civil Aeronautics Authority in Washington, beginning February 19, 1940. At present, All American Aviation's pickup and delivery services were simply experimental operations conducted solely under the aegis of the Post Office Department; at the hearings, the firm would present its case for a permanent certificate of public convenience and necessity that would give it the status of a full-fledged commercial air carrier operating under the regulatory authority of the CAA. But its hopes were even more ambitious than this, for in addition to putting its existing routes on a permanent footing it also wanted to win CAA approval of service to a considerable number of new communities and implant in the minds of federal officials the vision of a far-flung system of combined pickup, delivery, and passenger operations virtually blanketing the Middle Atlantic and southeastern regions. Throughout the fall and winter months, while the fledgling enterprise gained indispensable experience by conducting operations over its existing route structure and broke fresh ground by carrying out its successful experiments with night service, company officials were busy mapping out the details of no less than twenty potential new route systems and establishing contacts with hundreds of local business leaders and civic groups whose support would be required in order to make them operative. Pickup partisans hoped the CAA hearing would represent a significant breakthrough in the process of transforming Richard du Pont's visions and dreams into functioning realities.

The heart of the company's proposal, for which it presumably stood the best chance of obtaining approval, was a formal request that the CAA certify a network of six routes sprawling across seven states—Pennsylvania, New Jersey, Delaware, New York, Ohio, West Virginia, and Kentucky—and serving 224 communities. Included were 54 of the 58 points scattered along All American's existing system, regrouped in the interest of increased efficiency. Most of these communities were spread out over three new routes, whose overall shape closely resembled that of the company's two existing arteries. All six proposed routes converged on Pittsburgh. One of the three main routes went from Pittsburgh to Cleveland by way of such towns as Beaver Falls and New Castle, Pennsylvania, and Youngstown and Warren, Ohio; another went from Pittsburgh to Buffalo via a string of communities, including Butler, Grove City, Oil City, Titusville, Corry, and Warren, Pennsylvania, and Jamestown, Dunkirk, and Angola, New York; the third led from Pittsburgh to Newark, New Jersey, serving such places as Pitcairn, Vandergrift, Indiana, Punxsutawney, Du Bois, Clearfield, Philipsburg, State College, Bellefonte, Lock Haven, Williamsport, Sunbury, Danville, Bloomsburg, Wilkes Barre, Scranton, and Stroudsburg, Pennsylvania, and Morristown, New Jersey. All told, the six routes covered 1,817 miles and would provide service to an estimated 7,794,744 persons. Initially, service would be limited to airmail and air express, but it would subsequently include passenger operations to communities having adequate airports, in which case twin-engined planes would be used.[11]

While this six-route network was the only one formally proposed for CAA certification, others of an even more elaborate nature were informally suggested for that agency's scrutiny. Seven routes, for example, were plotted to blanket New Jersey, northeastern Pennsylvania, and upstate New York, most of them converging upon Newark, New Jersey, and Elmira, New York, with the exception of an extreme northern artery cutting a wide swath across New York, connecting Buffalo, Niagara Falls, Lockport, Rochester, Geneva, Auburn, Syracuse, Oswego, Pulaski, Watertown, Ogdensburg, and Messina. The entire system would involve ninety-one cities and towns, cover 1,588 miles, and serve 12,798,800 people. Yet another seven-route network would cover most of Virginia and Maryland, with arms extending into eastern and central Pennsylvania, the eastern panhandle of West Virginia, southern Delaware, and southwestern New Jersey; the nodal points of this system would be Philadelphia-Camden and Washington, D.C. Finally, All American projected yet another series of seven routes stretching across the vast southeastern region between Richmond and Atlanta, providing service to virtually every population center of consequence in the Carolinas and to a number of communities in southern Virginia and northern Georgia.[12]

This body of formal and informal proposals, aggregating twenty-seven routes and involving several hundred communities in an area that included eleven states and the District of Columbia, represented a dramatic new concept in American commercial aviation. It was supported by a rationale that had strong democratic and egalitarian overtones, well calculated to evoke widespread attention at a time in American history when the appeal of populist rhetoric was strong. Du Pont's concept of commercial aviation for everybody was also likely to stimulate interest among congressmen who represented districts lacking the major metropolitan centers that the established airlines served. It is easy to see why All American Aviation's plans stirred up enthusiasm among editors whose newspapers represented small cities and towns; their appreciative columns were diligently collected by Harry Stringer in his "Headline History."

All American's proposals were also in harmony with the prevailing receptivity to the lure of technological panaceas. These were years in which a creed (identified by historian Joseph J. Corn as "the winged gospel") proclaimed with messianic overtones that the age of flight heralded a new and beneficent era in human development. Such persons as Harold F. Pitcairn and Eugene L. Vidal were energetically promoting the concept of an "airplane for everyman," which would put the average citizen in the sky just as Henry Ford's Model T had put him on the highway.[13] The visions propagated by Richard C. du Pont fed on the same taproot of aerial enthusiasm, just as they represented the waning but nevertheless still vital spirit of the New Deal. However grandiose they later appeared, it was not unreasonable to think at the time that the CAA would find them persuasive.

On the other hand, there were equally cogent reasons why the CAA might be skeptical about the viability of the pickup system and about the wisdom of implementing it too rapidly on too large a scale, particularly insofar as combining it with passenger operations was concerned. The agency itself had come into being as the result of unsettled conditions within the commercial aviation industry and the desire of established carriers to protect their investments against the impact of sudden technological change in the form of such relatively new aircraft as the Douglas DC-3. It was intensely safety conscious, because of a wave of air crashes in the mid-1930s that had killed such persons as U.S. Senator Bronson Cutting, and was also influenced by the effects of a severe recession in 1937–1938 that was only now abating as the economy slowly responded to the preparedness drive that preceded America's entry into World War II.[14] All American Aviation had been in existence as a functioning entity for only a relatively few months, and could scarcely be said to have proved itself despite the public demonstrations its leaders had staged for the benefit of postal officials and other interested parties. Indeed, it was losing money at a rate of nearly five thousand dollars per month. Why adopt its methods on a large scale when it was not yet clear that it was succeeding on a small one? In particular, why approve a plan that contemplated carrying revenue passengers in planes engaged in daring maneuvers, when only a relatively few Americans could be persuaded to fly in normal commercial operations?

In its testimony before the CAA, All American presented information relating to its eligibility for certification as a "citizen of the United States" under the terms of the Civil Aeronautics Act and the soundness of its financial position as of December 31, 1939, indicating current assets of $63,982.35 as opposed to current liabilities of $9,342.36 and a total net worth of $174,215.10. By that date it had completed 283,100 miles of scheduled flying over its two routes, representing 94.5 percent of the scheduled mileage it had contracted to provide the Post Office Department—obviously a highly commendable completion rate considering the nature of the area it served and the officially experimental status of the techniques it used. Elaborate statistical data was presented relating to the costs of the new services All American were proposing to render and the additional equipment that would be required, including three new Stinson SR-10s, one twin-engine aircraft for the passenger service it hoped to inaugurate, much additional pickup and transfer apparatus, and miscellaneous spare parts, all aggregating to $87,972.00. Postal officials presented the results of surveys indicating the volume of mail that might be expected should the company receive certification for the six routes it proposed to serve and gave a good report with regard to the company's performance under its experimental contract. According to Graddick, All American "had definitely proved the feasibility of the pickup so far as the mail service is concerned," and the results of its operations "had been even more successful than had been anticipated by the Post Office Department." Other testimony by the company and various civic representatives indicated the need for the types of services All American was prepared to perform in communities that lacked air connections with the outside world and whose geographical circumstances impeded the rapid delivery of surface mail.[15]

As was to be expected, the company's proposal aroused opposition from larger carriers that operated on the fringes of the area covered by the six projected routes or that provided trunk line service to nodal centers within it. Eastern and TWA, as interveners in the case, argued that existing carriers should have a preemptive right to develop passenger feeder services between terminal points already served; they characterized All American's methods as unsafe; they denied that the public convenience and necessity required the services the firm was proposing; and they otherwise questioned its fitness and ability to perform them. Pennsylvania-Central Airlines, another intervener, joined Eastern and TWA in demanding that any certificate issued to All American must protect the established trunk line carriers from competition on routes they were already operating between terminal and intermediate points that du Pont's enterprise wanted to serve. On its part, All American disclaimed any desire to compete with the larger carriers and suggested that the CAA impose limitations on any rights it might confer upon the company that would obviate the concerns of its competitors.[16]

Of perhaps greater significance to All American, in view of its connection with Lytle S. Adams, was Tri-State Aviation's intervention in the case in opposition to the company's proposals. In a related proceeding conducted before the CAA at the same time, Tri-State was attempting to secure a "grandfather certificate" under the Civil Aeronautics Act that would give it the right to transport property by air—principally small packages sent by three Pittsburgh department stores and a Baltimore mail order house to their customers—between a number of towns and cities in West Virginia and Maryland. Tri-State wanted to continue the service it had rendered spasmodically from May 14 through August 22, 1938, which the Civil Aeronautics Act stipulated as a benchmark for a grant of permanent operating authority. On the grounds that a few of the communities involved in that proceedings were also served by All American's airmail pickup and delivery system, Tri-State sought to postpone any decision by the CAA on All American's application until a final determination was made on its own case. It also denied that public convenience and necessity required the services All American was proposing to render, and—quite importantly, considering the way the current hearing was to turn out—contended that the Civil Aeronautics Act did not give the CAA jurisdiction over the type of operations that All American was conducting.[17]

That Tri-State Aviation had intervened in the CAA hearings as an open adversary of All American indicates the deterioration in the relationship between Lytle Adams and Richard du Pont by this time. Ever since the pickup system had been redesigned at Granogue in the early months of 1939, All American's efforts to establish itself as a dependable and smoothly functioning enterprise had taken place against a backdrop of constant controversy between Adams, who claimed sweeping proprietary rights over the pickup system he had developed before his association with Richard du Pont, and a majority of the firm's directors, who contended that the system belonged to the company, which had the right to develop or improve upon it as it saw fit. Du Pont himself was particularly adamant in defending the latter point of view; in his estimation, the experiments conducted at Granogue had produced a pickup and delivery technique containing "only a few" of Adams's original principles, as he put it in one letter, and was therefore something virtually new. Whereas Adams saw invention as an individual achievement, du Pont looked upon it as a group activity made possible only because of the existence of the corporation as a whole. As he bluntly informed Adams at one point, "In my opinion, the company should receive all possible credit for the development of the present pick-up and delivery system, and I can see no reason why any one individual in the company should wish to receive special recognition for anything that might otherwise be included as additional credit to the company."[18]

Conflict engendered by these diametrically opposed points of view had reached a particularly crucial phase in the summer months of 1939, due partly to du Pont's concern that the company needed to secure the strongest possible patent position in case it ultimately decided to function primarily or exclusively as a manufacturing, licensing, and development firm. Disregarding a strong written protest by Adams, the directors appointed Henry A. Wise, Jr., a Wilmington lawyer, to assist All American in drawing up a comprehensive patent application embodying all features of the pickup and delivery system currently in use. In a letter to Adams written in early August, Wise asked for the inventor's help in studying a draft of the application "in an attempt to determine whether anything within the claims should be filed in your name as sole inventor."[19]

In a long and detailed response, Adams indicated a desire to help the firm in any reasonable way to strengthen its patent position but protested that in his 1938 agreement with du Pont regarding the assignment of existing or potential future patent rights to the company there had been "no provision for joint applications or of permitting others to obtain patents on improvements, refinements, or additions." He was particularly adamant in asserting his claims to any and all contributions made by Rintoul and Yesulaites in the course of the Granogue experiments, on the grounds that these men had been merely on loan to All American from Tri-State Aviation and that their ideas had stemmed from earlier work done with him. Furthermore, he insisted, he was also entitled to claim a right to anything for which James Ray or the technical personnel supplied by the Kirkham Engineering Company were responsible at Granogue, presumably because they had taken part in the process without his authorization. Adams then specified no less than eighteen categories of apparatus or methods, covering the entire gamut of pickup and delivery operations, as being of his sole invention, declaring that he could "produce adequate proof" of this if called upon to do so. Though readily acknowledging that his 1938 contract with du Pont obliged him to assign to the company "any and all patents" that might be useful to its operations and stating that he would be "glad to do so," he nevertheless refused to cooperate with Wise unless the claims he was advancing were "agreed to and approved" in advance.[20]

At stake was the corporation's right to control its own research and development activities; acceptance of Adams's terms was obviously unthinkable. Instead, another approach was used. At a board meeting that Adams apparently did not attend, a resolution was passed creating a technical committee to oversee engineering and development, with Adams as a possible member. Implementation of this plan would serve the firm's purposes by involving Adams in decisions affecting changing methods and equipment but relegating him to a minority position in which he could be outvoted if his judgment differed from that of other members. In a letter inviting Adams to serve on the committee, du Pont seized an opportunity to challenge him to document the claims he had made regarding proof that he had actually invented the various devices and techniques he had specified by asking Adams to

> supply to the company a full and complete description of any and all inventions, devices, improvements, or claims which may in any way pertain to pick-up and delivery equipment or service, including the original date of discovery, note books pertaining to work and study thereon, blue prints and all other matters which may aid in establishing the nature and character of the same.[21]

But Adams could not be so easily outmaneuvered. In his reply, he stated that he had "no particular desire" to serve on the newly authorized panel, though he would do so if it were "distinctly and definitely understood" that no action on its part could be regarded as "limiting, restricting, or binding upon me so far as my patent claims or work is concerned." As to du Pont's request for specific documentation, Adams responded:

> It is impossible for me to search my files and memory for every conceivable thing I have done with reference to pick-up and delivery equipment over many years, in advance of particular questions as they arise. As you must know, it is a substantial undertaking in time and effort to locate all ma-

terial concerning a known single well-defined patent issue. To attempt in addition to cover every conceivable issue is naturally beyond reason. I shall, of course, be glad to do my best to supply information to the Committee as issues are developed.[22]

In short, action on the patent issue had reached an impasse. Nor was this the only source of difficulty involving Adams's increasingly bitter relationship with All American. Well before the start of formal service in May 1939, suspicion had arisen in the minds of du Pont and other company officials that Adams had been padding requests for reimbursement of expenses incurred on official business and, particularly, that he had not actually contacted a number of local postmasters to make arrangements for the beginning of service even though he had submitted vouchers for such visits. At a special meeting on May 9, the board of directors passed a resolution that the company would not be responsible for any expenses incurred by Adams unless these were in connection with duties performed at du Pont's specific behest. In such cases, a preliminary estimate of the expenses had to be approved by du Pont in advance, and a subsequent request for reimbursement would not be honored unless it was submitted within fourteen days of the service performed. Adams was present at the meeting, but his attitude toward these stipulations or the reasons precipitating them is not revealed by the minutes.[23]

A dispute also arose concerning whether or not Adams had complied with the terms of a September 1938 agreement he had made to deliver to the company an assortment of steel poles, mailbags, and other equipment gathered in the course of his previous work on the pickup system. For a time the idea was entertained of withholding payment of Adams's salary as vice president of the company until he had completed the property transfer, or of removing him from that post altogether. In an indignant protest complaining of persecution by the firm, Adams implied that he had indeed held back certain items he had originally promised to deliver to it, justifying his action on the grounds that the company had destroyed pieces of equipment he had transferred earlier in order to discredit his claims to their invention. Before completing his part of the agreement, he wanted a guarantee that this would not happen to the items still in his possession.[24]

In the course of these developments, a wall of suspicion rose between Adams and the other officers of the company, which made effective cooperation in the best interests of the firm virtually impossible. A lack of coordination between Adams and du Pont was revealed by an episode of mid-1939 involving the efforts of W. P. Wilson, the Wheeling industrialist who had been a long-time friend of Adams, to have All American's Route 1002 extended to provide service to a number of communities in the northern panhandle of West Virginia and the southeastern corner of Ohio. Without consulting the other directors, Adams dictated a letter that Wilson sent to First Assistant Postmaster General W. W. Howes requesting inauguration of such service. While expressing interest in the idea, du Pont informed Wilson that Adams had "jumped the gun" in encouraging him to proceed without receiving permission from the company or adequately considering the costs involved. As a result, Wilson hastily withdrew from the project. Meanwhile, Howes responded to Wilson with a terse statement pointing out that the pickup service was still experimental and that no request for its extension could be considered until a report had been made to the Congress after its first full year of operation. Because of his many contacts in Washington, Adams had consistently served as the company's representative in dealings with the Post Office Department, and it is easy to see how he may have assumed the right to act in this way without prior approval from Wilmington. Nevertheless, he was clearly out of line in acting without authorization from the board, and the entire episode could not help but embarrass everybody connected with it.[25]

Unfortunately, such experiences became all too typical. That du Pont himself was not immune from "jumping the gun" in matters involving Adams was indicated by his haste in lending credence to a report, which subsequently turned out to be erroneous, that Adams had demonstrated the pickup system at an air show in Clarksburg, West Virginia, after All American had declined to participate in the event because of the demands it would have placed upon its maintenance schedule. The incident, which led to an accusation by du Pont followed by an indignant denial by Adams, stemmed from a rumor started after a crowd had gathered at Clarksburg the day before the show to see a routine pickup by Rintoul, who had taken advantage of being ahead of schedule by landing for a few minutes to let the spectators admire his plane. Word of this occurrence got back to du Pont in garbled fashion through a chain of informants who were apparently aware of the company's decision not to take part in the show, were confused about the precise date of Rintoul's impromptu landing, and assumed that Adams had been the pilot. Du Pont apologized to Adams for making a false accusation, but the episode must have put his own credibility in the company's persisting dispute with the inventor at least temporarily in a bad light. "I am very sorry we went off half cocked on this," one of his informants stated in a subsequent note to du Pont, "and that our doing so resulted in embarrassment to you."[26]

Convinced that du Pont and his colleagues were trying to deprive him of his rightful stake in an enterprise he had created, Adams fought back by using the one remaining instrument that remained under his control: Tri-State Aviation. Because Adams's personal finances were as badly strained as ever in the summer of 1939, this enterprise, never robust to begin with, was operating on a shoestring and actually suspended operations by early September. This, however, did not prevent Adams from continuing to push for a certificate of public convenience and necessity from the Civil Aeronautics Authority. Indeed, it was of crucial importance for him to do so, for the continued existence of Tri-State provided the most likely means of securing a satisfactory financial settlement from Richard du Pont in the event that Adams felt obliged to withdraw from All American entirely. As previously noted, under the terms of their August 1938 agreement, du Pont had the option of taking control of Tri-State in two years by canceling Adams's debt and paying him an additional forty-five thousand dollars in cash. Adams therefore took care to pump enough money into Tri-State to keep it alive, at least on paper. Indeed, there is evidence that he did so in part at the cost of his stake in All American, disposing of stock in the latter corporation as his only way of raising the necessary funds.[27]

Although Tri-State had initially applied for certification in October 1938, its case did not come up for disposition until

September 21, 1939, when hearings began in Washington before CAA examiner Robert J. Bartoo. Possibly because of Tri-State's desperate financial plight, the application, which had originally called for the transport of both passengers and cargo, was restricted to cargo, and a number of the communities it had asked authority to serve were eliminated. The resulting scaled-down proposal involved three routes, permitting the company to convey cargo between Pittsburgh and Princeton, West Virginia, by way of Morgantown, Wheeling, Parkersburg, and Beckley; between Morgantown and Charleston by way of Clarksburg and Elkins; and between Morgantown and Baltimore by way of Cumberland, Maryland, and Martinsburg, West Virginia. Even in this limited form, however, the proposal was ultimately turned down by Bartoo on the grounds that the service performed by Tri-State during the specified grandfather period had been "inadequate and inefficient."[28]

Facing liquidation of a key bargaining weapon in his struggle with the group controlling All American, Adams appealed Bartoo's ruling on various grounds, including the examiner's alleged failure to recognize that Tri-State was entitled to special consideration by virtue of the fact that it was merely seeking to transport property, not passengers. This maneuver won Adams a long reprieve, for the case was not finally decided until July 1940. Meanwhile, as previously noted, he used Tri-State's continued existence, however dormant, as a means of filing exceptions to the ambitious proposals submitted to the CAA by All American in February of the same year. As Congressman Frank W. Boykin of Alabama reported to Delaware lawyer George T. Weymouth in a letter written early that month, Adams was using his formidable network of contacts in the national capital to the utmost in his struggle with All American and was even threatening to launch an antitrust suit against Richard and Felix du Pont. According to Boykin's chief informant, a young attorney in the Washington law firm of Cummings and Stanley, Adams had the support of his powerful fellow Kentuckian, U.S. Senator Alben W. Barkley, and was also enlisting the help of such notables as Hugo Black, Thomas ("Tommy the Cork") Corcoran, and Eleanor Roosevelt herself. So far as Boykin could learn, Adams's goal at this point was to secure the most favorable financial settlement possible from the du Ponts. The letter was accompanied by a reasonably accurate brief account of the difficulties that had arisen between Adams and All American, ending as follows:

> The obvious solution for the entire matter is for the du Ponts, as they themselves have previously suggested, to purchase Adams's remaining interest in the patent corporation [All American] and also take over the operating field claimed by his Tri-State Corporation. The amounts involved are not large, but the dispute is bitter. Much litigation over a number of years is inevitable because Dr. Adams's friends are determined to protect him. . . . The du Ponts should make an immediate settlement before the situation becomes more serious. They could settle the matter in such a way that they would benefit themselves greatly and allow themselves to proceed with their aviation plans and the development of All American Aviation Corporation. Richard and Felix du Pont have previously discussed terms of settlement and understand quite fully the situation.[29]

But the matter was not settled at this time, and the hearings, which finally came to an end on March 7, were marked by bitter exchanges between Wise, who handled the legal presentation for All American, and William L. Denning, counsel for Tri-State, during the cross-examination of Lytle Adams and Richard du Pont. Under Denning's questioning, du Pont explained the details of the agreement into which he and Adams had entered in August 1938, and the various stipulations governing the assignment of patents by Adams to him. Responding to questions apparently connected to the threats made by Adams regarding the possibility of an antitrust suit, du Pont denied that any of All American's stock was held by the Elton Investment Company, described by one reporter as "one of the bouquet of corporations used for various purposes separately by different combinations of members of the du Pont family." He also described in detail the various types of apparatus and procedures used by All American, stressed the wide diversity of situations in which these could be used, and emphasized the way in which certification and expansion of the pickup system could aid the national defense by serving as a training ground for pilots.

Hope that the CAA might be impressed by the need for permitting All American to carry passengers as well as mail and express was weakened when Robert Hazen, a senior air carrier inspector for the agency, testified that navigational aids along the routes served by the company were not adequate for such operations. But the firm had grounds for satisfaction in the way in which the hearing enabled its message to reach important potential constituencies: the proceeding was followed closely by representatives of large retail merchandising concerns because, as one account put it, "the decision may afford an answer to their need for swift distribution of small parcels in areas now difficult to reach." According to the same source, persons were on hand from such places as Chicago, Detroit, Milwaukee, St. Louis, Denver, and New Orleans, while telegraph companies, railroad lines, express carriers, and trucking firms were also watching developments closely.[30]

Bartoo presided over these deliberations, as he had over the earlier Tri-State proceeding. His withdrawal to consider the issues in private after the hearing ended was followed by an anxious period of waiting, which became steadily more ominous as weeks and months went by without any decision being announced. Under the terms of its contract with the Post Office Department, All American's authority to carry mail would expire on May 13, and as that date approached officials of the company prepared to suspend operations. A flickering hope came and went when postal officials called for bids on a new contract and then rescinded the advertisement forty-eight hours before the bids were to be opened when the move was "suddenly challenged on the ground that it favored All American and precluded competitive bidding." According to the official explanation, "The service is no longer an experiment and consequently bids for its continuation as an experimental service could not legally be asked under the terms of the law."[31]

On the very day of the contract's termination, Postmaster General James A. Farley sent a report to the Congress praising All American's record of operations and recommending that the service be continued permanently. Despite "one of the worst winters in recent years," he pointed out, the company had maintained regular schedules with an extremely high number of completed flights, sometimes providing mail service when no other modes of transport were available. Despite the mountainous terrain over which the firm's two routes passed, its planes had operated for a full year "without a single casualty," which Farley characterized as being "without precedent when all conditions are considered." He described patronage of the service as "good," and predicted that usage could be augmented if night delivery were employed to permit mail to be dispatched at the close of each business day, pointing out that All American had "proved conclusively the feasibility of night operations" in the experiments it had conducted late in 1939. It was a ringing endorsement, but the Congress had no time to act upon it because the company's operating authority had come to an end. That very afternoon the gull-winged Stinsons made their final runs and the service was indefinitely discontinued. Eight days later, on May 21, Bartoo's report was issued. It confirmed what leaders of the firm had come to expect; echoing one of the primary contentions advanced by Tri-State Aviation in the hearing that had taken place in February and March, it denied All American's proposals on the grounds that the CAA lacked specific jurisdictional authority over the type of operations the company was conducting.[32]

A headline in an unidentified newspaper issued at some point during the course of these events provided a fitting epitaph for the year of experimental operations that had just passed, particularly when read in connection with Farley's endorsement. "Success Kills U.S. Air Mail Pickup Service," it declared. Voicing its agreement with the postmaster general's views, the Tarentum, Pennsylvania, *Valley Daily News* expressed mingled hope and disappointment by saying that "we'll be longing for the day when the red airplanes will again streak across our sky with a mail sack trailing behind." This more nearly corresponded to the mood of All American's own management, which, refusing to credit intimations that the pickup service was dead, had retained much of the company's staff in the expectation that its aircraft would soon be flying again. Within a short time a group of pilots, including Ray Elder, Holger Hoiriis, Tommy Kincheloe, and Cammy Vinet, were fanning out over Pennsylvania, West Virginia, and upstate New York making route surveys and speaking to local organizations about the need to support a resumption of operations. Meanwhile, the enterprise was mobilizing its forces on a number of other fronts to reverse the direction of events and to upset the judgment rendered by Bartoo.[33] Whatever the vexations he had encountered in the past twelve months, Richard du Pont still clung to his visions of what All American could become. In the months and years ahead, the struggle would continue.

4 • "The Biggest Little Airline in the World"

For twelve months the diminutive, gull-winged Reliants of All American Aviation had been part of the rhythm of life in scores of communities in Pennsylvania, West Virginia, and Ohio. The familiar throb of the Stinsons' Lycoming radials came with such regularity that some residents claimed they could almost set their watches by it.[1] But the failure of the Congress to take timely action to amend the 1938 Experimental Air Mail Act, coupled with Robert J. Bartoo's negative CAA examiner's report, forced the company's flight operations into a protracted hiatus. At the same time, congressional friends of the airmail pickup mustered in Washington to map a strategy that would get All American back into the air.

Before the end of May 1940, four bills to reinstate the pickup were thrown into the legislative hopper. On the twentieth, a day before Bartoo's recommendation, Congressman James E. Van Zandt, a Republican from Altoona, Pennsylvania, submitted a measure, H.R. 9826, to authorize the postmaster general to extend the experimental airmail service until June 30, 1941. Three other bills, however, went farther than Van Zandt's proposal in amending the 1938 Civil Aeronautics Act to give the CAA specific jurisdiction over nonpassenger airline operations. Clarence F. Lea, a Democratic representative from California and chairman of the House Committee on Interstate and Foreign Commerce, introduced his proposal, H.R. 9899, on May 27. Two days later, Democratic Senator James H. Hughes of Delaware presented a similar bill, S. 4061, while Senator Pat McCarran of Nevada added his own, S. 4075, on May 31.[2]

With two bills before the House and two more shortly to be advanced in the Senate, backers of the airmail pickup sought concerted action. At the invitation of Congressman Andrew Edmiston, a West Virginia Democrat, lawmakers from seven states attended a dinner at the Mayflower Hotel on May 27 to consider how best to direct the legislative effort. Patrick J.

Boland, of Scranton, Pennsylvania, the House majority whip, warned that the congressmen must act quickly "or you're liable to run into a legislative jam," and Republican Congressman Thomas A. Jenkins of Ohio concurred on the need to "get this through." The conference broke up with an informal agreement to seek passage of the Lea bill. Other measures, including Van Zandt's, promised to provide only a stopgap solution to the problem.[3]

If popular opinion carried any weight, there was reason for optimism that there would be positive developments in Washington. The editors of the Warren, Pennsylvania, Times-Mirror urged local residents to "get busy" writing to the CAA and their congressman to urge quick renewal of the pickup service. On May 14, the Oil City chamber of commerce sent a telegram to Senator Joseph F. Guffey and Congressman Benjamin Jarrett stating that "the curtailment of this [service] has worked considerable hardship on the business, commercial, mercantile and industrial groups throughout northwestern Pennsylvania." The chamber called upon the legislators to intercede with the CAA "to get immediate action and have this service restored even if on a temporary basis." The New York Times ran an editorial that claimed the pickup offered "great convenience" to the localities it served. "It is highly desirable," the Times concluded, "to continue this interesting innovation in civil flying."[4]

Wayne Parrish, editor of American Aviation, closely monitored events in the capital. He condemned Bartoo's report as "a miscarriage of justice and an abuse of the responsibility of a public agency toward the public interest." It was, Parrish wrote, a "serio-comic passing of the old-fashioned buck" and a "farce in these days when the development of aviation should be of primary consideration." Parrish sat in on the Mayflower Hotel conference as a representative of All American Aviation and reported on progress toward restoration of the pickup service.[5]

In the meantime, All American did not stand idly by while the Congress deliberated its fate. Halsey R. Bazley, who had become the company's operations manager at Allegheny County Airport after serving as acting director of the Pennsylvania Division of Aeronautics until May 1939, viewed the grounding as an opportunity to survey the new routes he expected the firm to receive. All American pilots also did their part to drum up support for the pickup. Norm Rintoul took a Stinson to Washington's Bolling Field for demonstration pickups during the National Aviation Forum, May 26–29. Tommy Kincheloe and Cammy Vinet spoke to the Kiwanis and Rotary clubs in Franklin on May 29 before flying to Indiana, Pennsylvania, later in the day to explain to civic groups that public pressure would be needed to restore the service. Rotarians in Weston, West Virginia, heard similar speeches by Ray Elder and Holger Hoiriis, while other pilots visited Jamestown, New York, and Wilkes Barre, Pennsylvania.[6]

The smoldering feud between Adams and du Pont, however, blazed into the headlines and threatened to delay swift action on the Lea and Hughes bills. In an interview in the *Pittsburgh Press*, Adams complained that du Pont was trying "to drive me from the field of feeder air line development. . . . My patents have been taken over, my company has been bankrupted, my labors have been frustrated, and all my work designed to perfect air line operation where it may serve rural and small-town communities has been made to serve only the du Pont interests." Adams correctly understood that the August 1938 arrangement with du Pont had limited All American's patent rights to the pickup system while leaving him free to run Tri-State Aviation, the parent company. But as 1939 wore on, Adams found that Tri-State was competing with All American Aviation and that du Pont wanted to terminate the 1938 loan arrangement. Moreover, Adams found little sympathy for his position on All American's board of directors. In increasingly desperate financial straits and on the verge of losing complete control of his invention and company, Adams sought to block legislation that would give the CAA authority over the pickup system.[7]

Richard du Pont could not let Adams's accusations go unanswered, for the inventor still had allies on Capitol Hill. "For purposes of his own," du Pont said, "Dr. Adams has assumed the role of the poor inventor who was robbed by the rich man. I think that anyone who takes the time to investigate the facts will agree that he plays it with exceedingly ill grace." He added that All American's records were open to anyone who wanted to determine if Adams had been "cheated of his rights and interests." Regardless of the rights and wrongs of the controversy, Robert H. Hinckley, chairman of the CAA, perceived that its continuance would send negative signals to the Congress and might possibly have adverse effects on how the CAA viewed the certification question.[8]

As Adams and du Pont sparred in the press, the congressional mill ground away in Washington on legislation to establish the pickup on a permanent basis. Lea received assurances from Hinckley on June 5 that H.R. 9899 would clarify the responsibilities of the authority in regard to the issuance of a certificate of public convenience and necessity to All American. Following hearings, the House Committee on Interstate and Foreign Commerce reported out the bill with unanimous approval on June 11. Six days later, the lawmakers briefly discussed the proposed law. John Jennings, Jr., a Republican from Tennessee, objected that the committee hearings had not been published and insisted he would not vote on the bill until they were. Lea responded that because the committee had expressed unanimity there was no reason to print the hearings. Congressman Van Zandt called for immediate adoption of the bill in order to restore airmail service as soon as possible. On the other side of the Capitol, Hughes's bill, S. 4061, which had gained priority over McCarran's S. 4074, received favorable treatment in the Committee on Commerce and reached the Senate floor on June 18.[9]

From that point on, the legislation to resume the airmail pickup proceeded briskly. On June 21, the House passed the Lea bill and sent it to the Senate, which the next day dropped the Hughes bill and voted in favor of the House measure. After being initialled by the vice president and the speaker of the House, the bill went on June 26 to Franklin D. Roosevelt, who signed it into law on July 2. The act was brief but full of meaning for All American. It had two sections. The first amended the Civil Aeronautics Act to broaden the definition of air transportation to include nonpassenger airmail and express operations and to permit the Civil Aeronautics Board (not the CAA) to regulate such services. In the second section, the legislation repealed those portions of the Experimental Air Mail Act of 1938 that had given the postmaster general authority to establish and supervise the operations of All American. This removed the pickup from the experimental category and eliminated the jurisdictional problem between the CAA and the Post Office Department that had led to All American's grounding.[10]

It was now up to the new Civil Aeronautics Board to decide All American's application for permanent certification. In the interval while the Congress made up its mind on the airmail pickup, President Roosevelt had pushed through a reorganization proposal that divided up the various functions of the two-year-old Civil Aeronautics Authority. As of May 14, the CAA and its administrator fell under the Commerce Department, while its safety and economic regulatory responsibilities became the business of the Civil Aeronautics Board. The CAB was a largely independent body with broad powers over commercial air transport. No carrier could operate without approval from the board, which also exercised control over routes, tariffs, mergers, and many other aspects of airline operations. Roosevelt's reorganization had been highly controversial, and, with the establishment of the CAB, portended a long era of intense regulation for the airlines.[11] All American would have to adjust to this strict regulatory environment if it was to grow and prosper in the years ahead.

Bartoo again was the examiner assigned to All American's case by the CAB, and he listened once more to the company's request to carry mail, express, and eventually passengers over six new routes totaling more than eighteen hundred miles. He was impressed by All American's performance during the year of experimental airmail operations and recommended continuation of the pickup. "It appears . . . that it is important that both the technical and the commercial development of service of the type proposed by the applicant should continue," he wrote. He determined that the company had safely executed its responsibilities and had demonstrated commendable financial stability. Although mail loads had been light, there was reason to expect increased poundage once regular pickups and deliveries were under way. And the service to the isolated West Virginia communities was important, for the Mountain State suffered from inadequate surface transportation, particularly between Charleston and the county seats to the north. Bartoo concluded that no existing air carriers could duplicate what All American proposed to do.[12]

On the other hand, the CAB took exception to a number of points in All American's application. Bartoo could find no justification for the company's proposed Route C, between

Pittsburgh and Cleveland, two cities that were already well served by existing air and ground transportation. The Williamsport-to-New York and Philadelphia-to-New York links made little sense either, for both paralleled well-established air routes. All American's Jamestown-to-Buffalo extension to its proposed northerly route out of Pittsburgh found little favor, either, because it was too close to existing connections flown by through carriers. Combined passenger-pickup operations, which the company acknowledged were not yet out of the experimental stage, were rejected entirely. Bartoo doubted All American could meet the high safety standards required for flying passengers and thought that the frequent stops would obviate most of the advantages of the pickup system. He therefore rejected the firm's bid to fly passengers between Pittsburgh and Cleveland and between Pittsburgh and Buffalo.[13]

The CAB decided the case on July 22 and issued a certificate of convenience and necessity authorizing All American to fly mail and express over five routes, designated A.M.49 by the Post Office Department. Route 49A between Pittsburgh and Huntington, West Virginia, included nineteen stops and pickup points, among them Mount Pleasant and Connellsville, Pennsylvania, and Morgantown, Fairmont, Clarksburg, Buckhannon, Spencer, and Charleston, West Virginia. Route 49B proceeded out of Pittsburgh through Canonsburg and Washington, Pennsylvania, to Steubenville, Ohio. It then connected ten towns along the Ohio River before jogging northwestward from Gallipolis to Wellston, Ohio, then southwestward to Portsmouth, Ohio, and back up the river to the Huntington terminus. Route 49D stretched north from Pittsburgh to Jamestown, New York, connecting various communities including Natrona, Butler, Oil City, Corry, and Warren, Pennsylvania. On Route 49E, which linked Pittsburgh and Williamsport, were eleven pickup stations at such communities as Indiana, Punxsutawney, Du Bois, State College, and Lock Haven. The last route, 49F, cut across Pennsylvania from Pittsburgh to Philadelphia, with twenty-one intermediate points, among them Latrobe, Johnstown, Altoona, Huntingdon, Harrisburg, Gettysburg, York, Lancaster, Coatesville, West Chester, and Wilmington, Delaware. All American's new routes added up to 1,365 miles, connecting eighty-six cities and towns with a total population of nearly two million. In a press release, All American trumpeted the CAB's decision as the "greatest expansion in [the] nation's domestic air transportation system that has ever been authorized at any one time." The new routes made All American "the biggest little airline in the world."[14]

All American's certification and its new routes spelled defeat for Lytle S. Adams. His Tri-State Aviation had been one of four interveners in the case; the other three (TWA, Eastern, and Pennsylvania-Central) had sought unsuccessfully the preemptive right to develop feeder lines similar to those eventually awarded to All American. The validity of Adams's contention that the Civil Aeronautics Act did not confer authority on the CAB to regulate the pickup service had evaporated with approval of the July 2 act. Moreover, the board decided that it could not withhold certification from All American pending a final determination on the case involving issuance of a grandfather certificate to Tri-State. This would have included three routes: between Pittsburgh and Princeton, West Virginia; between Morgantown and Charleston, West Virginia; and between Morgantown and Baltimore. Adams had been forced to admit that Tri-State's service, which included six stops on All American's routes 49A and 49B, could not adequately meet the public need for air transportation in West Virginia.[15]

Less than a week after awarding the new routes to All American, the CAB ruled on Tri-State's application. Based on a clause in the Civil Aeronautics Act that permitted the board to grant certificates to those companies that had been engaged in air transportation during the so-called grandfather period, the board issued a certificate allowing Tri-State to fly passengers and express over its proposed Morgantown–Charleston and Morgantown–Baltimore routes. The July 31 decision, however, was a hollow victory for Adams and Tri-State. In denying the Pittsburgh traffic, it effectively crippled any hopes Adams may still have harbored for financial success. A proviso that Tri-State had to begin operations within four months of receipt of certification was an additional problem, for by this time financial events had caught up with Adams and made it impossible for him to meet the deadline.[16]

The reasons for this relate to Adams's final break with du Pont and a settlement of the August 16, 1938, agreement. Precisely when this occurred and under what circumstances are difficult to determine, but it seems Adams resigned as vice president of All American in June, and within two months, du Pont exercised his option to cancel the 1938 loan arrangement. Du Pont, in canceling the note, acquired 51 percent of Tri-State's voting stock and 40 percent of the company's nonvoting class A stock, giving him a controlling interest in the firm. In return, du Pont had to pay Adams forty-five thousand dollars. The Wilmington Trust Company had prepared a cashier's check for the appropriate amount, but Adams balked, demanding immediate payment in cash. Because it was already late in the afternoon when the two parties concluded the agreement, the trust company's vault was closed. After much scrambling about, bank officials gained access to the cash section of the vault and Adams received his payment in ten- and twenty-dollar bills. He threw the money into a cardboard box, placed it in the trunk of his car, and drove off. Tri-State, curiously, did not immediately cease to exist. For more than two years, the CAB held its certificate in abeyance, granting an exemption to the original 120-day ruling and following that with a series of actions that delayed the revocation of the company's certificate until January 16, 1943. During that interval, Adams complained that du Pont never attended meetings of the stockholders and refused to cooperate in any way with the functioning of the firm.[17] But Adams could not have been surprised, for du Pont had long since determined that Tri-State's interests were at variance with those of All American, and in any case, Adams himself had turned from the pickup to new endeavors that seemed more in tune with his restless, inquiring personality.

A lonely, disillusioned inventor hauling away the remains of his dreams in an old automobile evokes a sense of profound melancholy. Since at least 1923, Lytle S. Adams had pursued the pickup as a means of bringing the advantages of air transportation to the majority of the American people. He had shepherded his invention through years of development, had promoted it in public and private, and had, almost singlehandedly, won for it important congressional friends. But like many individuals with promising ideas, Adams stumbled when it came to the hardheaded financing and painstaking engineering needed for complete success and public acceptance of a new technology.

Despite this major disappointment, Adams's fertile mind hardly paused. After Pearl Harbor, he proposed a rotary incendiary bomb dispenser and interested the National Defense Research Committee in a bizarre plan to loose millions of bats with miniature incendiary bombs over Japan's congested urban centers. In 1951, he left Irwin and returned for a while to his dental surgery practice in Seattle. Finally, in 1960 he moved to Tucson, where, as a consultant to the University of Arizona, he worked to adapt his incendiary dispenser to scatter seed and fertilizer pellets over remote desert areas. He died in Tucson on December 29, 1970.[18]

Three awkward months of watchful waiting ended for All American Aviation on August 12, when it inaugurated permanent service. While All American's planes were grounded, du Pont had made the vital decision to keep the company's organization intact pending action in Washington. This cost money —nearly twenty thousand dollars—but it enabled the pickup service to recommence with a minimum of delay. There was agreement to start with routes 49A, 49D, and 49F, which, because they overlapped to a large extent the old experimental connections, involved the least preparation. Following ceremonies presided over by du Pont, three planes left Pittsburgh at eleven A.M. bound for Philadelphia, Huntington, and Jamestown. Almost simultaneously, one of the company's Stinsons took off from Philadelphia with the westbound mail. Du Pont then climbed aboard another aircraft with CAB and Post Office representatives and followed the regularly scheduled plane to Jamestown, observing pickups along the way. At Jamestown, where a municipal field had been built six years before in anticipation of attracting commercial air service, du Pont's entourage joined a group of five hundred persons who had gathered to watch the arrival of the first pickup plane. Du Pont used the occasion to extol the company's long-range plans for a combined passenger and pickup service that would truly bring the air age to Jamestown and similar communities.[19]

Service over the rest of the network did not start until later. On the morning of November 12, one of All American's Stinsons was cleared from Allegheny County Airport for Huntington, following Route 49B along the general course of the Ohio River. Flights over the Pittsburgh–Williamsport route (49E) began on December 2. Henry A. Wise, Jr., All American's secretary, joined Harry R. Stringer and other company representatives to greet the first morning arrival from Pittsburgh, which was more than two hours late due to the heavy volume of philatelic mail. West Newton and Masontown on Route 49A, Slippery Rock on 49D, and Blairsville, Portage, and Williamsburg on 49F had to wait until the summer of 1941 to receive service. By the end of 1940, though, All American had virtually its entire system functioning. Early morning departures from Pittsburgh and Philadelphia carried mail that had come in on the overnight transcontinental and trunk line flights, assuring same-day delivery at points on the company's routes. Afternoon pickups were timed so that mail arrived at Pittsburgh and Philadelphia for transfer to the major airlines and, in most cases, next-day delivery.[20]

Although the usual problems associated with surveying new territory and assembling the necessary organizational structure were factors in delaying the introduction of service on the Ohio Valley and central Pennsylvania routes, the major reason All American waited until later in the year was to have sufficient time to effect improvements to the pickup system. Pickups had hitherto been made by hand-winching down a fifty-foot cable with a grapple at the end. The plane flew down, the grapple engaged the transfer line strung between two thirty-three-foot steel poles, and the flight mechanic/mail clerk then winched in the cable, transfer line, and mail container. Deliveries were made by dropping the mail container attached to the end of a separate line. It was an adequate arrangement, but it left room for more development. The air-oil shock-absorbing mechanism required careful timing by the flight mechanic, while severe oscillations in the trailing cable caused by air turbulence demanded precision flying as the plane flashed over the ground apparatus. The permanent steel poles on the ground were not only expensive but posed a potential danger to the low-flying aircraft and could foul the cable and grapple.

In Wilmington the engineers at All American's Manufacturing Division vigorously attacked these problems and by the end of the summer of 1940 had devised a system that ameliorated most of them. Now the flight mechanic lowered a fifteen-foot retractable steel boom hinged at a point forward of the plane's

All American's engineers made further improvements to the pickup system in the summer of 1940. A major change was the use of a retractable steel boom attached to the left side of the Stinson fuselage. Carrying the pickup cable and incoming mailbag in a slot on its trailing edge, the boom helped eliminate oscillations and further enhanced the reliability of the airmail pickup system. Here the company's black, Wasp-powered Stinson makes a pickup using the new gear. The new system also featured shorter and lighter uprights, which could be set up more conveniently than previous poles. (77-14723, Smithsonian Institution)

center of gravity. A hook, replacing the grapple at the end of the pickup cable, slipped down a groove to the lower end of the boom in a manner not unlike how the leading edge of a sail slides into place in the mast of a boat. When any part of the boom struck the transfer line stretched between the poles, the line ran down to the end of the boom and into the hook, which dropped off the boom along with the pickup cable. The cable, transfer line, and mail container were then reeled aboard. In place of the hand-cranked winch was an electrically operated one that incorporated an automatic energy-absorption mechanism. At the instant the hook engaged the transfer line, the winch freely

An electrically powered winch replaced the old hand-cranked unit following the 1940 revisions to the pickup system. Located on the left side of the cabin above and forward of the hatch, the winch greatly eased the flight mechanic's work load. (87-2473, Smithsonian Institution)

turned one complete revolution, paying out the pickup cable. Then a nut tightened a brake against the reel until it stopped turning, the electric motor took over, the winch reversed, and the cable was drawn in. To effect deliveries, the pilot pulled a switch that released the container and its transfer line from a point near the end of the retractable boom.

On the ground there were now two twenty-foot poles, with bamboo extensions resembling fishing rods fixed to their tops. Instead of being permanently sunk in concrete, the poles were attached to aluminum bases. They could be erected within a few minutes and when not in use were stored in a specially designed box. Because the boom largely eliminated the perturbations of the pickup cable generated by air turbulence, the poles could be set only twenty feet apart and still provide more margin for error by the pilot than the former setup. With the updated system, pickups rarely required more than one pass, and that could be at speeds of 110 miles per hour, in comparison to the previous 90 mile per hour limit. The more efficient shock-absorbing equipment and the electrically powered winch boosted the normal load capacity from twenty to fifty pounds. A radio set in the mail messenger's vehicle provided more convenient updates on flight schedules than the previous telephone-telegraph network, and a radio-equipped truck permitted emergency repairs in the field.

Though vastly improved, the system was not without shortcomings. The retractable steel boom was prone to aerodynamic flutter when fully extended, which excessively stressed the airframe. Fitted with a wooden airfoil on its leading edge, the arm vibrated less, but the problem was never entirely eliminated. Winch operation, though less complex, still was not fully automatic, for the flight mechanic had to make a manual inspection before switching it on to reel in the cable. This was intended as a fail-safe procedure to ensure that no part of the cable or hook fouled any part of the aircraft, but it required careful coordination between the pilot and the flight mechanic to guarantee a smooth pickup. A number of years passed, too, before the mail containers—which pilots usually saw well before the pickup poles—were painted a bright orange to increase their visibility.[21]

By November 1941, All American had installed the booms and electric winches in its aircraft and had replaced the old ground stations along its five routes with the new portable apparatus. Du Pont stressed that the investment, which amounted to more than sixty-five thousand dollars, would be offset by enhanced safety and by the capability of picking up increased loads at greater speeds. This underscored his goal of reducing operating costs and making the most efficient use of the company's equipment. There was little fat in All American's front offices, either; du Pont emphasized that managerial-level personnel received salaries no higher than six thousand dollars per year.[22] During All American's first year of operations after permanent certification, du Pont strove with considerable success to nurture the little airline through adolescence into a profitable maturity.

The CAB's award to All American was fundamental to the company's financial well-being, but it also revealed the economic limitations of the pickup operation. Airmail pay, according to critics, exceeded postal revenues and forecast perpetual subsidy for the pickup airline. Furthermore, the high cost tended to create uncertainties about the alacrity with which the CAB would proceed in granting certification for additional pickup routes—both to All American and to newcomers who had filed applications in Washington. Others defended the economics of the service. Congressman Jennings Randolph argued that the pickup had reached the point by 1941 "where it can be considered self-supporting insofar as its direct cost to the Federal Government is involved." He showed that airmail volume had increased markedly and calculated that the postal revenues exceeded costs by as much as five thousand dollars monthly. And that, he emphasized, did not include such indirect costs to the government as airways and airports, which the pickup obviated to a great degree.[23]

The fact remains, however, that profits in commercial air transportation were still largely determined by government financial support. Even the most efficiently run passenger carriers in the late 1930s and early 1940s relied upon mail payments—in effect a federal subsidy—to make up for losses. For All American, which had no passenger revenue, mail compensation was vital. On December 9, 1940, the company requested a hearing from the Civil Aeronautics Board to fix its rate of mail pay. During hearings in February and March 1941, the board's examiner heard All American's argument for a rate of forty-nine cents per revenue mile, which the firm expected would offset its considerable investment in establishing routes and developing equipment. The board finally determined on September 29 that, because the pickup was still in the early stages of evolution and revenues were difficult to predict, two rates were called for. From August 12, 1940, to August 31, 1941, All American would receive reimbursement at a base rate of forty-six cents per aircraft mile. Thenceforth, the rate fell to forty cents per mile, computed on a point-to-point basis for each flight and payable in monthly allotments. Later the CAB increased this to forty-two cents to cover the costs of the company's ground messenger service. Payments began before the end of October, and by the first week of November, All American had received most of the $387 thousand owed to it since the start of permanent service.[24]

Additional income for the company derived from air express. During the year of experimental operations, and before its status as a common carrier had been finally determined, All American had not actively sought this business. The CAB's July 22 ruling, however, eliminated any doubt about the advisability of doing so, and the company negotiated a contract with the Railway Express Agency, Inc. Under the terms of the agreement, All American received 15 percent of shipping charges for items issued from points on its own routes, plus a percentage based proportionately on total shipping distance. For goods originating off-line, REA paid the company only at a rate calculated on the percentage of total distance. Because express often included such fragile merchandise as phonograph records, eggs, flowers, and even baby chickens, it was necessary to use small parachutes for deliveries. Express began on Route 49E, Pittsburgh to Williamsport, on January 6, 1941, and was introduced on All American's other four routes later in the year.[25]

It was not enough for Richard du Pont to establish a young corporate identity on a profitable basis in an industry still fraught with considerable uncertainty. While overseeing the creation of new routes, the development of an improved pickup system, and finalizing arrangements for mail and express payments, du Pont kept an eye to the future. Almost since the start of experimental operations in 1939, he had envisioned an era when feeder lines would generate much of the traffic flown by the major trunk carriers. To ensure that it benefited from the boom in feeder lines forecast by du Pont, All American staked its claim before the CAB in 1940 and 1941 to serve hundreds of communities in the Middle Atlantic region and New England.

On September 23, 1940, All American applied for connections to seven new points in Pennsylvania and West Virginia located almost directly on its existing lines. An eighth community, the university town of Athens, Ohio, separately petitioned the CAB for approval of service. The board on August 14, 1941, approved the addition of Lewistown, Carlisle, and Shippensburg to Route 49F, while denying the other four points. All American inaugurated service to the three Pennsylvania towns by November 1941.[26]

Far more ambitious was All American's petition filed before the CAB in March 1941 to add six new arteries to its already far-flung route structure. Two of these would link New York City and Boston—one by way of New London, Connecticut, and thirty-three intermediate points, and the second by way of Greenfield, Massachusetts, with thirty-one pickup stations. Another route connected New York and Syracuse through twenty-eight intermediate points along the Mohawk Valley, while a fourth joined these two cities via Binghamton, Elmira, and twenty-two other localities. A fifth route was to connect Harrisburg and New York City by way of Williamsport and twenty-nine other communities in northeastern Pennsylvania and northern New Jersey. The company also planned to join Harrisburg and New York City by way of twenty-six intermediate points in south-central Pennsylvania and southern New Jersey. All told, the routes connected 175 cities and towns.[27]

All American followed up its New York and New England application with requests to the CAB for an even greater expansion of the pickup network. Specifically, the company filed to add sixty-four communities to its existing five routes radiating from Pittsburgh. Bradford and Kane, Pennsylvania, and Olean and Salamanca, New York, applied independently to be included in All American's system. Later in 1941, the company asked to connect Williamsport and Harrisburg and to extend its present Pittsburgh to Jamestown route to include Erie. Both requests were made in order to provide morning trunk line connections on routes 49D, 49E, and 49F, over which it had not always been able to guarantee next-day deliveries to major cities. Three new routes proposed by All American stretched from Pittsburgh to Cincinnati, through Columbus and sixteen other points in Ohio; from Pittsburgh to Columbus, with nineteen pickup stations in between; and from Jamestown to Buffalo, by way of sixteen communities in northwestern Pennsylvania and western New York.[28]

While planning for the future, du Pont and All American Aviation could not ignore the present. On August 12, 1941, the company completed its first year of operations following certification. Congressman Randolph reported with some paternal pride that All American's planes had logged nearly 700 thousand miles, completing 92 percent of their scheduled flights, and making more than thirty-two thousand pickups. As the flight activity went up, the company added four SR-10Cs to its fleet and set up an aircraft overhaul operation at the Manufacturing Division in Wilmington. Despite such considerable investment —and remarkably, given the relative youth of the firm and the unusual nature of its business—All American earned a small profit, $3,824.17, at the end of its first fiscal year, June 30, 1941. Profits are, of course, better than losses, but the company's current ratio (the ratio of current assets to current liabilities), an index to its financial health, was a disturbing −.81, indicating an immediate need for new capital. In October, brokers in New York and Philadelphia announced the imminent sale of twenty thousand shares of class A stock at four dollars a share.[29]

Flight operations in 1940–1941 were typical of the intensity that everyone came to expect after the airline received certification. All American's Air Transport Division offices in a wing of the art deco glazed-brick terminal building at Pittsburgh's Allegheny County Airport were busy six days a week. Radio operators monitored flights throughout the system, keeping a log of the position of each plane on horizontal strips of paper affixed to a flight-following board. Four inches of the strip were the equivalent of one-hour's flight time; by using this as a benchmark, the radio operators could pinpoint a plane's location on any of the routes fanning out from Pittsburgh. Once a year, the company required the radio operators to fly the entire route system in order to familiarize themselves with current flight conditions. Dispatchers at Allegheny County Airport kept track of plane movements, fuel loads, weights and balances, weather, and local and en route field conditions. No flight left until the dispatcher and the pilot agreed that it should proceed.

Under these circumstances, All American's mileage soared from 28,586 in August 1940 to 60,009 in December 1940 and to 73,191 in October 1941. The increase in mail poundage was even more dramatic—going up from 5,304 pounds in August 1940 to more than 17,000 pounds by the end of 1941. Air express, starting with more than 3,000 pounds in January 1941, fluctuated widely, but by the end of the year it was averaging close to the January figure.[30]

Meanwhile, All American's pilots and flight mechanics were out on Route 49. Most of the time they flew "contact"; that is, under visual flight rules. When the ceiling fell, they dropped close to the ground, skimming the ridges and making their way along rivers and streams. Etched in the fliers' memories were key landmarks—a barn, a radio tower, a road junction—that led to their destination, which could be an airport, a cemetery, a park, or merely a farmer's field. Veteran pilots devised their own navigational tricks. They constantly checked and reset their altimeters using the height of known topographical features as reference points, for an error of only a few feet could spell disaster in this kind of flying. Pilot Lloyd C. Santmyer was particularly innovative. A native of Greensburg, Pennsylvania, Santmyer joined the firm in December 1940 following employment successively as a pilot and mechanic at Latrobe, a stint as test pilot during the development of an instrument-landing system for the Bureau of Standards, and, briefly, service as a copilot for Pennsylvania-Central Air Lines. He developed a method of ridge hopping in bad weather whereby he headed for a landmark at a specific altitude, then pulled up into the overcast while timing his duration with a watch before descending into the valley beyond. When visibility was bad in the West Virginia hills on Route 49A, Santmyer used the radio interference hum of high-tension power lines as a makeshift airway between pickup points. He also found that the distinctive radio noise from the Delco power plants of most small towns made them convenient marker beacons in poor weather.[31]

Flying the pickup routes was rarely routine, and that was a

great deal of its attraction to the professional pilot. It demanded an aviator with a style and spirit that harkened back to the adventurous birdmen of the romantic era of flight before World War I. No one embodied that esprit more than All American's veteran pilot, Tommy Kincheloe. Coming into Allegheny County Airport one evening in the spring of 1941, he suddenly encountered weather conditions so bad that the Pittsburgh controllers had to hold all incoming traffic pending clearance for instrument landings. The controllers radioed Kincheloe to hold at the Highland Park Bridge up the Allegheny River some distance from downtown. Within minutes, complaints came into All American's offices of a plane flying under the bridge. Kincheloe later clarified the situation: "The top of the Bridge was in the soup and we were told to stay [in] contact. Besides, I didn't want to get into the overcast with all the airliners. The tower told me to hold at the Bridge, and hold at the Bridge I did. I don't know what the problem is—there's plenty of room between the pilings, and I stayed legal." On another occasion, an All American pilot was told that he would have to land at an alternate field because the ceiling was too low at his primary destination. The flier radioed back to ask for the ceiling. When the tower answered that it was 250 feet, the pilot responded: "Good Lord, if I ever got up that high I'd need oxygen."[32]

Flight crews quickly established a special rapport with ground personnel along the airmail route. Virginia Arnal was the mail messenger at Canonsburg, Pennsylvania, in the early 1940s. She recalled lighting kerosene lamps to help guide the pickup pilots in foggy weather. In West Virginia, a morning flight dropped a dime and a note asking for two soft drinks; when they made the return pickup they found two bottles of Coca Cola. In another instance, a flight mechanic delivered a message asking his grandmother to come out to see the next day's pickup. She did so, waving as the Stinson swept overhead. When the mechanic reeled in the mail container, he found it held a freshly baked peach pie, which he and the pilot hungrily consumed as they completed the leg to Huntington.[33]

All American's fliers came to have a particular regard for Mildred Albertson, or "Millie" as she was almost universally known. Millie Albertson was the wife of a farmer and lived between the pickup stations at Coatesville and West Chester,

Pennsylvania. She watched the Reliants fly low over her house on their twice-daily rounds and in 1942 began to listen to the chatter on her radio, which had an aircraft band. None of this was especially extraordinary until one afternoon it became apparent to her that neither the Wilmington nor the Philadelphia control towers could establish radio contact with All American pilot Junius M. ("Toby") West. Because Albertson could hear both the pilot's and the towers' transmissions, and recognizing that the rapidly deteriorating weather presented a possibly dangerous situation, she immediately telephoned Wilmington. The controllers were then able to radio instructions to West that enabled him to find the airport and land safely. On his next flight, West dropped a note thanking Albertson for her help. Thereafter, Millie became the guardian angel of the airmail pickup, and All American flight crews referred to her ground position as "Station 13."[34]

Mishaps were inevitable given the circumstances under which All American's planes flew and the type of service they provided. No mail containers were lost during this period, but ground messengers sometimes had to comb the underbrush near the pickup sites for those that overshot the mark. Richard du Pont himself headed a search at Wilmington for a container that fell into the Delaware River instead of the field near the city's marine terminal; it turned up in the water two and a half miles upstream, carried there by the tide. Near Pitcairn, Pennsylvania, the mail fell on a farmer's field and it took a group of Boy Scouts, farm workers, and airline people four hours to find it. Late in 1941, en route westbound from Williamsport to Pittsburgh on 49E, one of All American's crews ran into a blizzard. They turned back toward Williamsport but had to make an emergency landing at Bellefonte under appalling conditions. As the Stinson touched down, its wheels suddenly broke through a hard crust covering five inches of snow, stuck fast, and the plane nosed over. Luckily neither the pilot nor the flight mechanic was injured, and damage to the aircraft amounted to only several hundred dollars.[35]

That there were not more such incidents was a tribute to the skill of All American's flight crews and the thoroughness of the company's planning and preparation for the pickup. In a letter to All American's shareholders on November 7, 1941, Richard du

Pont looked confidently ahead to improving the firm's "position as a leader in this type of service" and to a time when it would "become an important factor in the commercial evolution of air transportation."[36] Yet only a month would pass before he and others in the company had to readjust their priorities in the face of the whirlwind that came out of the western Pacific and plunged the United States into global conflict. All American would have to direct its limited resources toward the war effort, and, temporarily at least, suspend du Pont's vision of a nation-wide pickup system.

5 • The Pickup Goes to War

There was a measure of optimism in 1941 that Britain and the Soviet Union, with American material assistance, could halt the Nazi steamroller in Europe and that the United States would be able to avoid war. Yet as events in the Far East lurched from crisis to crisis, thoughtful Americans had to concede that their country might well be drawn into an armed conflict with Japan. Even the most perceptive among them, however, were unprepared for the blow that came on December 7, when a Japanese carrier force launched a surprise strike against Pearl Harbor. The dawn assault crippled the American battle fleet and forever shattered any hope that the nation could somehow stay out of the conflict. All American Aviation, like the rest of the country's aeronautical industry, was drawn into the struggle and forced to adjust to the exigencies of the national emergency.

The war brought both opportunities and challenges to All American. Mail volume went up in proportion to the communication needs of the armed forces, while new points were added to the company's routes. An army cargo contract led to the acquisition of more planes and the establishment of a military operations base at Harrisburg. The company also signed an agreement to train army pilots, and its Manufacturing Division, which in 1943 became the Manufacturing and Development Division, worked out improvements to the pickup system that had important military applications. But these additional activities imposed enormous strains on the young corporation. Maintenance required innovative procedures as All American endeavored to keep its aging Stinsons in the air; key personnel were lost to the military services at the same time the company's manpower requirements went up. The board of directors fretted about the tenuousness of the firm's capital assets and worked ceaselessly to bolster them to deal with rising expenses and overhead. For some companies, the war signaled an end to hard times and was a springboard for expansion. For All American, it involved the sacrifice, albeit only for a relatively short time, of its long-range goal of bringing the benefits of the air age to the masses of the American people.

Although statistics cannot give an accurate picture of the magnitude of All American's commercial operations during the war, they do give some sense of how hard everyone in the company worked to cope with the demand for airmail and express service. The Post Office Department decreed shortly after Pearl Harbor that the domestic airmail postage rate for all items to and from military personnel would be six cents per ounce. Attracted by the inexpensive rate, more people sent mail by air. As a consequence, All American's monthly mail volume went up from 16,435 pounds in January 1942 to 24,758 pounds by the beginning of 1943, a 51 percent increase. By December 1943, the monthly total reached 53,001 pounds, an increase of 114 percent over that of January 1942. Monthly mail poundage, which had averaged 56,765 up to June 30, 1944, reached nearly 81,000 by June 30, 1945. Average mail volume per flight, which was 41.9 pounds in 1941, went up to 61.3 pounds in 1942, 89.6 pounds in 1943, 147.5 pounds in 1944, and 173.3 pounds in 1945. Annual revenue miles flown rose from 812,862 at the end of June 1942 to 943,627 on June 30, 1943, and broke the million-mile-per-year watershed before June 30, 1944.[1]

A sense of purpose permeated the atmosphere at Allegheny County Airport as workers at All American's Air Transport Division strove to speed the flow of mail and express over the company's sprawling route network. Most of the responsibility for this devolved upon Hal Bazley, who in the early spring of 1942 advanced to vice president in charge of operations. He assumed the vacated board seat of Jim Ray, who had left the company in December 1941 to assume a position with Southwest Airways in Fort Worth, Texas. Bazley's burden was somewhat eased by the assignment of Harry Stringer as vice president for traffic, advertising, and public relations. But everyone felt the pressure as they labored to expand mail and express service amid conflicting wartime priorities for people and planes. As did other airlines, All American endured losses to the military of key maintenance, operations, and clerical workers, whose places more often than not were taken by women. Particularly missed were the abilities of veteran pilots Cammy

Vinet, Ambrose Banks, and Lloyd Santmyer, who were called to active duty with the army air forces. Nevertheless, employment at the division kept pace with the need, growing to 150 by the spring of 1944. In contrast, the numbers of aircraft available to fly the mail were severely circumscribed—the fleet numbered eight in 1942, and expanded to only eleven by the middle of 1945.[2]

These aircraft and their young, dedicated flight crews accomplished some remarkable feats. An All American Stinson made eighteen pickups in seventeen minutes at Corry, Pennsylvania, where Air Associates, Inc., had a plant that manufactured small parts for aircraft instruments. By the end of 1942, it was not unusual for planes to make thirty pickups daily at Corry. In addition, company personnel performed various emergency services. Pilot Ray Elder in February 1942 spotted a house on fire near Gallipolis, Ohio, and radioed Pittsburgh to have ground personnel notify the proper emergency authorities. Later, Elder led an army fighter pilot to safety at Allegheny County Airport after he had become lost and was close to making a forced landing. When a man became stranded by ice in the Susquehanna River at New Cumberland in January 1945, pilot Harvey Thompson and flight mechanic Julio Verez flew to the scene and dropped a life jacket and rope to him. Later in the year, one of the company's planes delivered serum to Grove City for an emergency rabies treatment.[3]

Because of the relative paucity of aircraft, scheduling and maintenance became vital. In 1943, All American added second daily flights on routes 49D (Pittsburgh to Jamestown, New York) and 49E (Pittsburgh to Williamsport). A year later, the Post Office permitted the company to put second round-trips on routes 49A (Pittsburgh to Huntington, West Virginia) and 49B (Pittsburgh to Huntington by way of the Ohio Valley). The additional flights allowed All American to use its small complement of planes to best advantage. Under most circumstances, eight Stinsons (refinished in 1943–1944 in silver with blue and red trim) were kept in the air, while two underwent service and overhaul in the hangar and shops at Pittsburgh. The eleventh plane, an SR-10E with a more powerful Lycoming engine, was used for executive transport. About thirty people worked in All American's maintenance department. They overhauled aircraft at 4,500-hour intervals, the complete job involving stripping off the old fabric and replacing it, along with all major parts. Engines, hydraulic systems, propellers, and instruments received attention every 450 hours. Complete engine rebuilds occurred at specified intervals; some of the older Stinsons in the fleet had up to thirty-five engine replacements or rebuilds. The engine mechanics, according to Walter Sartory, a maintenance clerk and photographer with the company during the pickup years, "knew more about [the engines] than Lycoming, and knew more about the limits to which those engines could be pushed." With a small office force, All American's maintenance supervisor, Edward D. Musser, kept track of an inventory of more than eight thousand spare parts and coordinated maintenance schedules with an ingenious master-card file on each airplane. The procedure was important in meeting the arduous requirements of wartime operations.[4]

To enhance operational efficiency still further, All American added new pickup points to its current routes. The Civil Aeronautics Board's decision not long after Pearl Harbor to postpone all new route hearings forced the airline's prewar applications into a holding pattern. It did not, however, preclude consideration of additional service on the routes already being flown. On December 18, 1942, All American received permission to restore service at Nitro, West Virginia, which had earier been temporarily suspended. The CAB followed this on August 31, 1943, when it granted service to Ripley, West Virginia, located on Route 49A between Spencer and Charleston. All American began pickups at Ripley on September 27 with ceremonies that included the mayor, the postmaster, and members of business and civic organizations. Athens, Ohio, which had been denied the pickup by the CAB in August 1941, learned on April 27, 1944, that it would be included as an intermediate point on Route 49B. On the first day of service, May 15, All American picked up more than ten thousand pieces of mail at Athens—a record for inaugural flights up to that time and an impressive indication of popular enthusiasm for the pickup.[5]

The extension of Route 49F to Washington, D.C., in January 1944 gave All American access to a critically important metropolitan center that would play a key role in its corporate future. Service to the national capital came about through an unusual combination of circumstances. Fearing an accident at the munitions storage depot at Fort Mifflin adjacent to Philadelphia Municipal Airport, the CAB on December 23, 1943, closed the field to all but absolutely essential military traffic. Deprived of its eastern terminus, All American quickly shifted flights on Route 49F to Wilmington and fowarded mail to other points by rail—an unsatisfactory and time-consuming procedure. To obviate this, the company petitioned the CAB to designate Washington as its new eastern terminus, where direct connections could be made with the major trunk carriers; meanwhile, airmail service to Philadelphia could be resumed using the city's new Northeast Airport, whose runways, although too short for larger planes, were adequate for All American's Reliants. The CAB agreed to this proposal on January 11, 1944, and twenty-four hours later, Captain Roy Weiland landed at Philadelphia, took on a load of mail, and flew on to Washington's National Airport. The CAB's ban deprived Philadelphia of a passenger air connection until improvements at Northeast made possible limited service in June 1945, at which time All American reestablished its regular routes and schedules. The episode demonstrated the flexibility of the company's operations, and, for a time at least, raised its visibility in Washington, where federal bureaucrats pulled the regulatory strings that ultimately determined the firm's success or failure.[6]

Pilots and flight mechanics on Route 49, who seemed daily to tempt fate, had compiled an enviable safety record since they began flying pickups in 1939. But as their flight time piled up, especially when crews were permitted to be in the air ninety hours a month, the odds finally caught up with them. On April 12, 1943, pilot Russ Crow, accompanied by flight mechanic Ed Louden and Dick Bazley, a mechanic trainee and son of Hal Bazley, flew into a severe downdraft while crossing the mountains near Port Royal, Pennsylvania. Crow fought the plane through the turbulence to a crash landing in the scrub oak on the side of Tuscarora Mountain. The crew escaped without injury, and the cargo was unharmed, but the plane was badly damaged and it took considerable time to haul it down from the heights.[7]

Bad weather was a major factor in All American's next accident, too. Pilot Thomas E. Bryan and flight mechanic Victor J. Gasbarro had just made a pickup at Chambersburg late in the afternoon on October 25, 1943, and were headed toward Gettysburg. Bryan ascended through the low overcast to thirty-five hundred feet and timed a passage over the ridges separating the two communities, only to have his calculations thrown off by an extreme crosswind. As he let down, the two-thousand-foot eminence of Piney Mountain suddenly appeared through the gloom. At the last instant, Bryan pulled up, and the Stinson cut a half-mile swath through the thick underbrush, coming to rest with its starboard wing completely severed and the engine torn loose from its mounts. Bryan had a broken foot and Gasbarro a badly lacerated forehead. The two crawled from the demolished plane and found their way to a hunting cabin early the next morning. They took turns scouting the area looking for help, until they were finally found by a state police patrol late in the afternoon of the twenty-sixth. Gasbarro survived another accident a year later. He and pilot Millard Lossing were tracing the course of the Juniata River in a snowstorm when they slammed into a high-tension line that had been strung without their knowledge. The impact smashed the windshield and damaged the plane's control cables, but they managed to nurse the craft safely back to Pittsburgh.[8]

Despite such close calls, no All American fliers had yet been killed or seriously injured, and no mail had been lost. The string finally ran out on August 3, 1944. Climbing out from Yorkville, Ohio (the pickup point for Wheeling, West Virginia, and Bridgeport, Ohio) in a thick fog, a Stinson piloted by Gerald E. ("Red") Lindemuth of Vandergrift, Pennsylvania, hit a tree, plunged into a wooded hillside, and burst into flames. Flight mechanic Ralph Monaco was hurled from the aircraft on impact and sustained a severe hip injury, while Lindemuth, trapped in the wreckage, finally freed himself and clawed his way to safety with two broken ankles and a broken leg. Lindemuth and Monaco recovered, but the bulk of the mail was lost along with the airplane.[9]

Pilot Wilson A. Scott became All American's first fatality in an accident at State College, Pennsylvania, on September 29, 1944. A graduate of Parks Air College in St. Louis, Scott joined the firm in August 1942 as a flight instructor and flew military cargo before changing to mail flights. When the pickup cable parted on Scott's first pass over the field, he circled back to drop the broken segment and apparently let the plane's speed fall off. The Stinson stalled and crashed into a tree, killing Scott and badly hurting flight mechanic Robert H. Taylor. All American had completed nearly 3.7 million miles of airmail pickups before the mishap. The grim toll, however, did not end with Scott's death. On January 10, 1945, pilot Albert E. Holstrum, Jr., crashed his Stinson after an attempted pickup at Greensburg had fouled the plane's landing gear. The aircraft apparently stalled while Holstrum was turning to make an emergency landing. Suffering numerous broken bones and internal injuries, he died on January 12 at Westmoreland Hospital. Cecil Lingar, the flight mechanic, though also badly hurt, recovered. Inexperience with the pickup—Scott had flown it for a little more than two months, and Holstrum had come to All American only on November 8, 1944, after working for TWA and Monarch Air Service—may have been a contributing factor in the accidents, but it also seems that equipment failure played a part. In any case, the two deaths, coming in relatively quick succession, pointed up that flying the pickup line was still a risky occupation.[10]

All American's contribution to the war effort included arrangements with the army air forces to provide badly needed services during the critical early phases of the conflict. In July 1942, the company reached an agreement with the Air Transport Command to fly military cargo. Because the main operations base at Allegheny County Airport could not handle the resulting additional workload, All American leased facilities at Harrisburg State Airport in New Cumberland and assigned Norm Rintoul to get things going. All American's Air Transport Division acquired four Stinson SR-10Cs (or C-81s, as designated by the army) to fulfill the requirements of the cargo contract, but with this limited number of planes, it was necessary to transfer equipment from the company's already overburdened airmail operations. Later in 1942, the purchase of a Stinson SR-9 allowed one of the airmail planes to return to Route 49. By March 1943, the equipment situation had stabilized, and All American had seven planes flying military cargo over routes designated by the army.[11]

Before the army cargo contract ran out on July 15, 1944, All American had lived up to its slogan, "The Airway to Everywhere." Under the management of William B. ("Bill")

Moore and later Foster ("Foss") Thomas at Harrisburg, the firm's planes, painted olive drab for the ATC duties, flew a seven-day-a-week schedule, delivering nearly two-and-a-half million pounds of material from North Carolina to Maine. All American was guaranteed a profit of $10.00 per day per plane (later increased to $21.25 per day per plane), but the contract, despite its rewards, generated concern in the boardroom, particularly in arranging loans to buy additional equipment.[12]

The need for transport pilots and aircraft mechanics reached such proportions in 1942 that the army air forces turned to the scheduled airlines for assistance in their instruction. All American responded in August 1942 by instituting training programs at its Wilmington base. To get started, the company's board approved the lease of a Link trainer and other ground facilities and the purchase of two Piper J-5 Cub Cruisers and a Stinson SR-6. In addition to instruction in instrument flying and other skills, All American established a transition course at Harrisburg where its own pilots received training on twin-engine Lockheeds. Richard du Pont believed this was important, not only to meet immediate requirements but because "twin engine equipment will be used in the future, and the company must prepare itself so as to be capable of operating such equipment." Graduates from All American's flight training courses went on to Air Transport Command jobs, flying cargo and personnel throughout the world. At Harrisburg, too, the company began an instruction program for aircraft and engine mechanics in February 1943 that was capable of graduating five hundred trainees a month.[13]

Those engaged in the delivery of vitally needed military air cargo and the instruction of pilots and technicians received well-deserved praise for their part in the war effort. But possibly the most dramatic direct benefit came from All American's continued development of the pickup system and its adaptation to military uses. Despite the progress made before the war in improving the airborne and ground pickup apparatus, the company's Manufacturing and Development Division at Wilmington kept working on refinements. Among these was a tapered pickup boom made of ash to replace the one made of steel. The new boom was mounted farther forward on the fuselage, featured a more robust retracting mechanism, and exhibited less aerodynamic flutter than the old boom. Equally significant was the modification of the entire system to handle appreciably greater loads.[14]

Du Pont was the driving force behind the rapid advances in upgrading the lifting capacity of the pickup equipment that were made by the company's Wilmington division. As an experienced glider pilot, du Pont had closely followed the Germans' employment of these aircraft in the invasion of the Low Countries in the spring of 1940 and later in the swift takeover of the island of Crete in May 1941. He initiated experiments at Wilmington to determine if the pickup system could be used to tow gliders. A Piper J-3 Cub was modified to a glider configuration with its engine and propeller removed. Du Pont himself sat in the cockpit of the improvised glider for the first tests on September 23, 1941, while Cammy Vinet flew the pickup plane. The problem of shock absorption that had plagued the pickup in its early days resurfaced when the transfer line snapped on three attempts to snatch the glider aloft. Overnight, engineers produced a new line made of undrawn nylon that had far superior elasticity, and on the twenty-fourth the motorless Cub soared into the air behind the Stinson towplane.[15]

After Pearl Harbor, military authorities took a closer look at gliders for airborne assault and were quickly attracted to the possible applications of All American's pickup system. At Wilmington, du Pont made further successful glider pickups in May 1942 and followed them on June 4 and 5 with a demonstration before army air forces officers at Wright Field in Dayton, Ohio. More important was a series of tests at Wilmington on July 28, during which the towplane, making successive passes, picked up two gliders, each carrying three men. Among those present were the commanding officers of the army Airborne and Troop Carrier commands, both of whom were impressed by the potential shown by the company's pickup experiments.[16]

It was, however, necessary to augment the capacity of the pickup gear if it was to be used for large transport gliders. All American's Wilmington engineers, headed by Arthur B. Schultz, concentrated in 1942 and 1943 on strengthening the mechanism and adapting it for installation in a wide spectrum of operational aircraft. By the fall of 1942, the company had built a unit capable of lifting a fifteen-hundred-pound glider and had negotiated a

All American's black, Wasp-powered Stinson SR-10F picks up a modified Piper J-3 Cub with engine and propeller removed in a test performed at Wilmington in 1941. (76.410.43, Hagley Museum and Library)

fixed-price contract to manufacture eighteen of the devices and install them in training aircraft. Further contracts called for the construction of units with a capacity of two tons and for modifying C-47s (the military designation for the airlines' Douglas DC-3) to be equipped with them. Even more powerful mechanisms followed. For larger aircraft—heavy and medium bombers—All American perfected equipment that was able to pick up and tow gliders loaded to gross weights of eight thousand pounds and sixteen thousand pounds. The sixteen-thousand-pound unit advanced from the experimental stage to production in 1943 and 1944, with the backlog on orders for several hundred of the devices reaching four million dollars by the spring of 1944.[17]

Not only did All American tackle the engineering and development of the glider pickup, but its personnel were important in the flight-testing phases. Lloyd Santmyer, now an army captain, transferred from duties training night fighter pilots at Orlando, Florida, to work with the glider pickup. The tests began in 1943 at Clinton County Airport in Wilmington, Ohio, which had been selected by the army air forces because of congestion at its big experimental facility at Wright Field. Santmyer, who was soon joined by Norm Rintoul, oversaw a program that progressed from cargo glider pickups with a twin-engine Douglas B-23 to C-47s, and ultimately to pickups with four-engine B-17 bombers. Trains (two or more gliders linked to a single towplane) and tandem tows (using two C-47 towplanes) were part of the extensive flight-testing effort at Wilmington. There were also trials using All American's black Wasp-powered Stinson, with its propeller replaced by a tow hitch to simulate the pickup of a disabled aircraft.[18] The work of Santmyer, Rintoul, and others was instrumental in proving the company's equipment and perfecting the techniques necessary for the effective operational use of combat gliders.

All American's pickup equipment enhanced the flexibility of Allied glider operations. It transformed the glider, which had been conceived as expendable, into an aircraft that could be flown over and over again, so long as it did not sustain serious structural damage. This capability was demonstrated for the first time in Burma in February 1944, when a Tenth Air Force glider came down in a clearing, offloaded its cargo, and was picked up for the return flight to India. A number of British and American gliders that landed airborne troops behind the beaches at Normandy were picked up and flown back to England in the days after the June 6, 1944, invasion. The ill-fated Arnhem operation, during which Allied airborne forces unsuccessfully attempted to secure river crossings in Holland in September 1944, also saw the pickup used to retrieve downed gliders.[19]

Glider pickups made possible the speedy air evacuation of wounded troops from areas inaccessible to conventional aircraft. The Tenth Air Force prepared six gliders as ambulance ships in support of a British offensive in Burma in February and March 1944, while a year later gliders flew seven hundred to eight hundred American casualties daily from the bridgehead at Remagen on the Rhine to field hospitals behind the front lines. But surely the most extraordinary rescue occurred following the crash of a C-47 on May 13, 1945, in a beautiful, remote valley in the mountains of New Guinea. There were only three survivors—two men and a Women's Army Corps corporal, Margaret Hastings, who was badly burned in the accident. Although a B-17 search plane found the trio not long after the crash, a forty-nine-day ordeal ensued while workers who had parachuted in carved a clearing large enough for a glider to land and be picked up. Corporal Hastings later visited All American's facilities in Wilmington, where she took part in a Victory Bond drive and watched a demonstration of the company's pickup techniques.[20]

Combat employment of gliders using All American's pickup system engaged most of du Pont's time during the early months of the war, but he did not overlook the benefits to the company that would accrue from the peacetime application of the glider pickup. At a meeting on December 2, 1942, of the American Society of Mechanical Engineers in New York, du Pont read a paper in which he outlined his vision of the future of the glider in commercial air transport. Stressing the limitations of modern airliners, which operated most efficiently on long-range through routes between major metropolitan centers, du Pont sounded a familiar theme by showing that air transportation bypassed three-quarters of the nation's population. All American's airmail pickup network, which penetrated into the hinterland of Pennsylvania, Ohio, West Virginia, and Kentucky, helped remedy that situation, but it reached only a small percentage of those communities that needed air links and, despite considerable recent improvement, had limitations in lifting capacity. But by "employing the air pick-up by which gliders can be picked up and delivered in the same fashion that air mail and air express are handled today . . . we could provide with flexibility a much needed cubic capacity for greater payload."[21]

In du Pont's vision of the future, the glider would bring a new dimension to short-haul commercial air transportation. Based on military experience with gliders, du Pont calculated that a short-haul cargo-passenger airline was economically feasible. The pickup allowed a wide variety of towplane and glider combinations. It also permitted gliders to be dispatched to intermediate points where it had not been cost effective to render air service. For example, a DC-3 towing three gliders could maintain a scheduled rate of 120 miles per hour over a four-hundred-mile route with three intermediate points at one-hundred-mile intervals, where gliders would be dropped off and picked up. Because pickups were made at cruising speed or above, no significant diminution in average speed would occur regardless of the number of intermediate points, thus taking advantage of the principal attributes of modern airliners—range, payload, and speed—while offering service to communities with modest landing fields and ground support facilities. Warning that "we should not discard new ideas just because they seem fanciful," du Pont foresaw an alluring postwar world knitted together by glider trains using All American's equipment and techniques.[22]

Du Pont's concept, inspired not only by recent military developments but also by the railroad, fired the imaginations of public officials and journalists who saw the glider as the answer to the problem of providing low-cost air transportation to significant numbers of Americans. In a press release, Postmaster General Frank C. Walker noted the progress that had been made in picking up large military gliders and forecast an era of commercial freight and passenger gliders. L. Welch Pogue, chairman of the CAB, visited Wilmington to witness the company's experiments and rode as a passenger in a three-place glider piloted by du Pont. He concluded that short-haul freight gliders were "a very distinct possibility." Far less restrained was writer Robert

M. Hyatt. He predicted that trains of sky Pullmans would whisk hundreds of travelers swiftly and silently through the air in near-perfect safety. The short-field landing characteristics of gliders enabled them to put down almost anywhere in the event of an emergency and, because they carried no fuel, there was negligible danger of fire or explosion. Existing military gliders, some of which had load capacities of six tons or more, pointed the way to economic peacetime passenger and cargo operations.[23]

People at All American exuded confidence that the glider pickup would solve the problem of short-haul air transport. For a five-day period in October 1945, the company experimented with commercial glider service, using a Schweizer TG3A to haul live lobsters from Hull, Massachusetts, to Bendix Field in Teterboro, New Jersey. According to one account, the glider pickup was intended to provide cost estimates and to demonstrate time advantages over other forms of air or ground transportation.[24] Although it had showed some promise, the regularly scheduled commercial passenger and cargo glider pickup envisioned by du Pont and other All American executives never materialized. In the postwar years, the availability of surplus military equipment (like the Curtiss C-46, Douglas C-47, and converted twin-engine trainers based on the Beech 18), followed by the production of more economical short-range aircraft, effectively eliminated the glider pickup from competition in the short-haul market.

A development related to the glider pickup was the adaptation of All American's equipment to carry aloft human beings. At least one air express pickup before the war had included live baby chickens, leading one imaginative wag to suggest trying the same thing with a parrot, who could then report orally on the experience. The army air forces, after seeking for some time a means of rescuing downed fliers from difficult terrain, finally turned to All American's pickup system. In July 1943, engineers of the Air Technical Service Command, headquartered at Wright Field, began experiments at Wilmington, Ohio, using instrumented containers. These recorded accelerations of up to seventeen Gs—plainly in excess of what the human body could withstand. Changes to the transfer line and a modified parachute harness brought these forces down to a little more than seven Gs, well within the body's limits. Following tests with containers, bundles, and dummies, the engineers turned to live sheep, because of their docility and supposedly fragile bone structure. The first test failed when the harness twisted and strangled the animal, but thereafter all went well. An occasional astonished observer on the ground was treated to the sight of a sheep soaring overhead while the pickup plane passed unseen and almost unheard through the overcast. But the next phase—a test with a chimpanzee named Barbette—was vetoed by pickup pilot Norm Rintoul, who declared that the ape had better learn to fly, " 'cause when she comes in one side, I'm going out the other."[25]

After well over a hundred pickups, the locus shifted to Wright Field on September 5, 1943, for the initial trial with a human being. Lieutenant Alexis Doster, a paratrooper, volunteered to be the first, donning the modified harness, which held his knees tight against his chest. He also wore a crash helmet, goggles, and a small chest parachute, and he carried a knife to cut himself free should anything go wrong. Half-reclining on the ground, facing away from the pickup poles and transfer line, Doster waited as Rintoul swooped over in the Stinson at 125 miles per hour. The rest was almost anticlimactic, as Doster was lifted vertically from the ground and then soared off like a glider behind the pickup plane. In less than three minutes he clambered aboard the aircraft with the assistance of the flight mechanic. More than a year passed before others tried the pickup, which gave the army time to make further improvements, most notably introducing a harness that could be strapped on without assistance. On September 23, 1944, army Staff Sergeant Harry C. Conway and Captain John Peter Lee-Warner of the British army were picked up by a Noorduyn Norseman flown by Lieutenant Norman S. Benedict. Sergeant Constantine Stiakatis followed on October 7. None encountered any difficulties, although the plane missed on the first attempts to pick up Conway and Lee-Warner.[26]

Despite the development effort at Wright Field, the human pickup was not widely used. In fact, the helicopter, which in the postwar era came to be the preferred aircraft for most rescue missions, soon superseded the human pickup. Nevertheless, the British used the system to extract intelligence agents from occupied Europe. A low-flying aircraft dropped a package with telescoping poles, transfer line, and harness, along with instructions for their use and a message indicating the time and place of the pickup. Usually within a matter of hours, another plane picked up the agent and flew him and his presumably valuable information back to Allied territory.[27]

Another job that involved All American's engineers and

Certainly the most spectacular wartime adaptation of the airmail pickup was to carry human beings aloft. In September 1943, Lt. Alexis Doster became the first person to be snatched into the air using the technique. Here, in September 1944, British Capt. John Peter Lee-Warner prepares to be picked up in further tests of the equipment. (76.410.41, Hagley Museum and Library)

manufacturing people was the Brodie device. The war had demonstrated the value of light planes for spotting artillery fire, liaison, medical evacuation, and a host of other activities. In order to take off and land these aircraft from areas close to the fighting, where adequate airstrips were not always available, the army pushed the development of an apparatus conceived in 1942 by Captain James H. Brodie that consisted of a wire cable suspended from four sixty-five-foot steel masts. An overhead trolley and a three-loop nylon web sling were attached to the cable. To land, a plane with a hook located above the wing flew under the wire cable and engaged the nylon sling. Takeoffs reversed the procedure, with the pilot releasing the hook after running some three hundred feet along the cable. Attracted by the short takeoffs and landings that were made possible by the device, the navy installed it on an LST in the summer of 1944 and used it during the Iwo Jima and Okinawa campaigns in 1945. All

An army Piper L-4 on the Brodie device. Invented by Army Capt. James H. Brodie, the mechanism was used to land and launch light observation planes during World War II. All American helped develop the arresting-brake reel used to decelerate the planes after they hooked on to the overhead cable. (76.410.45, Hagley Museum and Library)

American assisted with several key components of the Brodie device. In late June and early July, the Wilmington engineers concentrated on the Brodie arresting brake reel, which as originally designed had been the cause of numerous cable breakages. Experiments using a dynamometer led to improvements in the brake-reel delay mechanism. These resulted in much smoother deceleration of the aircraft and fewer cable problems.[28]

The Brodie device was only one of dozens of projects that occupied All American's Wilmington group during the war. They experimented with undrawn nylon, exploring its elastic qualities in various applications relating to the pickup and as the principal material in aircraft crash barriers. The army air forces carried out flight tests in the summer of 1944 using a B-24 Liberator bomber to prove the feasibility of towing extra fuel tanks using techniques derived from the pickup. In April 1945, the company received a substantial contract from the navy to develop and manufacture equipment for towing antiaircraft targets.[29]

These and other projects brought changes in Delaware. As the Manufacturing and Development Division took on more contracts, the company leased hangar, shop, and office space at Du Pont Airport from Atlantic Aviation Service. Later, it became necessary to build a new eighty-foot by eighty-foot hangar at Du Pont Airport, which was used for converting both commercial and military aircraft for flying pickups. In the fall of 1943, Dr. Edward E. Minor, Jr., formerly a development and design engineer with the Glenn L. Martin Company, came to Wilmington as head of the division, which by then comprised seven departments organized according to such functions as production, engineering, contracts, personnel, and accounting. All American's technical representatives ranged far and wide, supervising the installation of the firm's pickup equipment and advising military personnel on its operation. Security, never of much concern in the prewar years, took on added importance, particularly because much of All American's work with the pickup was classified as restricted or secret.[30]

Concomitant with All American's increase in air transport and manufacturing activities was a significant growth in employment. From fewer than one hundred workers in January 1942, All American expanded to 355 employees in the middle of

1943, and to 370 by June 30, 1944, including significant numbers of women. Approximately three-fifths of the company's personnel were at Wilmington in the Manufacturing and Development Division. In Delaware, too, were most of the firm's administrative workers; as they grew in numbers, All American shifted its headquarters in the spring of 1943 from Ninth Street to more commodious offices on Greenhill Avenue. Internal communications and morale were also concerns at the burgeoning company. Publication of the *Pick-Up,* a four-page newsletter, began in 1941, at first on a bimonthly, and then, in 1944, on a monthly schedule. It was written in a lively style and included information on marriages, births, and former employees in the armed forces.[31]

Relations between management and employees were superb throughout the war years. Despite the marked increase in numbers of workers, the company retained its close knit, almost familial character. Part of this was due to the feeling of common purpose created by the war and part was a result of the camaraderie built up over the years of operating the unique airmail service. All American personnel were not unionized, nor did there seem to be any compelling movement toward organization. Corporate policy concerning employee welfare was a major factor in holding off unionization. As early as August 1942, Grover Loening suggested at a special meeting of the board of directors that a certain amount of stock be set aside for purchase by employees. At their September 1943 meeting, the company's stockholders agreed to distribute twenty thousand shares of common stock at $2.50 per share in quantities determined by the employees' length of service and pay scale. All American also offered various incentive plans and bonuses, and in December 1943 added a group accident and health insurance plan for its hourly employees that was entirely paid for by the company. Though a corporate-sponsored sports and fitness program did not exist, employees at Wilmington did organize a three-team baseball league in the summer of 1944. Games were played on Mondays and Wednesdays at Du Pont Airport, and received thorough coverage in the *Pick-Up.*[32]

Higher up in the company, a similar sense of commitment prevailed. Two key officers and directors who had been with the company since its inception in 1938 stayed on through the war years: Charlie Wendt, as vice president and treasurer, provided important continuity, as did Arthur P. Davis, whose loan to Lytle Adams in early 1937 had led directly to the creation of the firm. Those who had come to the company in 1939, notably Harry Stringer and Hal Bazley, performed crucial roles during the war. But there were also changes and additions in Wilmington. In March 1943, Richard P. Dunn's place on the board was taken by W. S. Carpenter III; by September 15, 1943, the board included Frank M. Donohue, George S. Leisure, and Charles F. Benzel. On January 25, 1944, Grover Loening stepped down as director. Yet the greatest loss had occurred on April 24, 1943, when company founder Richard C. du Pont had submitted his resignation as president to take over the army's glider program as a special assistant to Army Air Forces Chief Henry H. ("Hap") Arnold. After the board of directors reluctantly accepted du Pont's resignation at its April 24 meeting, Wendt nominated Bazley to succeed him as president. The board voted unanimously in his favor.[33]

No one at All American could foresee that du Pont's departure from Wilmington would set in motion a fateful chain of events that ended in tragedy. Du Pont received his new appointment on April 27 and reported for duty in June. He observed Allied glider operations in North Africa and Sicily before proceeding in August to March Field, California, where the army was testing experimental gliders. On September 11, 1943, he and five others were towed aloft in one of the new motorless ships. Shortly after the tow line was released at three thousand feet, the craft fell into a spin from which recovery was apparently impossible. Du Pont bailed out with two others, but his parachute malfunctioned and he plunged to his death. The remaining three, including Colonel P. Ernest Gabel, deputy director of the army's glider training program, died when the aircraft impacted in a plowed field a mile southeast of the air base. Du Pont was only thirty-three years old. News of his death deeply saddened everyone at All American, for they had hoped to see his return to the company following his wartime tour of duty. Du Pont's young widow, Helena Allaire, accepted the posthumous awards of the army's Distinguished Service Medal and the Franklin Institute's John Price Wetherill Medal for his contributions to the war effort and his pioneering work with the airmail pickup.[34]

Not yet forty-seven when he took over as All American's chief executive officer, Halsey R. Bazley had considerable administrative experience. Born in Boston on May 7, 1896, he had attended Northeastern College (now University) before joining the Aviation Section of the Signal Corps in 1917. After flight instruction at Hicks Field in Texas, he joined the American Expeditionary Force in France with the rank of second lieutenant, finishing the war as a flight instructor. From 1921 to 1929, he worked for Atlantic Air Service, Inc., in Boston, and then managed the Curtiss-Wright Flying Service at Pittsburgh's Bettis Field. He spent four years (1932–1936) as aviation director for Allegheny County, and another year as chief of the Works Progress Administration's Pennsylvania department. Before coming to All American in May 1939, he had been acting chief of the Pennsylvania Division of Aeronautics. Employees remembered him as a man they could talk to on a first-name basis and who took a personal interest in their work. Jennings Randolph saw Bazley as a particularly "vigorous advocate" of the pickup, and so he remained during the boardroom battles that lay ahead over whether or not the company should become a conventional passenger carrier.[35]

For the moment, though, Bazley was busy enough seeing to the management of the company. He inherited a nagging problem—the need for capital sufficient to cover the day-to-day operations as well as to meet the obligations incurred by the firm's expanded flight and manufacturing activities. Hitherto, all capital requirements had been met by loans. A $400 thousand advance from A. Felix du Pont, Sr., in late 1942 helped the company pay for aircraft and the expenses associated with manufacturing pickup equipment. In January 1943, All American obtained $200 thousand from the Equitable Trust Company in Wilmington. Following this, in the summer of 1943, was a guaranteed V-loan, totalling $1 million and secured by the company's claims to payment under three military production contracts. Considerable discussion also took place in Wilmington about the desirability of selling the Manufacturing and Development Division. Discussions opened with the Bendix Aviation Corporation in 1942, and an offer was made to sell the division for $800 thousand. Richard du Pont, however, had never given his wholehearted support to the separation of the division, maintaining that it was necessary to keep a close relation between engineering the pickup and operational experience with it. The proposal fell through in October.[36]

Yet other measures were still necessary to cover All American's need for working and equity capital. In addition to loans and to exploring the idea of selling its manufacturing facilities, All American's directors decided to make a major stock issue. Aside from the offering of a small number of shares of class A stock in October 1941, there had been no issuance of securities since 1938. By early 1943, it had become obvious that this was not enough to meet the company's needs. On March 17, the stockholders approved the board's plan to amend the charter to eliminate the distinction between class A and class B stock and authorize the distribution of one million shares of common stock at $1 per share and forty thousand shares of preferred stock at $25 per share. Blyth and Company of New York handled the stock offering, which began in August and which by the end of February 1944 had brought in more than $950 thousand. On March 1, the company paid its first dividend—fifty cents a share to holders of preferred stock.[37]

The outcome of rate negotiations with the Civil Aeronautics Board directly affected All American's finances, too. In September 1941, the company had been awarded a rate of forty-six cents per mile, which fell to forty cents after the completion of one year of flight operations. No one at All American was comfortable with this, particularly because the bulk of the firm's revenues derived from airmail compensation. On April 15, 1942, All American filed a petition before the CAB requesting a substantial increase in compensation. The board responded with a proposed rate of a little more than fifty-three cents per mile for part of 1942 and 44.58 cents per mile thereafter. Wendt found these rates "entirely inadequate to provide for the breakeven need of the company." Hearings ensued in the spring of 1943 to determine as precisely as possible All American's financial requirements. The CAB ruled on June 29, 1943, that All American would receive fifty-four cents per mile from April 10, 1942, to March 31, 1943, payable on a point-to-point basis; starting on April 1, 1943, the rate dropped to a little more than fifty cents, based on total aircraft miles. An additional twenty-seven cents per mile could be collected for miles in excess of the average computed monthly total.[38]

Largely as a result of the CAB's decision to increase All American's rate of airmail pay, the company's balance sheet showed a gratifying turnaround. After a small surplus of $6,127.69 in the fiscal year ending June 30, 1941, All American suffered a loss of $22,407.40 the following year. On September 15, 1943, Bazley reported to the stockholders that All American in the preceding fiscal year had earned $27,689.68 after taxes. This jumped to $188,587.50 in 1944, and $191,771.13 in 1945, although the increases were due not so much to augmented mail pay as they were to almost exponential gains from military contracts placed with the Wilmington division. In fact, the Air Transport Division suffered a loss of nearly $74,000 in the fiscal year ending June 30, 1945, which prompted another appeal to the CAB for upward revisions to its rate of airmail compensation. The company's current ratio improved from a dismal −.96 in 1943 to 3.71 in 1944 and 3.52 in 1945, but it was still lower than its executives would have liked in an industry as volatile as aviation. Nevertheless, the war years, during which business exceeded $3.5 million annually, helped fuel general optimism for expansion and continued progress in the postwar era.[39]

A surplus in the company's treasury was an encouraging sign, but All American's future lay with expanding its own route structure and promoting the nationwide growth of the pickup system. Even before the Civil Aeronautics Board reopened applications for domestic air routes on June 21, 1943, All American's directors had discussed the need to identify future markets for the pickup. A day after the CAB's decision to entertain new route cases, the company's board approved the retention of the services of Ross M. Cunningham, a professor of marketing at the Massachusetts Institute of Technology, to help prepare for the impending hearings. By the middle of September, the CAB had before it applications to extend Route 49 by 1,362 miles, including sectors from Corry to Erie and Buffalo, two arteries to Columbus, and an additional leg to Cincinnati. Six more routes in Pennsylvania, New York, New Jersey, and four New England states, essentially duplicating the petition filed in March 1941, totaled 2,252 miles and included 182 cities and towns. Also pending from before the war were proposals from twenty-one airlines in eighteen states for twenty-five thousand miles of pickup routes touching fifteen hundred communities.[40]

Due to the tremendous number of applications for local and pickup routes, the CAB decided to hold a series of public hearings. In preparation, William J. Madden and Albert F. Beitel, the board's examiners, came to Pittsburgh to study All American's operations. They inspected the company's maintenance facilities and ground operations, and they accompanied pickup flights. Their firsthand observations formed the backdrop to the CAB's new route investigation, which began on September 28 and extended until October 25. All American dispatched a major contingent to Washington: Bazley, Stringer, Cunningham, general counsel Austin M. Zimmerman, and chief pilot Tommy Kincheloe. On October 5, Bazley presented a summary of All American's pickup operations, complete with a statistical analysis of costs, actual and anticipated revenues, estimates of the time saved by dispatching first-class mail with the pickup, and projected increases in mail volume. Bazley said that his company's experience proved beyond a doubt the practicability of the service, concluding that "by Air Pick-up the Government almost overnight, could extend the benefits of direct air mail and air express service to every nook and corner in the country."[41]

Madden and Beitel were considerably less bullish about the long-range prospects of the pickup. While they found that service should be expanded to smaller communities by newly classified feeder air carriers, they urged the board to examine thoroughly the economics of each new route application before granting its approval. Despite All American's contention that postal revenues exceeded mail compensation by as much as seventy-four thousand dollars monthly, the Post Office Department still found the costs of the pickup to be relatively high and recommended its extension only to those routes where the mail volume was such as to "indicate early self-sufficiency." Moreover, the Post Office foresaw major growth in road transportation in the postwar period that would preclude a considerable local expansion of air service. "There will be few . . . proposals for local and feeder air service," the Post Office Department predicted, "that will meet the searching tests of practicability and economy in competition with surface transportation." Madden and Beitel found that there should be "no general expansion of air services incorporating only pick-up operations," except in "unusual cases" where the Post Office had no alternatives. On the other hand, the examiners were convinced that a combination passenger-pickup service was safe and practical and recommended its adoption on new routes.[42]

As a result of the CAB examiners' report, the possibility of a combination passenger-pickup service drew more attention in Wilmington and Pittsburgh. In its original application for certification in 1940, All American had requested approval to carry passengers. The CAB had rejected this, but it had done so "without prejudice," meaning the company was free to reapply at a later date. Whenever possible, All American invited government officials and representatives of the press to fly the pickup. Early in 1944, Edward J. Slattery, chief of the CAB's information bureau, and James J. Strebig, Associated Press aviation editor, flew two pickup routes. Both were highly impressed. Eric Bramley, a writer for *American Aviation*, rode along on a flight from Pittsburgh to Williamsport in May. He said he "wouldn't mind being a passenger, provided some of the pickup stations were relocated to permit a better approach and a slower climb after pickup." But he thought some flights would be "mighty bumpy," and he reserved judgment on whether or not in the future passenger service could be provided with an acceptable degree of safety and comfort.[43]

It was clear to All American's executives that a new and larger aircraft would be essential for the combined passenger-pickup service. At the CAB's hearing on local and feeder air service, Bazley had specified the type of plane that would be best suited for this application; he wanted a twin-engine, high-wing monoplane capable of hauling ten to twelve passengers. Later, the technical committee of the Feeder Airlines Association, which had been created in April 1944 with Harry Stringer as its chairperson, refined Bazley's concept for a new airliner. The committee specified a twin-engine craft with tricycle landing gear, a cruising speed of 170 miles per hour, a range of more than five hundred miles, and a seating capacity of twelve to twenty-two passengers, depending on the volume of cargo anticipated on the various routes. The pickup mechanism, rated at three hundred pounds, would be an integral part of the design. All American approached several manufacturers with these specifications and by the end of 1944 had received replies from three of them— Hughes Aircraft, Consolidated Vultee, and Boeing—indicating an interest in supplying such a plane in the postwar years.[44]

While studying the combination service and exploring the possibilities of new aircraft, All American aggressively pursued new route applications during the last eighteen months of the war. A planning committee chaired by Bazley and including Stringer, Wendt, Minor, and Zimmerman, was formed early in 1944 to consider the company's strategy for the postwar years. New routes received high priority, in spite of the CAB's demonstrated coolness toward the expansion of the pickup. In short order, All American placed before the board a request for ten new routes and extensions to existing Route 49, adding 297 points and 4,129 miles. The company also resurrected and resubmitted its March 1941 proposal to extend connections into upstate New York and New England, presenting its case at CAB hearings in Boston in December 1944. Eight new routes radiating from New York and Boston would encompass about 220 communities and more than 2,300 miles. Three of the proposed connections— Albany to Boston by way of Springfield; New York to Syracuse by way of Albany; and Albany to Syracuse by way of Burlington, Vermont—were to include combination passenger-pickup service. All American's most ambitious application was for twenty-three routes covering 7,440 miles and 405 points in Virginia, North Carolina, South Carolina, Kentucky, Tennessee, Georgia, Alabama, and Mississippi. Another twenty-five pickup routes totaled 5,992 miles and 320 communities in the Great Lakes region. The CAB heard the company's proposal on May 31 and June 1 during proceedings in Greensboro, North Carolina. Rather than considering each of the airline's proposals separately, the board lumped All American's requests into four major area cases that, when they were decided after the war, reshaped the country's commercial air map for years to come.[45]

All American's chief booster in Congress, West Virginia's Jennings Randolph, hoped to prod the CAB into speedy and positive action. On June 22, 1945, he introduced a concurrent resolution calling upon the Congress to express its support for the expansion of the nation's commercial air transport network to include smaller communities. He followed this with a speech on July 9 in which he urged the Congress to make a "vigorous expression" in favor of the maximum possible growth of air transportation in the postwar period. Citing All American's superior performance, he said that the pickup system was "self-sustaining and is now producing a substantial profit" for the federal government.[46] Randolph's concept of a nationwide air system joining thousands of isolated hamlets meant, of course, a major diffusion of the pickup technology with far-reaching implications for All American in terms of licensing, marketing, and manufacturing components of the pickup.

Charlie Wendt's vision was even broader than Randolph's. He foresaw large potential markets for the pickup outside the United States. For more than a month in August and September 1944, Wendt, his wife, and Helena Allaire du Pont held discussions with Brazilian government and airline authorities in Rio de Janeiro. A huge country with notoriously poor ground transportation, Brazil was seen as fertile soil for the pickup. Wendt negotiated an understanding whereby All American engineers assisted in the conversion of a Junkers Ju52 for tests of the pickup gear in the fall of 1944. The next year, the company set up a subsidiary, Equipamentos Aeronauticos All American S/A, to provide technical support for a Brazilian freight airline, Services Aereos Cruzeiro do Sul, that planned to use Ju52 trimotors over an eleven-thousand-mile route penetrating the country's remote interior. In addition to the Brazilians, Swedish, Norwegian, British, Canadian, and Colombian officials, by the summer of 1945, expressed interest in adopting the pickup.[47]

Wendt's Brazilian venture was indicative of All American's commitment to postwar expansion. World War II had set back the company's ambitious program, and its demands had diverted the firm's still less than ample energies and capital. But by 1944, All American was back on its original heading. The CAB's go-slow approach to wholesale approval of new pickup routes and the looming issue of passenger service forecast possible turbulence. But, on the whole, All American's people looked ahead with confidence to an era of peace and prosperity in which air transportation in general and the pickup in particular would play major roles.

6 • Changing the Flight Plan

Looking back nearly two decades later upon All American's situation at the end of the Second World War, writer Page Shamburger recalled that the company "sat at the peak of the glory at this time." The characterization was apt. Certainly the firm could take pride in its contributions to the war effort, symbolized by an Army-Navy "E" production award given to the Manufacturing and Development Division in October 1945; the accompanying citation singled out for special praise the glider pickup system, the human pickup system, and the Brodie wire-assisted takeoff and landing system. Similarly, the latest annual report, issued in August 1945, contained financial information satisfying to stockholders: net current assets, for example, were approximately $980 thousand, representing a gain of $105 thousand over the preceding year and "placing your Company in an excellent liquid position." The recent formation of the new Brazilian subsidiary, Equipamentos Aeronauticos All American S/A, was another heartening development, and optimism was expressed that airmail pickup and delivery service would be inaugurated in Colombia and Canada within six months. Also indicating faith in the future were decisions to construct a new hangar at the Du Pont Airport in Wilmington, purchase and renovate a building at 210 Greenhill Avenue in the same city for a new corporate headquarters, and issue a million additional shares of common stock.[1]

On the other hand, as the directors of the firm were all too aware, any careful analysis of All American's prospects in the light of its wartime performance was bound to be disquieting. To a dangerous degree, its profits during the war had depended heavily upon income from the development and sale of materiel for the armed services. In fiscal 1944 and 1945, for example, the Manufacturing and Development Division had amassed earnings totaling nearly $850 thousand; over the same two-year period, by contrast, the Air Transport Division had lost approx-

All American's Manufacturing and Development Division's wartime achievements won for the company an Army-Navy "E" production award in October 1945. Mrs. Richard C. du Pont, standing next to the flag pole, holds the award pennant. Hal Bazley is at right. (76.410.42, Hagley Museum and Library)

imately $58 thousand. The latter figure was particularly disturbing, because the company's pickup and delivery operations had expanded greatly under the spur of wartime demand; in fiscal 1945, its aging Stinson Reliants had flown 137,208,039 pound-miles of mail as opposed to 25,682,221 just three years earlier, and carried 26,856,205 pound-miles of express as compared to only 6,331,977 in fiscal 1942. Obviously, despite periodic upward adjustments, the rates of compensation set by the Civil Aeronautics Board had been totally inadequate to reward the firm for excellent performance; what reason was there to suppose that the situation would be different in the future? Under such circumstances, the inevitable termination of wartime development and manufacturing contracts that came with the cessation of hostilities in 1945 could not help but be a major source of worry to company leaders, particularly because All American had not been an established producer of goods prior to the war and therefore had no traditional customers to fall back upon.[2]

The degree to which the company's announced future policies addressed these problems at the end of the war was, to say the least, open to debate. In his annual message to stockholders, President Hal Bazley stated that plans were under way to expand the operations of the Air Transport Division so as "to provide for straight Air Pick-Up and combined passenger Pick-Up operations." Within the past year, hearings had been held before the CAB in which All American had asked for the creation of eight new routes in New York and New England and twenty-three in the Southeast. Other applications were pending for the establishment of thirty-five new routes in the Great Lakes and Middle Atlantic states. All told, the company was seeking sixty-six new arteries covering 18,481 route-miles and serving 1,156 communities. In addition, on three routes the firm was engaged in its perennial quest to carry out night operations. Should all its applications be successful, it would need to acquire 128 new aircraft. In an experimental move, it had already purchased a Noorduyn Norseman with a payload capacity three times that of its Stinson SR-10Cs and would soon put it in service on Route 49. Plans were also afoot, as a drawing in the annual report indicated, for the design and acquisition of a new twin-engined plane that could carry ten passengers and still have space for a roomy mail-sorting compartment. Meanwhile, the company had launched an advertising campaign to enhance public enthusiasm for the pickup system.[3] But of what use would it be, an unfriendly critic might ask, to expand straight pickup operations when existing ones were already losing money for reasons that bore no relation to volume of service? And, so far as combined passenger and pickup operations were concerned, what grounds existed for believing that the CAB would be any more inclined to authorize implementation of this idea than it had been in the past?

Bazley's message provided no answers for such questions, but at least one important company leader was already pondering them. This was Charlie Wendt, who had been the firm's chief financial expert from the beginning and who now bore an even greater responsibility for its future in the wake of Richard du Pont's death. Commanding the support of shareholders holding a majority of the company's stock, Wendt spent a great deal of time throughout the summer and early fall of 1945 thinking about All American's prospects and came to the conclusion that it would be unwise to remain so firmly committed to continuation of the pickup service as to exclude consideration of other options should circumstances make this advisable. In his own mind, Wendt doubted that the CAB would ever authorize the combination passenger and pickup service for which All American had been striving since Richard du Pont first broached the idea in 1939. Wendt also believed that Bazley was too deeply identified with pickup operations and too emotionally involved in perpetuating the pickup concept to be capable of the fresh and objective attitude that the firm's situation demanded. It followed that new leadership was required. Wendt could have assumed the presidency himself but felt unqualified for the job on the grounds that he did not know enough about aviation, however skilled he might be in financial matters. Instead, he launched what he later called a "very private investigation" and interviewed a number of potential candidates whose names were suggested to him by persons he respected. By the end of the year he had found his man and the company had a new president.[4]

Wendt's choice fell upon Colonel Robert MacLure Love, a veteran aviation administrator who had been recommended by a member of the C. D. Barney brokerage firm. A native of Brooklyn, Love had been educated at Princeton and MIT and had learned to fly in 1929. In 1932, he organized Inter City Airlines, Inc., which flew between Boston, Springfield, and Albany. In May 1933, he went on to various other careers, including running a flying school, conducting a charter service, and operating the Boston airport. For a time, Love also served as a member of the Massachusetts State Aeronautical Commission. After the United States became involved in World War II, he became a key official in the Air Transport Command, supervising the operation of its West Coast Wing and assisting its overall director, American Airlines executive C. R. Smith. Following the war, Love was thinking of starting a passenger operation in New England when Wendt contacted him about the possibility of assuming the presidency of All American. After receiving Wendt's assurances that he would have authority to make whatever moves he felt might be in that firm's best interests, he accepted the job. The first public indication of his accession to power came at a meeting of the board of directors on November 26, 1945, when he was given an option to buy fifteen thousand shares of the company's common stock. At the next meeting, on December 18, Love was officially elected president and a member of the board, effective January 7, 1946.[5]

This crucial development was accompanied by a series of changes that established a new administrative framework for the immediate postwar era. Stepping down from the presidency, Bazley became vice president for operations and moved to Pittsburgh to direct the day-to-day functioning of the airline. In announcing this development, he stated that, in accepting the helm of All American several years before, he had done so on the understanding that his presidency would be on a "temporary basis for an indefinite period." Continuing as vice president and treasurer, Wendt formally assumed charge of the Manufacturing and Development Division, "subject to the understanding that he was primarily concerned with the extension of the routes of the Air Transport Division, which he indicated was the most important business of the corporation immediately at hand," as the minutes of the December 18 board meeting stated. To facilitate Love's membership on the board, Arthur Davis, as ever a firm supporter of the controlling du Pont interests despite his previous affiliation with Lytle Adams, temporarily resigned as a director but was quickly reelected under a new arrangement in which the composition of the board was fixed at eleven members in an apparent move to broaden the firm's administrative base. In addition to Love, A. Felix du Pont and Harry W. Lunger, a Wilmington attorney who was related to the du Pont family by marriage, joined the eight previous board members, while Harry R. Stringer retained his post as vice president in charge of traffic.[6]

These moves fortified the company for what was obviously going to be a difficult period of reevaluation and transition. The deeply cherished traditions associated with the pickup system—the very basis of the company's identity since its inception—might ultimately go by the board. Bazley's announcement indicating that he had intended to relinquish the presidency all along obviously masked what must have been intense disappointment and regret about the possible abandonment of the pickup system. It could not have been easy for him to watch developments from Pittsburgh knowing that the destiny of the firm was being decided in Wilmington by a new administration lacking his emotional commitment to the techniques that made the company unique. As Wendt later observed, Bazley's situation was "not exactly pleasant," but, according to Wendt, he recognized the realities All American faced and played a "valuable, cooperative role." Intensely popular among the rank and file of the company's pilots and other employees, he provided indispensable assurance to long-time personnel that, in Wendt's words, "their interests would be protected as long as he was there."[7]

Nor did Love have an easy role, even though he occupied the seat of power. He was regarded with suspicion by many of the firm's employees, who took it for granted that he had come into the organization determined to convert All American into a conventional airline. Wendt later denied that this was the case; Love, he said, began his presidency with an open mind, wanted only what was best for the company, and did not assume that the pickup service must end. Nevertheless, Love's background in the Air Transport Command, along with his close ties to C. R. Smith, fostered a conviction among veteran pickup personnel that "their company was going to be run like the Army or like the big business of trunk airlines," as Page Shamburger later put it. This impression was strengthened when, shortly after assuming office, Love appointed the New York aviation consultant Charles A. Rheinstrom, whose roots were in American Airlines, to prepare a report embodying recommendations for future policy. Shamburger recalled that Love had grave reservations about the "hair-raising aspects of the pick-up lines" and the "wild, individualistic tactics" of some of the company's pilots. On their part, the pilots considered themselves an elite and resented being regarded as "canvasback cowboys." From the beginning of his administration, therefore, Love found himself in an adversary relationship with the rank and file of his employees, who in turn looked upon Bazley as their guardian.[8]

Certainly, the opening months of Love's tenure indicated that All American was in trouble. There was, to be sure, one conspicuous bright spot: under a temporary exemption order issued by the CAB, the company inaugurated service on April 29, 1946, on a route from Huntington, West Virginia, to Cincinnati by way of two intervening points, Maysville, Kentucky, and Georgetown, Ohio, thus gaining access for the first time to a potentially lucrative Midwestern market. Once again, however, an expanded volume of operations resulted only in a larger deficit at the end of the fiscal year. "As of June 30, 1946," the firm's annual report indicated, "the Air Transport Division was flying 6,096 scheduled miles per day in comparison to 5,000 scheduled miles flown per day in July, 1945," but the reward for this effort was a loss of over ninty-five thousand dollars. Moreover, there was an even more ominous note: although the company's planes were flying more revenue miles, the actual volume of mail they were carrying, which had risen steadily throughout the war years, was shrinking precipitously from 137,208,039 pound-miles in fiscal 1945 to 94,317,820 pound-miles in fiscal 1946. Express, also, was down from 26,856,207 pound-miles to 16,798,627. As usual, All American was involved in proceedings before the CAB to secure a higher rate of compensation for its services as an airmail carrier, and hope of a retroactive increase was held out to the stockholders. But how realistic was it to expect the government to spend more and more money for the delivery of less and less mail, particularly if the drop in pound-miles registered in fiscal 1946 became a continuing trend?[9]

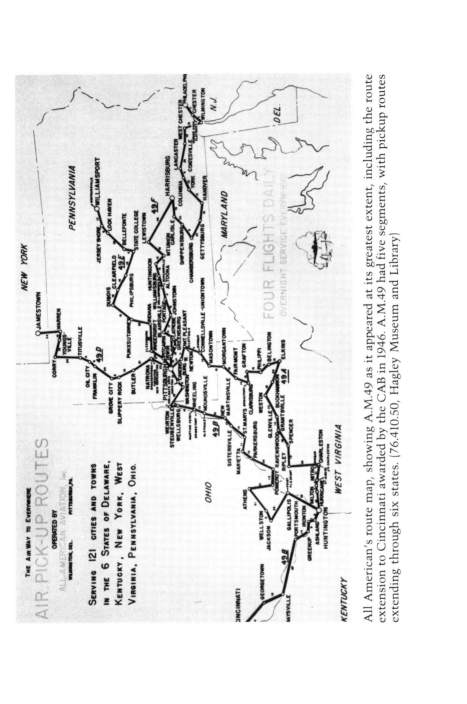

All American's route map, showing A.M. 49 as it appeared at its greatest extent, including the route extension to Cincinnati awarded by the CAB in 1946. A.M. 49 had five segments, with pickup routes extending through six states. (76.410.50, Hagley Museum and Library)

A more hopeful note was the performance of the Manufacturing and Development Division, which earned an operating profit in fiscal 1946 slightly in excess of $59 thousand. But this was down from earnings of more than $230 thousand the previous fiscal year, and the future was forbidding. The effect of the cancellation of wartime contracts had been partly offset by continuing military interest in Unylon, a special type of undrawn nylon developed by the All American engineering staff that had uniform stretching characteristics at all normal temperatures and humidities and provided excellent shock absorption when used with such aircraft safety apparatus as belts, harnesses, and parachutes. In two other developments foreshadowing the direction it would take in years to come, the division completed work on an arresting mechanism for emergency landings of light aircraft and a restraining barrier for use by airports in connection with the landing of large planes.[10]

But the shape of the future for what had been the firm's only really dependable source of earnings was highly problematical, particularly in view of ongoing efforts in Washington to trim postwar military spending. Under the circumstances, All American's management had been forced to search for new sources of revenue. Some of these, such as developing a sample railway mail pickup unit, for which the board of directors authorized an expenditure of $3 thousand, or a move to acquire a Piper Cub with which to conduct experiments related in part to aerial crop-dusting, were at least tangentially in line with the firm's past research and development efforts, but others, such as manufacturing a sample egg boiler or making refrigeration equipment for the Wilson Cabinet Company, were not. In another money-making gambit, an agreement was signed with Ludington-Griswold, Inc., under which All American would receive a 10 percent royalty on the sale of "Air Pick-Up toys," and it was subsequently announced that production of 500 thousand to 1 million model kits would begin May 29, 1946. Despite such moves, however, the Manufacturing and Development Division had a backlog of only $400 thousand worth of business at the end of fiscal 1946 instead of the $1 million for which Wendt had hoped, and the stockholders were warned to expect short-term losses pending the beginning of work under new contracts.[11]

The company also suffered a major disappointment related to the failure of its Brazilian subsidiary, for which great hopes had been entertained, to commence operations. Shortly before Love's appointment as president was announced late in 1945, Wendt made a discouraging report to the board of directors concerning the Latin American venture, blaming its lack of progress on poor management by the Brazilian officers and stating that a letter had been sent to its chief operating executive, Dr. Benito Ribiero Dantas, setting a deadline of November 15 for the inauguration of pickup service and warning Dantas that if this were not met, All American would dispose of its 51 percent interest in the project. According to Wendt, this was "the only suitable means of directing attention to a very unfortunate and unfavorable situation," but it failed to produce results. After more than six months had elapsed following the expiration of the deadline, Equipamentos Aeronauticos All American S/A, remained as dormant as ever, and patience in Wilmington finally came to an end. At its May 23, 1946, meeting the board unanimously passed a resolution directing that the subsidiary "be sold at the best terms possible." There were no immediate takers, and in his annual report to the stockholders at the end of August, Love merely noted that the South American arm had "not become active, primarily because of the shortage of aircraft for air pick-up purposes."[12]

Despite the Brazilian fiasco, hope persisted that All American might yet be able to market its pickup system abroad. In November 1945 the board authorized the signing of a contract with the Laister-Kauffman Company granting it the right to demonstrate, sell, and rent pickup equipment in all Latin American nations except for Argentina, Brazil, and Colombia. Wendt also conducted negotiations with D.N.L., a Norwegian airline, looking toward the establishment of pickup service in that country. Although these steps proved fruitless, heartening news came in May 1946 when Wendt announced that orders for pickup equipment had been received from Sweden and South Africa. Apparently these were not large, however, for Love did not even mention them in the annual report that came out a few months later. Thus far, All American had all too little to show for a great deal of effort aimed at what had once been envisioned as a major outlet for its products.[13]

Meanwhile, the firm went through a series of adventures and misadventures connected with its search for suitable new aircraft to replace its obsolescent Stinson SR-10C Reliants. It is not clear that the Noorduyn Norseman had ever been looked upon as anything but a stopgap while the company looked for a satisfactory multiengine plane, but even in this temporary capacity the single specimen of this strut-braced, high-wing monoplane acquired by All American turned out to be a disappointment. Superficially, the Norsemen seemed better suited for All American's needs than the Stinson SR-10C. Built by Noorduyn Aviation, Ltd., in Montreal, it was designed for service in the far north and appeared to be equally well suited to the mountains of western Pennsylvania and West Virginia. During World War II, it had been extensively used by the army in pickup operations. Its single nine-cylinder Pratt and Whitney Wasp air-cooled radial engine was rated at 550 horsepower, more than twice the 260 horsepower rating of the SR-10C's Lycoming power plant. The Norseman was also considerably larger than the SR-10C; empty, it weighed 4,250 pounds as opposed to the Stinson's 2,725, and it had a disposable load of 3,150 pounds as opposed to the SR-10C's 1,425.

Nevertheless, the Canadian plane proved ill suited for the demands imposed by the highly specialized type of service performed by All American. At its meeting of May 23, 1946, Love gave the board a detailed report on the Norseman's deficiencies based upon an analysis by Bazley, who was unable to attend. Essentially, the plane's "lack of aileron sensitivity," in Bazley's words, rendered it unsuitable for the frequent descents and ascents required for pickup operations. For this reason, as Love had previously informed the board, it was currently being used only as a spare by the company's Air Transport Division and as a craft for checking out pilots. No objection was raised when Wendt announced that the plane would be put up for sale at an asking price of $34,500, although this was much too high an estimate of its actual market value.[14]

In another move of much greater significance, the board had already authorized the purchase of two Beechcraft D-18C aircraft especially designed to carry both airmail pickup equipment and four passengers. A sleek, low-wing monoplane with a twin tail, this experimental craft had two Wright-Continental en-

The Noorduyn Norseman V, a rugged Canadian-built plane, seemed to provide the answer to All American's needs in the early postwar era, but failed to perform satisfactorily. (76.410.46, Hagley Museum and Library)

gines, each capable of delivering 525 horsepower at takeoff, and was expected to provide block-to-block speeds of 160 miles per hour as opposed to the 110 miles-per-hour performance of the Stinson SR-10Cs. With the approval of the Post Office Department and the Civil Aeronautics Board, some of whose members were said to be "privately enthusiastic" about the undertaking, All American intended to conduct nonrevenue tests with these planes looking toward the establishment of combined pickup and passenger service between Huntington, West Virginia, and Cincinnati and conventional passenger service between Pittsburgh and Huntington. Not surprisingly, in view of their experimental nature, production delays occurred after the aircraft were ordered on November 15, 1945, but the first one arrived in Wilmington in early May 1946 and the company was soon familiarizing pilots and maintenance personnel with its operation. By the time the 1946 annual report was submitted to the stockholders, the CAB had still not issued a license for the plane, and difficulties were being experienced with its hydromatic propeller system. Nevertheless, Bazley indicated that pilots were making progress in "improving the performance of the pick-up operation" with the new ship and that it would continue to be used for training purposes until licensing was completed. By the end of 1946, the firm expected to have at least four or five D-18Cs in service.[15]

Whatever irritation company officials were feeling because of the problems they were encountering with the Beechcraft was tempered by their enthusiasm for yet another plane for which they held even greater hopes. This was the Lockheed 75 Saturn, an aircraft designed especially for operation on feeder lines connecting relatively small centers of population with large cities located on major trunk routes, just as Richard du Pont had envisioned before World War II. Preliminary plans for this new ship had been announced to the public late in 1944 on the basis of elaborate market surveys conducted by Lockheed, and development work got under way in earnest after V-J Day in 1945. A massive engineering effort resulted in a high-wing monoplane with a single tail and a pronounced dorsal fin, powered by two nine-cylinder Continental radial engines, each of which were capable of delivering 600 horsepower.

It is easy to see why the Saturn project was so well received by

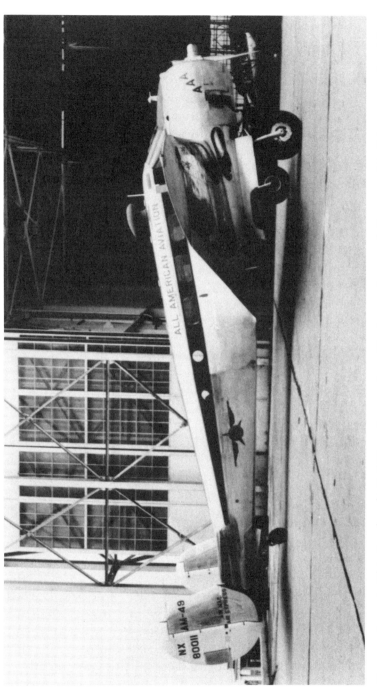

New equipment. This Beechcraft D-18C, and two others like it supplemented the venerable Stinsons on the pickup routes starting in 1946. (Lloyd C. Santmyer)

such airlines as All American; for an initial asking price of $85 thousand, it offered seats for up to sixteen passengers, the ability to take off from short, unpaved runways, a cruising speed of 225 miles per hour, and a range of 600 miles. All American ordered five of the craft on July 26, 1946, by which time a prototype had already been flown and the unit price had gone up to $100 thousand due to the discovery that the plane needed larger engines and other refinements. All American's ships would cost even more—$125,600 each—because of the company's need for a special design permitting the installation of pickup equipment, but Love and other company officials believed they had found a "winner." In addition to committing themselves to accept delivery of five craft between April and July 1947, they took out options to acquire twenty more planes by late November of that year. "As a result of being the first Company to buy the first specially designed feeder type aircraft, an excellent priority position has been established," Love informed the stockholders, looking forward to utilization of the planes "in combination passenger and air pick-up operations in scheduled service over existing routes or new routes, whichever presents the first opportunity."[16]

The possibility that All American might actually achieve its long-cherished goal of establishing a combination passenger and pickup service, using planes specially designed for this purpose, appeared to have been brightened considerably by the outcome of a CAB proceeding known as the West Coast case, decided on May 22, 1946. Two of the applicants, Southwest Airways Company and West Coast Airlines, Inc., had sought authority to conduct feeder operations connecting a large number of relatively small communities in Washington, Oregon, and California and providing both pickup and passenger service. In approving various parts of their respective proposals so as to establish two new feeder networks converging on Medford, Oregon, the CAB, in language that must have been music to the ears of All American's management, specifically authorized the two Pacific Coast firms to provide combination service if and when a suitable plane had been certified for such a purpose. Stating that the idea of such service "seems to have much to commend it," the CAB justified its decision in part by referring to All Ameri-

All American officials pressed hard for the combination passenger-pickup as a means of preserving the company's traditional service to rural areas as well as breaking into the postwar feeder line market. The Lockheed Saturn, shown here in a retouched photograph with All American livery, seemed to be the ideal aircraft for All American's proposed passenger-pickup operations, but it never went into production. (Lloyd C. Santmyer)

can's long record of pickup experience and the successful military use of the pickup technique in World War II.[17]

Any hope that the promise inherent in what appeared from All American's perspective to be a landmark decision might be quickly realized to All American's benefit were dashed within less than a month, however, by the outcome of the New England case, in which the firm had a heavy stake. In this proceeding, decided June 13, 1946, All American had sought to provide pickup service to 168 communities scattered over 2,338 miles of routes connecting such major centers as Boston, Hartford, New York City, Albany, Syracuse, Rochester, and Buffalo. Even more important, given the company's long-range hopes, it had proposed to conduct combination passenger and pickup operations over a smaller network of routes, totaling 992 miles, among most of these centers. In both respects it came away empty-handed, losing out to two established trunk carriers, Colonial and Northeast, and to an aspiring feeder line, E. W. Wiggins Airways, Inc.

There was some consolation for All American in that the CAB specifically denied backing away from the earlier West Coast decision insofar as the possibility of authorizing future combination passenger and pickup service was concerned. The rationale for the decisions favoring Colonial and Northeast was strictly economic, based on the argument that various points requiring new services of a conventional type fit better into their respective route systems. The CAB selected Wiggins for other awards, likewise of a conventional nature, because it had been an established fixed-base operator in New England since 1930. There was also a ray of hope in that decisions involving points in New York located west of the Hudson River were deferred pending the outcome of a related case involving proposed new services in the Middle Atlantic region. Nevertheless, All American could not help but regret that a proceeding in which it had invested a great deal of time, effort, and hope had turned out badly.[18]

Regardless of what the future held in store for the pickup service, whether performed alone or in combination with passenger operations, the company urgently needed fresh capital to replenish funds expended for the two new Beechcraft planes, to purchase the Lockheed Saturns, and to finance its expansion plans in the event that the CAB acted favorably on its remaining new route proposals. At the board of directors meeting of June 25, 1946, Love presented a plan calling for the sale of 100 thousand shares of common stock at not less than $9.50 per share. This was unanimously approved, and on July 1 an agreement implementing the new issue was consummated with the brokerage firms of Van Alstyne, Noel, and Company, Francis I. du Pont and Company, and Courts and Company, acting on behalf of a consortium of underwriters. The stock was actually sold at $9.75 per share, and All American ultimately netted $877,500 after commissions and other related expenses had been paid. Of this, $177,500 was returned to working capital to replace funds expended for new equipment, principally the $160,000 cost of two Beechcrafts, while the remaining $700,000 was temporarily invested in short-term certificates pending anticipated future outlays, including $560,000 earmarked for the Saturns.[19]

In the end, the reserve funds were not allocated exactly as the firm had intended, but the financial transfusion nevertheless proved indispensable in getting All American through the next fiscal year, which turned out to be extremely difficult. By the time the company published its 1947 annual report, the shape of the future had come into much clearer focus, and it was increasingly obvious that the pickup service, however deeply cherished by All American's rank and file, was doomed. During the twelve months commencing July 1, 1946, the weary Stinson Reliants and the newly acquired Beechcrafts amassed a record total of 1,780,162 revenue miles flown and achieved the second-best percentage of maximum possible performance in the firm's history, a remarkable 93.78. Altogether, an unprecedented 93,903 pickups were made; other peak figures were the number of communities served, 122, and the total pounds of express transported, 368,071. Clearly, the Air Transport Division was performing at a very high level, as All American's dedicated pilots, flight mechanics, and ground personnel fought doggedly to save an aeronautical way of life they had come to love. But it was all in vain, for the financial result was a net loss of $94,038.80, based on operating revenues of $858,801.25 and expenses amounting to $952,840.05.[20]

The cause of the debacle was not difficult to identify: the

public was simply not using the company's services to the degree it had during World War II. Since mid-1945, All American's annual mail poundage had sagged from 969,698 to 527,943, while pound-miles had shrunk correspondingly from 90,571,302 to 71,774,104. Obviously, making record numbers of pickups was of little or no avail when the mailbags themselves were getting lighter and lighter. The firm could justly complain that some of its problems were caused by the persistent failure of federal authorities to approve night operations, which they still deemed potentially unsafe despite All American's best efforts to prove otherwise. There was a natural tendency for mail to be posted most heavily at the end of the day, but because of its inability to fly at night the company could not pick up most of this accumulation until the next morning except for the few communities located near the end of a route, which were served during twilight hours. This negated to a considerable extent the benefit of speed that the pickup system was otherwise uniquely qualified to render, a fact that was not lost upon businesses and private citizens in considering whether or not it was worthwhile to pay the difference between regular postage and the cost of an airmail stamp. On the other hand, it was difficult to argue that this alone accounted for the alarming drop in mail traffic. As federal postal authorities pointed out, the gradual improvement of roads and highways, combined with the growing use of mobile postal units, made it possible for mail to move more quickly by ground transportation than it had once done, making the benefits of the pickup system less and less persuasive. In any case, the company faced a badly deteriorating market situation.[21]

Temporary relief of All American's financial woes was possible if the Civil Aeronautics Board could be persuaded to raise the rate of compensation received by the company for carrying mail. A proceeding aimed at securing a higher rate had been instituted in May 1945, but the matter was still unsettled in October 1946 when, in a procedural move aimed at expediting the case, the firm specified approximately 55 cents as a "fair and reasonable" rate. In February 1947, the CAB issued a tentative ruling providing for a retroactive mail pay adjustment giving All American a prospective yield of $236,911.89 in added revenue. Badly needed as this was, the company nevertheless held out for more. By the time the annual report to the stockholders went to press in the summer of 1947 a final decision was still pending, but the firm seemed sure of a settlement that would provide a healthy infusion of cash even if it did not get everything it wanted. On the other hand, how long would the CAB want to continue paying the company escalating rates for a service that fewer and fewer postal patrons seemed interested in using? This was the ultimate stark question confronting Love and his fellow managers, and its existence placed the entire future of the enterprise at profound risk.[22]

A major reason why All American did not want to settle for the rate tentatively proffered by the CAB was that the Air Transport Division's deficit for fiscal 1947 accounted for less than half of the red ink in which the company was wallowing as a result of its previous twelve months of business activity. Once a mainstay of the corporate health, the Manufacturing and Development Division was now in desperately bad straits, having posted a staggering loss of $156,661.07 for the year. Its need to take any business it could get, whether or not it was connected with aeronautics or any other activity with which the company had been historically identified, was now firmly established. Throughout the year it had been particularly dependent upon two clients: the Richmond Radiator Company, for which it made machined casings, and the William H. Harman Corporation, for which it made rafter assemblies for prefabricated houses. As of late January 1947 it was producing 100 water heater casings per day for the Richmond enterprise and had just secured a new contract from that firm for 4,570 additional casings at a total figure of $168 thousand, but subsequent difficulties in obtaining steel forced a temporary shutdown of the assembly line. Production resumed during the summer, but by that time Harman had suspended purchases on its 140-thousand-unit contract in a move to "adjust inventories to lower levels," compounding the division's problems. At least one of its other projects, that of machining and assembling components for the Glenn L. Martin Company, did pertain directly to aviation, but this, too, was cut back when that firm experienced delays in developing its new commercial airliner, the Martin 2-0-2.[23]

An important component of the Manufacturing and Development Division, the Engineering Department, continued to do pioneering work for the armed forces, much of it highly classified, in the research and design of equipment associated with problems involving acceleration and deceleration, such as arrester gear, pickup devices, and aerial lifting apparatus. Under a contract with the CAB, it was also developing improved crosswind landing gear for heavy, multiengine aircraft, aimed in part at permitting cost-conscious communities to build airports with single runways instead of having to invest in costly multi-runway facilities. The company heritage of technological creativity was thus being perpetuated, but like every other facet of the firm's operations, Engineering, too, felt the impact of hard times. In October 1946 the board of directors ordered a cutback in its operations involving previous expenditures of between four and five thousand dollars a month, and it subsequently curtailed research and development connected with All American's own equipment and activities.

One of the Engineering Department's last in-house projects had been the development of a modified pickup mechanism for the new Beechcrafts, using a retractable boom hinged to the underside of that aircraft's nose and permitting simultaneous pickups and deliveries at speeds of two hundred miles per hour. Here was the maturation of a system that began with the earliest efforts of such pioneers as Lytle Adams and Godfrey Cabot to develop a workable method of in-flight airmail pickup and delivery, a fact underscored by the publication by the company at about this time of the *Air Pick-Up Handbook,* giving a detailed account, with numerous illustrations, of the various types of mail, cargo, glider, and human pickup devices it had developed since 1940. Ironically, insofar as the pickup and delivery of mail was concerned, the system had reached its technological apogee at precisely the point at which changing economic circumstances were undermining its profitable application.[24]

During this difficult period, as the future of the pickup system became increasingly dubious, an unexpected development complicated the company's hope of being able to combine it with passenger operations. At the board meeting of October 22, 1946, Love informed the directors that Lockheed had canceled its contract to supply All American with the Saturn aircraft "due to difficulties with production of proper engines." The true explanation was somewhat more complex; although the nine-

One of All American's Beechcrafts making a pickup. The plane had significantly greater carrying capacity than the Stinsons, and was capable of maintaining higher average speeds over the pickup routes. (Hagley Museum and Library)

cylinder Continental GR9-A radial engines with which the Saturn had been equipped during its initial trials in June 1946 proved unsatisfactory due to insoluble cooling problems, the substitution of more powerful seven-cylinder Wright engines in the second prototype flown in August of the same year eliminated the difficulty. Nevertheless, Lockheed decided to cancel the project because the postwar transport market was glutted with such surplus planes as the Beech C-45 and the Douglas C-47, readily available at prices with which the $100-thousand-plus Saturns could not compete.

The move was a blow to All American, which had been working closely with Lockheed engineers in adapting the projected new craft to the needs of the pickup service. There was a fleeting hope that Boeing might develop a plane, slightly larger than the Saturn and known as the Model 417, which appeared suitable for All American's needs, but this, too, faded as the Washington firm refused to accept orders and suspended its short-haul aircraft program in December 1946. Douglas was also contemplating the possibility of replacing its celebrated DC-3 with a new plane to be known—interestingly enough, in view of what was to happen in the far future—as the DC-9, but this would not be available until the end of the decade, if indeed it were ever produced at all.[25]

Yet another possibility evaporated when the Beech Aircraft Corporation failed to develop a new airliner that appeared potentially suitable for the needs of both short-haul and trunk line carriers, embodying what Love referred to as "a somewhat radical airplane design, involving four engines geared to two propellers." Although Love informed the stockholders that "it should be ready to fly in the very near future and quantity production is promised for 1948," this venture collapsed as the postwar market for new aircraft continued to sag. Beech had introduced some highly successful airplanes, notably the famous Bonanza, but even it could not prop up sales, and the company turned by 1949 to the temporary manufacture of such products as corn harvesters, vegetable crispers, and meat preservers, merely to survive.[26]

For the time being, therefore, All American had to be content with its two recently acquired Beechcraft D18Cs, which it hoped the CAB, putting into practice the enthusiasm it had expressed in the West Coast case, would certify for combined passenger and pickup operations. Members of that body, along with other federal officials, had been given a chance to make good on their words in late September 1946, when All American's first Beechcraft, suitably modified for mail pickup and delivery, was taken to Washington's National Airport for two days of demonstration flights. Altogether, eighty-six passengers were taken aloft, including CAB chairman James M. Landis, representatives of the Civil Aeronautics Administration and the Post Office Department, and the company's perpetual legislative cheerleader, Jennings Randolph. No fewer than eighteen flights took place, including pickups and deliveries at Hyde Field in Clinton, Maryland, and at Hybla Valley in Alexandria, Virginia. Referring to the Lockheed Saturns that were still on order at this point, Love stressed that the Beechcraft was "simply an interim plane to prove the service and to make way for the larger planes which will be used later in this type of service." Brimming with enthusiasm, Randolph stated that "the combination passenger and air pick-up plane has become a reality." Of more interest to Love and other All American officials were the words of Landis, who described the flights as a "new and pleasurable experience."[27]

Despite this apparent encouragement and previously published reports that other CAB members were "privately enthusiastic" about combined passenger and pickup operations, the authorization All American wanted so intensely never came. Before the Washington demonstrations, the CAA had already approved the firm's Beechcrafts for regular pickup service, and toward the end of 1946 they had joined the venerable Stinson Reliants in this type of activity. The inaugural flight took place on November 21, with Tommy Kincheloe at the controls, on the Pittsburgh to Huntington route. Transporting passengers on such flights, however, remained an elusive goal, and the company never acquired the additional D18Cs it had once contemplated adding to its fleet.

Other approaches to promoting the firm's ambitions flickered briefly and then died. Pursuing an idea that was particularly appealing to long-time All American Director A. Felix du Pont, Sr., an enthusiastic proponent of helicopters, the company applied to the CAB for permission to create five new routes serving fifty-five communities in the Pittsburgh and Philadelphia-Camden areas, using this type of aircraft to carry both passengers and mail. But the regulatory agency was unresponsive, and the proposal was eventually withdrawn in June 1947. According to Love, the move had been merely a "protective measure" aimed at forestalling competition from other firms that might try to introduce helicopter service in All American's territory. Meanwhile, on March 3, 1947, the company had presented a formal proposal to CAB Examiner Curtis B. Henderson requesting authority to transport passengers between Pittsburgh, Elkins, and Huntington during the course of scheduled pickup operations. At the conclusion of the hearing later that month, Henderson waived further procedure and forwarded the matter directly to the CAB for decision, but these steps were destined to be as futile as all the other efforts the company had made to combine the two types of service.[28]

Given the increasingly obvious reluctance of the CAB to approve joint passenger and pickup operations and the shrinking volume of mail collected and delivered on the firm's existing routes, company officials had to think hard about alternatives that would enable All American to survive. So far as both Love and Wendt were concerned, the most promising possibility was that of abandoning the pickup service and becoming a conventional feeder-line operator. By selecting Wiggins over other applicants for feeder routes in the New England case, the CAB had shown that it would look with special favor upon firms that had pioneered other types of aeronautical services in a particular region. It made sense to believe that it would use the same rationale in the ongoing Middle Atlantic case, in which All American's long operational record in such states as Pennsylvania and West Virginia might win it preference over other contenders, particularly if the airline were willing to surrender its pickup role and thus relieve both the CAB and the Post Office Department of any further need to support a service that had become increasingly uneconomical. This logic appealed to a growing number of All American's directors, including W. S. Carpenter, Frank M. Donohue, Beverley B. Howard, and Harry W. Lunger, who together with Love and Wendt composed a majority of the board.[29]

Some of the firm's other officers and directors had a more difficult time reconciling themselves to this course of action.

Bazley's deep emotional identification with the pickup service, along with his unofficial role as watchdog for the interests of rank and file employees who clung devotedly to the system, made him extremely reluctant to support the policy contemplated by Love and Wendt, but his equally strong loyalty to the company guaranteed that he would ultimately go along with whatever seemed to be in its best interest. Arthur Davis generally sided with Wendt on important financial issues, but he retained a sentimental identification with the pickup system stemming from his prior association with Lytle Adams. Also, he had a number of outside business involvements that made his continued participation in the firm's inner councils less likely than that of Bazley. Every other leader in the company had similar conflicts to ponder as a crisis atmosphere developed and deepened in response to the ongoing course of events.[30]

Because of the tensions inevitably engendered by this process, it is not surprising that a series of resignations and administrative changes took place as time wore on. The first to go was Secretary and General Counsel Austin M. Zimmerman, who had represented the firm in a number of proceedings, including the unsuccessful New England case; he tendered his resignation in July 1946. Early the next month, Arthur Davis departed from the board of directors, this time permanently. In November, Harry Stringer, who had served All American in such capacities as head of advertising and public relations and vice president in charge of traffic since 1939, announced that he was leaving the company to take a position with the Sea-Air Committee of the National Federation of American Shipping. Predictably, Bazley stayed on under the terms of a five-year contract to manage the Air Transport Division, which had been approved shortly after Love became president. But there was an indication of possible ill feeling against him when, at its November 26, 1946, meeting, the board adopted a resolution pointing out that the vote on the contract, previously reported as unanimous, had actually been four in favor and two opposed.[31]

The administrative changes that took place along with these developments naturally reflected Love's accession to power as the company's chief executive. Zimmerman's successor as general counsel, for example, was Hamilton ("Ham") O. Hale, with whom Love had become acquainted through his wartime association with C. R. Smith. Hale had been legal counsel to American Airlines and was far more experienced than Zimmerman in the ins and outs of government regulatory proceedings. In addition, Love was now leaning heavily for advice upon Charles Rheinstrom, who had been a marketing executive for American before resigning shortly after the war to become aviation consultant to the New York investment firm of Dillon, Read. These developments lent additional credence to the conviction held by old-line All American employees that the small, intimate, and technologically unique pickup firm they loved was being made over in the image of a conventional airline, with American, then the nation's largest trunk carrier, serving as the model. Hale was quickly appointed a director and assumed a leading role in planning strategy for the future. Early in 1947, he was appointed by Love to a four-man executive committee whose other members were Carpenter, Lunger, and Love himself.[32]

Beginning in the spring of 1947, a succession of key developments rapidly sealed the fate of the pickup service and steered the company in the direction of becoming a conventional feeder line securely based in the Middle Atlantic region. One of these was the decision reached by the CAB in the Southeastern States case, which was publicly announced in early April. All American had not applied for any passenger-carrying rights in this proceeding, seeking instead to establish a characteristically vast network of pickup routes, although it did state that it was willing to furnish a combination passenger and pickup service if this were deemed desirable.

Instead, the CAB decided that public convenience and necessity in the Southeast required the establishment of two new conventional feeder lines, and followed the precedent laid down in the New England case by awarding the certificates to a pair of enterprises that were securely based in the region: Piedmont Aviation and Southern Airways. Addressing itself squarely to the changed circumstances that had rendered All American's pickup service increasingly uneconomical, the CAB admitted that the company's proposal in the current case "would result in a considerable expedition of movement both for incoming mail from, and outgoing mail for, other airline flights," but pointed out that All American had neither shown the probable volume of mail to be carried nor taken into account how the Post Office

Department's use of mobile postal units might offer the same advantages. Furthermore, it asserted that the southern areas that All American wanted to serve had less than one-fourth the traffic-producing potential of the Middle Atlantic and adjacent territories covered by the company's Route 49.[33]

The same reasoning was followed several months later when, in a decision made public on September 3, 1947, the CAB settled the Great Lakes Area case, in which All American had applied for exclusive pickup rights to serve 320 communities scattered over a network of twenty-five routes and involving the creation of approximately six thousand new route miles. In denying the merits of the company's proposal, the CAB once again asserted that the benefits to the middle western states of All American's pickup service could be more economically rendered by mobile post offices using that region's highways, particularly considering that the area had relatively level terrain and one of the best systems of surface transportation in the country. Instead, the CAB awarded a number of new destinations to such established trunk lines as Chicago and Southern, Delta, TWA, and United, and certificated yet another locally based enterprise, Roscoe Turner Aeronautical Corporation, to supply conventional feeder services of the type it had previously awarded to Piedmont, Southern, and Wiggins.[34]

This decision effectively killed any lingering prospect that All American's pickup system might be transplanted outside the area it currently served. Moreover, by this time the system was facing extinction in that very part of the country. On May 2, 1947, the CAB finally got around to settling the All American Mail Rate case, in connection with which it had set forth the tentative rates in February that the company had rejected as inadequate to meet its needs. In its decision, the CAB specifically raised the ominous question whether public convenience and necessity required suspension of All American's certificate to operate its existing Route 49 in view of the present and potential airmail volume on the route, the limited benefit derived by the public and the Post Office from its operation, and the present and probable future cost to the government of maintaining the pickup service. "The increasing cost to the Government of the pick-up operations on No. 49 without any apparent corresponding benefit to commerce, the postal service, or the national defence," it stated, "is a matter of grave concern to the Board." In one sense, the company did win a victory, for the CAB raised its previously announced tentative award by specifying a retroactive rate of 48.5 cents per mile for the period from May 28, 1945, to August 31, 1946; 54.7 cents per mile on and after September 1, 1946, for route segments flown on a twice-per-day schedule; and 79 cents per mile on route segments flown on a once-per-day basis. The issue of suspension was held over until the CAB rendered a final decision in the ongoing Middle Atlantic area case, but the board had made clear its conviction that All American was being subsidized and that continuation of this subsidy was unlikely.[35]

In another decision made public on August 7, 1947, the CAB resolved yet one more long-standing issue in a manner constituting further bad news for All American. Despite all the hopes the company had entertained over the years of implementing the idea since Richard du Pont had first advanced it in August 1939, the concept of combined passenger and pickup flights was finally laid to rest. In its arguments before Examiner Henderson for the authority to provide such service between Pittsburgh and Huntington by way of Elkins, using Beechcraft D18Cs, All American contended that, due to the circuitous nature of ground transportation between these points, its proposed service would provide substantial savings of time for travelers, and described how it had modified the Beechcrafts by installing pickup gear and mail bins in the area normally occupied by the four front seats, leaving space for four passengers in the rear. Company representatives admitted that in the long run the ships were not economical for combined operations but claimed that they were satisfactory for experimental service pending the acquisition of more suitable aircraft.

Responding to the All American proposal, the CAB acknowledged that it had expressed hope concerning combined operations in its West Coast case decision, based upon a belief that the type of service contemplated in that part of the country, the likelihood that airports would not be available at a number of the communities that would need to be served, and the lack of strong traffic potential at various points would justify application of the idea "as soon as it can be conducted consonant with the maintenance of safety standards." Unfortunately, however, the CAB had never been convinced that such standards could be adequately upheld in this type of operation, even on an experimental basis. Commending All American for the "initiative and energy" that it had displayed in trying to put the idea into practice, the agency nevertheless had to place the public welfare above all other considerations:

The Board in the past has authorized air transportation services which were experimental in their economic aspects, but has consistently taken the position that it would be contrary to the public interest to authorize experimental services where passenger safety was directly involved. The type of operation contemplated by the present applicant requires frequent descents to low altitudes for property and mail pickup which would expose passengers to hazards which do not attend the operation of conventional aircraft. Although the present applicant has actually conducted demonstration flights in this type of equipment since the Board's earlier denial of its application to perform combination passenger and pick-up service [here was cited the CAB decision of 1940 in which All American was enjoined from conducting such flights while being authorized to conduct ordinary pickups], we cannot find on the basis of evidence presently available to us that the state of the art has progressed to such a point as to give adequate assurance that the high standards of safety requisite in all scheduled air transportation can and will be preserved.[36]

This decision, rendered unanimously despite the guarded enthusiasm that such CAB members as Landis had earlier expressed for the combination idea after taking part in demonstration flights, was a crucial defeat for All American. Coupled with the recent suspension threat contained in the mail-rate decision published in May, it gave the company no choice but to abandon the pickup service. As yet the firm had no aircraft with which to transport passengers, cargo, and mail; it was hoped the CAB would be willing to wait for a reasonable time until it had acquired such equipment. A recent examiner's report in the unfinished Middle Atlantic area proceeding had recommended that All American be certificated to render conventional feeder service between Pittsburgh and Buffalo on a north-south axis and between Cleveland and New York–Newark on an east-west line, by way of fourteen intermediate points in Pennsylvania, Ohio, and New York. This, combined with the clear precedents that had been established in the three cases involving the certification of feeder lines in New England, the Southeast, and the Great Lakes area resulting in route awards to long-entrenched local operators, gave grounds for believing that All American might win out over the firms against which it was competing in the Middle Atlantic case. In any event, it seemed to represent the company's only hope as the autumn of 1947 approached.[37]

Truly, All American had passed through an extraordinarily rough period since Love's accession to the presidency. Two events accentuated the atmosphere of crisis. On April 29, 1947, Flight 17 crashed and burned at Bellefonte, Pennsylvania, costing the lives of Captain Gearhart H. Porter and flight mechanic Robert F. Schneider; and less than a month later, Allaire du Pont, Richard's widow, resigned from the board of directors, snapping a symbolic tie with the firm's past.[38] Through such sobering events, All American moved toward an uncertain future in which its will to survive and flourish would be further tested.

7 • The Transformation

Throughout much of 1947 the fate of All American Aviation hung in the balance as the Civil Aeronautics Board moved slowly toward disposition of two key proceedings that would determine whether the enterprise lived or died. The first of these was an investigation ordered by the board in May, when it had dealt with All American's chronic mail pay needs, to determine "whether the public convenience and necessity require that Route AM 49 be suspended in whole or in part." The order was quickly amended to stipulate that the inquiry should be conducted "without prejudice to pending applications of All American before the Board," an obvious reference to the other proceeding in which the company was vitally interested, the ongoing Middle Atlantic area case. In late June, Love pointed out to the firm's directors that in presenting arguments before the CAB, Ham Hale might well be asked what All American's position would be with regard to continuance of the pickup service should the federal regulatory agency confirm the recent examiner's report recommending that the company be authorized to operate a series of conventional feeder-line routes. The directors lost no time in reaching a consensus that "in the event of the granting to All American of the conventional passenger route service, the company should not be opposed to the suspension of the Air Pick-Up service for the duration of the conventional passenger certification."[1]

Things did not stand still as officers of the firm waited to see what the CAB would do. In September, continued and unexpectedly heavy losses on the part of the Manufacturing and Development Division, once All American's financial mainstay but now a costly liability, forced the directors to think seriously about jettisoning the manufacturing functions of the division. The executive committee soon decided in favor of such a move, and less than six weeks later Love gave the directors "tentative production schedules leading to the termination" of the company's manufacturing operations by January 1, 1948. The executive committee was authorized to obtain offers for equipment and other assets, but none of the bids obtained was satisfactory. At its final 1947 meeting, Love informed the board that the sheet metal shop would cease operations by the end of the year, while the machine shop would continue to the end of January in order to finish its contract with the Glenn L. Martin Company and to complete some miscellaneous work. In February, most of the equipment and accessories were sold at public auction by the Industrial Plants Corporation of New York, yielding a net return of approximately $141 thousand, which, according to Love, was $39 thousand more than the private offers received prior to the sale.[2]

This move did not affect the Engineering Department, which remained in operation and received plaudits from Love for its development of a crosswind landing gear for a twin-engined Beechcraft plane owned by the federal government, the first time such equipment had been installed on an aircraft this large. In addition, Engineering won a "substantial contract" to provide pickup apparatus to the Canadian government and assisted military authorities in various projects involving experimental rescue operations.[3] The department subsequently became the core of the new Engineering and Development Division in Wilmington.

Confident that the CAB would act favorably in the Middle Atlantic area case, Love achieved further economies by abandoning a number of patent applications the firm had been pursuing involving pickup methods tangential to the company's basic techniques. A badly needed financial boost came with the announcement that All American would receive $461 thousand in retroactive mail pay from the federal government, wiping out previous deficits and enabling the Air Transport Division to strike a new balance, showing a modest profit of approximately $22 thousand for fiscal 1947. In its current operations, however, the company was still having trouble making money even with the higher rates recently authorized by the CAB. Within a few months the company was again petitioning for another pay increase amounting to nearly 7 cents per mile. From the government's point of view, All American's mail operations were costlier than ever; pieces of mail dispatched per revenue mile over its system in 1947 plummeted to 4,202, the lowest level since 1942, while its rate of pay per revenue mile rose to approximately 53.6 cents, the highest figure in the company's history. It was increasingly inevitable that federal officials would balk at paying higher and higher subsidies to maintain a largely unwanted service.[4]

By now Love was firmly in control of company policy. In November 1947, he added substantially to his voting power by acquiring 86,345 shares of All American common stock from A. Felix du Pont, Sr., whose son, A. Felix du Pont, Jr., was obliged during the same month to vacate his place on the board when the CAB refused to permit him to hold interlocking directorships in All American and the Piasecki Helicopter Corporation. Although Piasecki was currently involved exclusively in military work, the CAB believed it might seek commercial markets, particularly for its large PV-3 helicopter, designed originally for air and sea rescue missions with the navy. Despite the fact that All American had withdrawn its application for helicopter service in the Pittsburgh and Philadelphia areas, the possibility of conflict of interest was sufficiently strong in the eyes of the CAB to forbid du Pont to serve both companies.

Du Pont's place on the All American board was taken by James P. Mills of Long Island, New York, a stockholder whose interest in company affairs had been shown by searching questions he had asked concerning the firm's shrinking mail poundage and other matters at a recent annual meeting held at Wilmington in September. By the time the next annual report was issued in mid-1948 the composition of the board had changed even more due to the resignations of Beverley E. Howard and David F. Rawson and action taken to fill the seat previously held by Mrs. Richard C. du Pont. The three vacant positions went to Martin Fenton and Hugh R. Sharp, Jr., both familiar figures on the Wilmington financial scene, and to David L. Miller, who had replaced Frank J. Trelease, Jr., as assistant secretary and who had subsequently been promoted to secretary, a position he continued to occupy. More and more, the firm's destinies were being mapped by new leaders who had no connections with the early years of the pickup service and consequently no strong attachment to its continuation.[5]

On December 6, 1947, the company suffered its second fatal

accident of the year when one of the recently acquired Beech-crafts crashed at Wellsburg, West Virginia, due to the failure of a right-wing spar cap, costing the lives of pilot Thomas E. Bryan and flight mechanic Burger N. Bechtel. In addition to the pain associated with the loss of such valued personnel, the company faced the necessity of acquiring further equipment in order to maintain a full schedule of operations, particularly because the incident led to the temporary grounding of its remaining Beechcraft. Until a replacement Beechcraft was obtained, the antiquated Stinsons had to take up the slack. At a meeting held six days after the crash, Love discussed these difficulties with three members of the CAB, chairman James M. Landis and members Josh Lee and Oswald Ryan. Later that same month, he reported to the directors that the CAB was "very sympathetic" to the company's plight.[6]

The full measure of the CAB's concern about the increasingly untenable position of All American was manifested in its long-awaited decision, announced February 19, 1948, that finally decided the Middle Atlantic area case and assured the firm of survival as the operator of a conventional feeder-line system. In this historic verdict, the CAB pointed out that as long as All American's Route 49 remained in operation it would be impossible to justify regular feeder-line service in the same area because duplication of mail service could not be permitted and a new service limited to the carrying of passengers could not possibly succeed without mail revenue. On the other hand, the CAB declared, evidence indicated that there was abundant need for feeder-line service to many smaller cities in the Middle Atlantic region. The terrain between Pittsburgh and Buffalo, for example, required at least nine and one-half hours of rail travel, whereas the same distance could be covered by air in less than two hours. East of Pittsburgh, where some of Pennsylvania's most rugged mountains are located, the relatively short distance to such places as Johnstown and Altoona made the inclusion of these cities on trunk routes uneconomical. West of Pittsburgh, service to such centers as Wheeling, Parkersburg, Athens, and Chillicothe could be justified en route to Cincinnati; similarly, a number of communities located between Pittsburgh and the Baltimore-Washington area merited air connections with these centers. Finally, a group of towns and cities scattered along or near the Atlantic Coast would benefit from inclusion within a new feeder network. One of these was Atlantic City, which Eastern Air Lines currently served but which it could not integrate effectively into its long-haul route pattern. Others included communities situated in the Delmarva Peninsula, cut off from the more populous areas to the west by the Chesapeake Bay.[7]

There was an obvious way out of the dilemma, and the CAB quickly seized upon it. Pointing to the possibility that the concurrent investigation of the need for continuance of All American's Route 49 might "result in the suspension or substantial modification of the air mail pick-up service," the commissioners stated:

> We find public convenience and necessity for the local feeder system (persons, property, and mail) discussed above, subject to a condition that the certificate shall be issued only in the event that the Board finds, within not more than 1 year from the date hereof, that, as a result of the alteration, amendment, modification, suspension, or abandonment, in whole or in part, of All American's certificate for route No. 49, the conventional local feeder route discussed above will not substantially duplicate the mail and property service provided over the Pittsburgh–Jamestown, Pittsburgh–Philadelphia, and Pittsburgh–Huntington–Cincinnati segments of route No. 49. The proceeding will remain open in order that appropriate findings can be made with respect to the fulfillment of the condition. In the event the Board is unable to make such finding within the specified period, the finding of public convenience and necessity made herein will be deemed to be of no further force and effect.[8]

Here, in the ponderous language of the federal bureaucracy, was All American's charter for the future. If, over the next twelve months, it phased out its existing pickup service, it would become the conventional feeder-line carrier for the Middle Atlantic area. This result would be consistent with the CAB's previous decisions in favor of Wiggins, Piedmont, and Southern in the New England and southeastern states cases, and would, it was hoped, free the federal government from the increasingly unmanageable airmail subsidies it was paying to All

American. Assuming that All American would consent to this solution, the CAB saw no need to delay its final verdict. After discussing the qualifications of the seven prospective carriers competing in the Middle Atlantic proceeding—Hudson, Hylan, Mutual, All American, Columbia, Mason-Dixon, and Atlantic Central—it pointed out that All American possessed "long experience" in the area; that it was well known there, obviating the need for expensive promotional efforts on its part; and that the speedy inauguration of feeder service would be promoted by the existence of its present personnel, many of whom would be absorbed into the new service.

As a result, the CAB summarily denied the claims of all other parties in the proceeding and issued All American a certificate of public convenience and necessity to transport persons, property, and mail for three years on six feeder lines. The first of these ran from Washington and Baltimore to Pittsburgh by way of Frederick, Hagerstown, Martinsburg, Cumberland, Connellsville, and Uniontown; the second, from Washington and Baltimore to Atlantic City by way of Dover and Bridgeton-Millville-Vineland. The next three arteries covered mostly familiar territory so far as All American was concerned: they ran from Pittsburgh to Atlantic City by way of Johnstown, Altoona, Harrisburg, Lancaster, Wilmington, Philadelphia, and Camden; from Pittsburgh to Buffalo by way of Butler, Oil City-Franklin, Warren, Bradford, Jamestown, and Dunkirk-Fredonia; and from Pittsburgh to Cincinnati by way of Wheeling, Parkersburg, Athens, and Chillicothe. Finally, the CAB awarded All American a meandering route from Washington to Wilmington by way of Baltimore, Easton, Cambridge, Salisbury, Ocean City, Georgetown, Rehoboth Beach, Cape May, and Dover, with Ocean City, Rehoboth Beach, and Cape May to be served only during summer vacation periods. Two conditions were attached to the award: All American was required to conduct a survey demonstrating the adequacy of airports serving the specified communities, and, more important, phase out existing pickup services so as to satisfy the CAB within a year's time that a duplication of mail services would not result from implementation of the board's decision.[9]

Predictably, All American reacted positively to this momentous development, which amounted to a vindication of the policies Love had pursued since assuming leadership of the company two years before. When the directors held their first regularly scheduled meeting about two weeks after the decision had been announced, Charles Rheinstrom reported in detail on the costs and revenues that could be anticipated in operating the routes granted by the CAB, which were estimated to aggregate fifteen hundred miles. Within another month, plans were under way to submit a report to the CAB demonstrating the adequacy of airports to serve three-fourths of the designated communities by the time conventional feeder operations were inaugurated, and expressing All American's "willingness to suspend air pick-up service where it paralleled the new routes." The firm, however, took exception to the recent decision by asking that the CAB reconsider having omitted points along its existing Route 49E, stretching northeast of Pittsburgh in the direction of New York City; it wanted not only a feeder line between these two cities but also an extension of the Washington to Atlantic City route all the way to New York. Looking ahead to operation of the new system, Love was authorized by the board to spend $250 thousand to acquire four Douglas DC-3s and to have them suitably modified for the services All American would render.[10]

Approximately seventy-five war surplus C-47s were available, and of these All American selected six for purchase at what Love described as "a good average market figure" of about thirty-three thousand dollars each. These had to be modified for commercial passenger service. After considering various options, All American officials decided to let Douglas itself undertake the task even though its bid was higher than the others received by the company, on the grounds that as the original builder of the planes, it was "obviously best qualified to do the work." Final decisions about the specifications were made by late July 1948, including selection of dark green and what Love called "a high visibility yellow" as the firm's color motif. Interior decoration would be in two shades of green, with russet curtains and carpeting and matching leather arm rests. In August, Love disclosed that the modifications would cost seventy-eight thousand dollars per plane and that the company would need to acquire at least two more aircraft before the start of passenger operations in February or March. Two was too low an estimate—by the time

All American reached the starting gate it had eleven DC-3s in its fleet.[11]

In addition to acquiring aircraft, All American faced a massive reorganization and retraining effort to get a company that had never done anything but pickup operations ready for the totally new demands of passenger service. Looking back on the situation many years later, Wendt described it as "a whole new world." Insofar as possible, Love and his fellow officers wanted to utilize existing personnel; no other policy could be seriously entertained, given their desires to retain the close-knit family feeling that had chracterized the firm and to avoid a loss of morale among its employees, many of whom were nothing short of heartbroken about the impending demise of the pickup system that had given All American its identity. Among employees promoted to new positions of responsibility was Ray Garcia, who had come into contact with All American as a young man working at the Latrobe airport for twenty-five dollars a week and who had been hired by Bazley as a flight mechanic in 1942. Seven years later, he became the firm's new head of passenger service after amassing twelve thousand hours in pickup operations. Another major responsibility, that of retraining All American pilots to fly DC-3s instead of Stinsons and Beechcrafts, was entrusted to Frank Petee, a pilot who had previous experience with TWA. Meanwhile, flight mechanics who had sorted the mail between pickups were now retrained as stewards to attend to the needs of passengers. In yet another important area involving the effective coordination of flight operations, Karl Tewell, previously chief dispatcher at Pittsburgh during the pickup era, was requalified to play a similar role with regard to dispatching passenger flights. Inevitably, some new people, like Petee, had to be added to the organization; often these were identified and recruited with the help of Charles Rheinstrom, whose advice remained indispensable throughout the transition period. Among other persons brought into the firm was Walter Short from Capital Airlines, which, as its previous name of Pennsylvania-Central Airlines indicated, constituted an excellent training ground for passenger operations in the Middle Atlantic area.[12]

All American's directors decided upon a rite of passage befitting an enterprise going through a change of identity. At a meeting held in July 1948, the board settled upon the name All American Airways, Inc., as being more suitable to the firm's emerging status as a passenger carrier than its old one, All American Aviation, Inc. As Love explained in the annual report for fiscal 1947–1948, "This change provides a continuing identity with the organization which has so efficiently provided some twelve-million miles of air transportation in the Middle Atlantic Area and yet reflects the change to its principal activity." Love added with a touch of humor that "The simplest and most descriptive name could not be made available due to its very close similarity to that of another domestic carrier." This reference to the mammoth enterprise headed by Love's former wartime associate, C. R. Smith, may not have been appreciated by some members of All American's rank and file, who resented the degree to which the firm was being modeled upon American Airlines. But the new name had clear sailing when submitted to the stockholders at their annual meeting on September 20, 1948, and was duly filed at the office of the secretary of state in Dover on October 4.[13]

Now that All American had assumed a change in both purpose and identity, Love came to the conclusion that Wilmington was no longer a suitable location for the firm's headquarters. Although Pittsburgh remained a key operational center, proper administrative facilities were lacking at the Allegheny County Airport, which in any case was about to be replaced as the city's main air terminal by a large new facility that was as yet unfinished. After considering other alternatives, Love presented an administrative report to the directors at their October 26, 1948, meeting, announcing plans to move the firm's general offices and operational headquarters to National Airport in Washington, D.C. While a number of persons, including Wendt, were unhappy about the prospect of leaving Wilmington, particularly because of its deep associations with the du Pont family and heritage, a move to Washington offered maximum closeness to the regulatory arena in which so many decisions crucial to the company's welfare were made. As Love also pointed out, the capital city was the terminal point of no less than three of the passenger routes granted to the firm under the recent CAB decision. Perhaps most of all, relocating there would give All American a chance, as Wendt later expressed it, to "start a brand new operation in a new location," free of emotional ties to the past.[14]

Yet one more factor played a part in the selection of National Airport as the site of the company headquarters. Like a number of other airlines, TWA had overexpanded its operations in the postwar era and found itself encumbered with a building there, known as Hangar 12, which it could not utilize effectively. Under the terms of the CAB decision in the Middle Atlantic area case, All American would initially operate its new route system on a three-year trial basis, and its pickup routes would be under suspension for a like period. Under the circumstances, a rental arrangement made a great deal of sense, and TWA's willingness to extend All American a three-year lease worked to the firm's benefit. Such an arrangement was readily negotiated, yielding All American 80 percent of Hangar 12's floor space—nearly forty thousand square feet—for slightly less than $30 thousand per year. In a related move, All American put its existing headquarters at 210 Greenhill Avenue in Wilmington on the market, hoping to realize $215 thousand on the transaction after realtor's fees had been paid. The sale took much longer than the company anticipated; not until September 1949, was a firm offer of only $150 thousand from the Wilmington Appliance Company accepted. Long before this, however, All American was established in its new Washington headquarters. The first meeting of the board of directors to take place there occurred on February 1, 1949.[15]

By this time, the CAB had cleared up two remaining questions involving All American's future. On January 11, 1949, it issued its long-delayed verdict in what was now called the All American Airways, Inc., suspension case. Although it had appeared nearly certain that the pickup system was doomed to extinction, it was still not technically clear whether All American would be permitted, or even required, to continue pickup service to the many small communities on Route 49 that would not enjoy passenger service on the company's new route system. In responding to the CAB's decision in the Middle Atlantic area case, All American had taken the position that it "would be willing to continue pick-up service in areas not covered by the conventional routes should the Civil Aeronautics Board find need for such service, and upon the willingness of that body to meet the high costs of small scale pick-up operations."[16]

In its new January 11 ruling, the CAB put this question to rest once and for all. First, it dealt with arguments to the effect that suspension constituted revocation and that the CAB lacked legal authority to revoke a certificate of public convenience and necessity unless a carrier had intentionally failed to comply with the terms of its certification. Here the board simply denied that suspension constituted revocation and, equally flatly, asserted that it did have the power to suspend. From here on, responding to pleas advanced by representatives of communities that stood to lose their airmail service if suspension were put into effect, the CAB dealt in considerable detail with the question of whether the constantly increasing cost to the government of the pickup service, together with the "steady decline of patronage by the public since the war," warranted continuation of the service. Its answer, buttressed by testimony presented by the Post Office Department in support of suspension, was emphatically negative; after rehearsing a great deal of statistical and financial evidence, it argued that "the present pick-up service gives a relatively small amount of benefit to a relatively small amount of mail in return for a substantial expenditure of Government funds."

Acknowledging that patronage of the pickup system might intensify if All American were permitted to engage in night operations, the CAB reasserted its earlier findings that the safety of such operations had not been demonstrated. As things stood, communities enjoying pickup service were being subsidized by the taxpayers in the rest of the country who enjoyed no such benefit, an obviously unjust situation. On the basis of all the evidence it had heard, the board concluded that All American's certificate authorizing pickup service on Route 49 should be indefinitely suspended, effective July 1, 1949, unless All American began conventional service on routes radiating out of Pittsburgh sooner, in which case the date on which such service began would become the date on which suspension of pickup operations went into effect. The pickup service had now been officially sentenced to death, and all that remained was to conduct the funeral ceremonies.[17]

On the same day that this historic verdict was rendered, the CAB also resolved the remaining issue still hanging over from the Middle Atlantic area case, namely All American's plea that it be permitted to conduct conventional passenger operations between Pittsburgh and New York, serving a string of smaller communities en route, and also be given a route connecting Atlantic City with New York. The CAB decided that Eastern was rendering adequate service on the latter segment and therefore turned down All American's Atlantic City to New York proposal. The other part of All American's plea, however, was convincing, for the corridor between Pittsburgh and Williamsport was bypassed by the main line of the Pennsylvania Railroad to the south and the New York Central to the north, making such communities as New Kensington, Indiana, Du Bois, State College, Bellefonte, and Lock Haven dependent upon circuitous surface transportation. East of Williamsport, better connections were available to New York by means of TWA and American, but in the interest of the communities to the west All American was certified to conduct flights between Pittsburgh and New York so long as it stopped at a minimum of three places and did not conduct nonstop operations between those two cities or between Scranton-Wilkes Barre and New York. The decision did not give All American everything it wanted, particularly in that the CAB eliminated a few of the smaller cities the airline had targeted. But the company did nevertheless win a victory by receiving on a temporary three-year basis a route from Pittsburgh to New York–Newark via Indiana, Du Bois, Bellefonte–State College, Williamsport, Scranton–Wilkes Barre, and Stroudsburg–East Stroudsburg.[18]

Throughout the winter and spring months of 1949, All American proceeded on a variety of fronts to prepare for the abandonment of the pickup service and the beginning of operations as a conventional carrier of passengers, airmail, and cargo. One by one, newly modified DC-3s arrived and were added to its steadily growing fleet, while arrangements were made to dispose of the Stinsons and Beechcrafts, all of which were put up for sale. Legal proceedings were instituted to qualify the firm to conduct local business in the various states served by its newly awarded route system, and new banking arrangements were made to facilitate the transfer of administrative and operational offices from Pittsburgh and Wilmington to Washington. Executives maintained a watchful eye on the company's capital reserves, which shrank steadily as new aircraft were acquired and preparations for the future proceeded apace. Despite a number of recent economies, it became increasingly obvious that additional cash would be required, and the company negotiated a loan of $800 thousand with the Reconstruction Finance Corporation, secured by collateral in the form of liens on the firm's aircraft, land, and buildings.[19]

Much thought was given to devising an orderly schedule of suspensions and inaugurations as conventional operations replaced pickup services. At a meeting held in early February 1949 at the company's new Washington headquarters, the board decided that the suspension process would begin on March 5, when pickups on the portion of Route 49A between Pittsburgh and Charleston would be terminated. The next segment to go would be Route 49F, from Pittsburgh to Philadelphia, the suspension of which would take effect on March 26. Route 49B, from Pittsburgh to Cincinnati, would follow on May 7; Route 49E, from Pittsburgh to Williamsport, on May 28; and Route 49D, from Pittsburgh to Buffalo, on June 18. Meanwhile, in a series of seven steps, the inauguration of conventional passenger service would take place, beginning with operations between Pittsburgh and Washington-Baltimore on March 7 and proceeding at intervals to open the Pittsburgh to Atlantic City, Washington to Atlantic City, Washington to Philadelphia, Pittsburgh to Cincinnati, and Pittsburgh to New York City connections, until the firm's entire system would be in operation by June 20 with the inauguration of service between Pittsburgh and Buffalo. A brochure providing detailed timetables and information on airfares was soon released; its cover showed an All American DC-3 winging its way over hills and valleys from one urban-skylined destination to another, in a series of graceful hops. Heralding "A New Air Service Covering the Industrial Heart of America," it listed no less than fifty-two cities and towns that would be included in the company's network of routes, and identified the airports serving each. A map of the system showed a sprawling web of arteries fanning out in various directions from eight major centers, and detailed information was given concerning such matters as reservations, baggage handling, and insurance, for the benefit of prospective passengers who would "fly at 3 miles a minute in modern twin-engined airliners."[20]

During the late winter and early spring of 1949, All American and its people strove to meet the company's self-imposed deadlines for the inauguration of passenger flights over the seven segments of newly designated Route 97. Love and others saw a well-planned and orderly changeover as imperative, particularly because the company had only a three-year temporary operating certificate from the CAB. Unfortunately, tardy deliveries of modified DC-3s, the complexities of pilot transition training, and the need to establish passenger services at scores of airports generated delays that marred the carefully thought-out schedule.[21]

Of special concern was integrating the newly hired personnel into All American's operations and familiarizing the older pilots with passenger flying. Norm Rintoul, the company's chief pilot, insisted that the new people fly the pickup at least briefly. He wanted them to gain an appreciation for All American's unique style of flying and get to know some of the veterans of the pickup routes. It proved a wise policy that helped smooth over the inevitable tensions between the two groups of individuals. Most of the pickup pilots and the flight mechanics (many of whom became copilots under the new scheme) moved easily through the transition process and completed the required two qualification flights over each route segment. As chief test pilot, Lloyd Santmyer worked extremely hard with flying personnel during the route familiarization and qualification period.[22]

It took an almost herculean effort, but All American was ready to start passenger services as planned over the first of the new routes—Pittsburgh to Washington-Baltimore—on March 7. A handful of company executives, headed by President Love, saw off the seven A.M. inaugural flight from Washington's National Airport. In the cockpit of the DC-3 were Norm Rintoul, who served as check pilot, Captain Tommy Kincheloe, one of the senior pickup pilots, and First Officer Frank Petee. Another official assemblage gathered at Pittsburgh's Allegheny County Airport despite cold, blustery weather and a limousine strike that had inconvenienced travelers for weeks. After brief ceremonies, the DC-3, captained by Ray Elder and with Don Mitchell in the right seat, took off for Washington. Among the passengers was Betty Sayre, a Pittsburgh nurse. Almost twenty years before, she had been on one of Cliff Ball's planes when his company began passenger flights between Pittsburgh and the nation's capital.[23]

Everything went smoothly with the inaugural flights. There were brief celebrations at stops along the route, notably at Cumberland and Hagerstown, Maryland, and at Martinsburg, West Virginia. The other two round trips also went off without a hitch. But only two days later, the company had a brush with disaster when one of its DC-3s out of Pittsburgh suffered a fire in its left engine shortly after takeoff from Hagerstown. Captain Byron Moe reacted quickly to extinguish the blaze and made a safe emergency landing at Frederick, Maryland. Although no one was injured and the passengers took another plane to Washington, the mishap, had it occurred only forty-eight hours earlier, might have been a serious blow to the company and its efforts to compete as a passenger carrier.[24]

With the decision finally to abandon the pickup and launch a conventional local feeder passenger airline, All American began the acquisition of DC-3s. Here the company's chief test pilot Lloyd C. Santmyer is shown in the cockpit of one of the company's new planes. (Lloyd C. Santmyer)

Inaugural passenger flights began from Washington's National Airport on March 7, 1949. Left to right: Robert M. Love, Halsey R. Bazley, Malcolm McAlpin, Hamilton Hale, Martin Fenton, Charles Wendt, Harry Lunger, Michael Donahue, and David Miller. (76.410.47, Hagley Museum and Library)

Try as it might, All American had a difficult time adhering to its schedule for implementing passenger service on its other routes. Flights began as planned on March 28 over the Pittsburgh to Philadelphia to Atlantic City route. The Washington-Baltimore to Atlantic City connection opened on April 11 with a pair of daily flights, followed two weeks later by the circuitous Washington-Baltimore to Wilmington link. Operations between Pittsburgh and Cincinnati began on May 23, but the start of the important Pittsburgh to New York route, with its eastern terminus at bustling Newark, had to be postponed from June 9 to June 20 because of a shortage of aircraft. The seventh and last connection, between Pittsburgh and Buffalo, scheduled to begin on July 1, was delayed until July 25. By then, All American's DC-3s were handling nearly twelve thousand passengers per month.[25]

Few airlines made as intensive use of their equipment as All American. Three round trips daily on most routes meant that the company's green, yellow, and silver DC-3s were in the air an average of nine thousand hours a month. It was not uncommon to make eighteen landings and takeoffs in an eight-hour period; on some routes, twenty-four were needed. This number of stops demanded a minimum of time on the ground. All American crews perfected a drill to cut stops to two minutes or less. Using new "air stair" doors, strategically located baggage hatches, preflight checks while taxiing, and radioing ahead with passenger lis, they were able to minimize delays. Sometimes, the company's agent handed small bags of mail to the copilot while the plane sat on the end of the runway awaiting clearance for takeoff.[26] The two-minute routine exemplified the innovative character of the company in its efforts to gain a foothold in the feeder-line market.

Seemingly forgotten in the rush to inaugurate passenger service was the pickup. Because the CAB had ruled that passenger and pickup flights could not coincide, All American phased out the pickup in progressive stages as the new passenger routes were added. On April 11, All American removed its Beechcrafts from the pickup routes and began retiring the Stinsons from service. Only a month later came a shocking reminder of the inherent danger of flying Route 49. On May 11, a Reliant piloted by Captain Bill B. Burkhart, and with William J. Steinbrenner aboard as flight mechanic, crashed near the Harrison County Airport in Clarksburg, West Virginia. Burkhart and Steinbrenner were killed and the Stinson was destroyed. The accident cast a pall over the company as it was bringing the pickup era to an end. Frank Petee recalled that it was "devastating" and a "blow" to All American, which justifiably had prided itself in the excellence of its safety record. On June 30, the last airmail pickup flight left Pittsburgh for Jamestown, New York, on Route 49D. Norm Rintoul was the captain and Victor Yesulaites was the flight mechanic. Both had worked with Lytle Adams in the early days of the pickup, and both had amassed thousands of hours in the sturdy Reliants. On the return leg of the flight, Rintoul and Yesulaites made the final pickup at Natrona Heights, where ceremonies sponsored by the local aero club marked the passing of the pickup era.[27]

The last airmail pickup elicited nostalgia among those familiar with All American's accomplishments. The *Pittsburgh Press* on July 1 lamented the "end of a saga in world aviation history and airmail service to the 'common people.' " More than 628 thousand pickups had been made over the years, and some 11,559,000 miles had been accumulated by All American's fliers. Norm Rintoul was determined that there be a physical as well as statistical reminder of the pickup. Fulfilling a pledge made to Richard du Pont before his death, Rintoul bought the black Wasp-powered Reliant used for many of All American's experiments and presented it to the Smithsonian Institution less than a week after the pickup service had been brought to an end. The plane is currently in the collection of the National Air and Space Museum's Paul E. Garber Preservation, Restoration and Storage Facility at Silver Hill, Maryland.[28]

It was one thing to look to the past; it was another thing to concentrate on the real challenges that faced All American during the critical years of 1949 and 1950. For one, opening the new passenger routes severely strained the company's finances. Through the first nine months of 1949, All American lost $587,000 and its fleet of DC-3s averaged a discouraging load factor of 22.5 percent. Love took corrective measures to staunch the flow of red ink. He secured permission from the CAB to suspend service at Frederick, Maryland, and Martinsburg, West Virginia, and to reroute flights from the Delmarva Peninsula to

The pickup came to an end on June 30, 1949. From that day on, the company was a conventional passenger carrier with a route system firmly set in the Middle Atlantic area. The company also changed its name to All American Airways to reflect its altered focus. This view shows one of All American's DC-3s at Easton, Pennsylvania, in the early 1950s. (76.410 PO 21-341, Hagley Museum and Library)

Dover, Delaware. He also cut the payroll to 392 people and appealed to the CAB to extend All American's temporary increased mail pay rate through March 1950. These efforts brought results in early 1950. Passenger load factors began an upward swing that pointed to even better results that summer. By the end of the fiscal year, June 30, 1950, All American had reduced its losses to $251,700.[29]

All American's strides toward improved operating efficiency gained momentum during 1950 and carried over into the succeeding year. In April 1950, Love initiated a more vigorous marketing campaign in the communities served by the airline, and the following month he announced that All American had reached an agreement with Capital Airlines to confirm reservations on connecting flights between common points on the two carriers' routes. Load factors reflected these changes, increasing to nearly 40 percent in the fall of 1950. Most important, in 1951 a route between Newark and Atlantic City was established, which enhanced revenues from summer tourist traffic. Another new link, between Harrisburg and Scranton-Wilkes Barre, opened later in the year. Considerably brightening the financial picture in mid-1951 was the receipt of nearly a million dollars in retroactive mail pay, which allowed All American to retire the large debt to the Reconstruction Finance Corporation.[30]

Merger with a second feeder airline seemed, at least for a time, to be another means of enhancing All American's operations. Negotiations began in early 1951 with Robinson Aviation, Inc., a small carrier that in 1948 had received a certificate to fly routes from New York City to Albany, Buffalo, and Niagara Falls. All American had for some time been running Robinson's airport facilities at Newark, so there was a history of cooperation between the two firms. Love spearheaded the preliminary discussions with Robinson and kept his own board of directors apprised as the talks progressed through the winter. A break occurred while the CAB pondered permanent mail subsidy rates for the two potential partners, and the discussions were not resumed before the fall of 1951. Though unsuccessful in uniting the two airlines, Love's efforts helped to lay the groundwork for later negotiations that yielded a merger between All American and Robinson's successor company, Mohawk Airlines, more than twenty years later.[31]

If All American's break with the past was not made sufficiently clear by the shift to passenger carrying and by management's attempts to improve the level of operations, the changes came into sharp focus on April 1, 1951, when Hal Bazley submitted his resignation as vice president of the company. Bazley had been with All American since 1939, was a favorite with the pickup fliers, and had assumed charge of the company upon the death of Richard du Pont in 1943. He left All American to take a position with Aerodex, Inc., an aircraft maintenance company in Miami. On January 22, 1952, he hitched a ride on one of that firm's Lockheed Lodestars to observe a test flight following maintenance procedures. The craft lost power in its right engine and crashed on takeoff, killing Bazley and four others. The loss of two former All American presidents in air crashes is one of the tragic coincidences of the company's history.[32]

Employee demands for wage and salary increments, combined with the establishment of union representation, were further evidence of All American's transformation in 1949–1950. Because of the sense of common purpose engendered during the pickup years, the company had never been fertile ground for union organizers. With the advent of passenger service and the influx of new pilots, many of whom were already members of the Air Line Pilots Association (ALPA), that special relation changed. In the spring of 1949, maintenance personnel joined the International Association of Machinists, while dispatchers were affiliated for a time with the Air Line Dispatchers Association. At the same time, the ALPA moved aggressively to secure contracts with companies operating new four-engine equipment and to reach agreements with the emergent feeder lines. Negotiations between the ALPA and All American opened in the fall of 1949, but little progress was made. Although money was an issue, many of the pilots had also developed a dislike for Colin H. McIntosh, the new vice president for operations, whose heavy-handed style proved a major irritant. When an impasse developed in late 1950, the issue went before the National Mediation Board. There it lay for nearly a year before a strike threat by All American's eighty pilots and copilots in November 1951 forced the company's management on December 1 to grant 12 percent pay hikes.[33]

Love's attempts to shore up the company's finances brought

mixed results. In All American's 1951 annual report, he said that he had the "pleasure . . . to show a marked change" and stressed that the small annual profit of $4,660 disclosed in the report forecast a turnaround. Passenger revenues were up nearly 50 percent over those recorded in 1950, while operating expenses increased only marginally. The Engineering and Development Division in Wilmington showed a good profit and had a healthy backlog exceeding $1.2 million, mostly in government contracts connected with the demands of the Korean War. But Love's optimism could not have lasted long, for the 1952 financial picture was far from rosy. Passenger revenues leveled off at the same time the new pilots' contract markedly increased labor costs. By the middle of the year, All American had accumulated nearly $291 thousand in losses.[34] This unsettling trend became submerged, however, in momentous developments in 1952 that forever changed the character of the company and its activities.

Since at least 1942, All American's board of directors had considered splitting the firm into two companies, one to engage in airline operations and the other to carry out research, development, and engineering. The concentration of airline activities in Washington and the demise of the pickup stimulated further board interest in dividing the company. At its regular meeting on December 27, 1949, the board discussed the matter and agreed to establish a special committee to investigate it further. The committee recommended to the board on December 12, 1950, that the two divisions be separated, but the board took no action to implement this recommendation until 1952.[35]

The postwar years had brought a major shift in the work of the Wilmington division. During the war, the group had concentrated more than 90 percent of its effort on the design and manufacture of pickup equipment, mostly for use in Allied glider operations. The bulk of these contracts were canceled in 1945. Thereafter, the Wilmington division concentrated on acceleration and deceleration devices based on the pickup technology. These included aircraft barriers, arrester gear, catapults, ejection seats, and specialized landing gear developed under military auspices. A major subcontract for airship handling equipment from the Goodyear Aircraft Corporation helped guarantee at least two years of work for the division's sixty-five engineers and other employees. Because its activities were for the most part military in nature and unrelated to the business of air transport, the Wilmington division enjoyed a great deal of autonomy within the corporate structure.[36]

It made sense, then, to push ahead with plans to separate the Engineering and Development Division from the Air Transport Division. The board came together in Wilmington on September 9, 1952, to discuss a detailed proposal for dividing the company. The plan involved stock transfers that were arranged so as to obviate taxable capital gains among shareholders in the airline. It received the overwhelming approval of the board, which, following a vote of proxies, sent it on to the stockholders in the form of a resolution outlining the proposed reorganization of the company. The parting of the ways came on October 28. At their annual meeting, All American's stockholders approved a complicated process involving the sale of the Wilmington division to a wholly owned subsidiary, which would then be spun off as a new company, All American Engineering and Research Corporation. Payment was in the form of the transfer of 256,830 shares of stock at a par value of ten cents per share. The new firm, which was incorporated on October 31, had as its president Charlie Wendt, who, under the terms of the agreement, divested himself of his holdings in the airline. To avoid confusion, the name of the airline had to be changed. By this time, the company had established a definite regional orientation, with routes crisscrossing the Allegheny Mountain chain. Therefore, the board recommended, and the stockholders approved at their annual meeting, the name Allegheny Airlines, Inc. The change became effective on January 1, 1953.[37]

Taken together, the end of the pickup, the unionization of the airline's employees, the splitting off of the Wilmington operations, and the name changes demarcated the sharp break the company had made with its past. Robert Love's decisiveness in moving into the passenger era had not come without friction, and it had been costly. Yet it also had been necessary. The future of commercial air transportation lay with passengers, not with airmail; in fact, the long-term trend in Washington was to end airmail pay subsidies to the larger, more prosperous carriers. For All American—now Allegheny—to establish itself as a profitable competitor in the airline passenger business, it would have to anticipate and adjust to the technological and economic changes taking place within the industry.

All American's Manufacturing and Development Division, which engineered the pickup equipment used during World War II, was located at Du Pont Airport in Wilmington, Delaware. This view is from the early 1950s after the separation of the division as an independent firm, All American Engineering. (76.410.44, Hagley Museum and Library)

Epilogue: Widening Horizons

After 1953, All American Engineering and Allegheny Airlines went their separate ways, each adapting to the technological and economic fluctuations that lay ahead. Both companies achieved stability after difficult financial times, and both now have carved out what appear to be secure niches in their respective fields.

Of the two companies, All American Engineering is probably less well known to the general public, despite its continuance of the founding firm's name. All American remained in Wilmington and, for the most part, concentrated on the development of the basic pickup technology and its various military spinoffs. Charlie Wendt, president of the firm, was responsible for much of its continuity until his retirement in the 1970s. As in the past, All American Engineering received a number of military contracts for equipment derived from the pickup. Most closely related to the old technology was its work with air and sea rescue gear and satellite and drone aircraft recovery. The company devised an air-dropped system that allowed downed fliers and shipwreck survivors to be picked up at sea. It consisted of a lightweight Y-shaped pole with the pickup line attached to it that could be engaged by a hook on the aircraft. A similar system used for rescuing individuals from the jungles of Southeast Asia during the Vietnam War incorporated a balloon to lift the pickup line above the dense forest canopy, where it could be snagged by a specially equipped C-130 aircraft.

A variation of the pickup was also used to recover intelligence data from satellites. American Discoverer and SAMOS reconnaissance satellites ejected special photographic and instrument capsules from orbit. To recapture these, All American designed and built a mechanism that used two poles splayed out in a Y-pattern from the nose of C-119 or C-130 transport planes; this apparatus grabbed the reentry package in midair while it was descending under a parachute. After several missed attempts, the air force succeeded with the first aerial pickups from satellites in August 1960. Thereafter, the procedure became routine. The MARS (midair retrieval system) was also employed during the Vietnam War to recover reconnaissance drones.[1]

Among other, though less spectacular, activities of the Wilmington company have been high-capacity, lightweight winches; arrester gear and tail hooks; catapults; and aircraft crash barriers. All American's fifty-pound Mighty Mite, derived from pickup winches, could lift a deadweight of six thousand pounds. Air and sea rescue helicopters have relied on such equipment since the 1950s. Arrester gear have been supplied to the armed forces, as have tail hooks, which are now standard equipment on nearly all high-performance military aircraft. All American's Turbocat Tiger Tosser was a catapult system supplied to the marines to launch jet aircraft from short runways; through its use, a marine fighter could be thrown skyward after a takeoff roll of only three hundred feet. In 1974, the company offered a nylon and dacron crash barrier known as the LEN (load equalizing net), which could be used to decelerate crippled airplanes safely and with a minimum of damage.[2]

While still retaining much of its old identity, All American Engineering underwent significant corporate changes in the 1970s and 1980s. Through an arrangement consummated in January 1970, the company became a partially owned subsidiary of the International Controls Corporation. During the first part of the seventies, the company, now known as All American Industries, Inc., suffered from general cutbacks in military contracts and incurred huge operating deficits. But profits returned in the late 1970s and early 1980s with major orders for military gas turbine engines and bodies for Mark-82 bombs. In May 1982, International Controls absorbed All American as a wholly owned subsidiary by buying the remainder of its outstanding common stock.[3]

Allegheny Airlines, meanwhile, has passed through its own evolution in the last three decades. It grew from a regional carrier to one of the nation's major airlines, with a large fleet of jets and a route network covering most of the country. Not long after Allegheny acquired its new name in 1953, Robert Love became chairman of the board, and his job as president fell to

Leslie O. Barnes. As with so many of the company's executives at the time, Barnes had come from American Airlines with considerable knowledge of airline operations and an understanding of what was needed to keep the firm competitive in the passenger business. Barnes quickly secured Allegheny's position as a regional carrier with the addition of flights to Erie and Butler, Pennsylvania, and from Philadelphia to Newark. He also worked out an agreement to share offices and other facilities with Mohawk Airlines in Newark and entered into a cooperative advertising campaign with Capital Airlines. Within a year, the company recorded major increases in passenger mileage.[4]

More passengers and new routes dictated an expansion of Allegheny's fleet, which in 1954 numbered thirteen DC-3s. Early in 1955, Allegheny bought the assets of California Central Airlines, which included four twin-engine Martin 2-0-2s. By May, the forty-four-passenger Martins went into service over the Pittsburgh to Newark and Pittsburgh to Atlantic City routes. Additional Martins came into service before the end of the decade, but of more importance was the acquisition of Convair 340/440s by 1960. These highly efficient, short-range, twin-engined planes proved to be excellent replacements for the company's aging DC-3s, which were gradually retired from service. In an interesting experiment, Allegheny fitted five of the Convairliners with Napier Eland turboprop engines. Although they did not work out well in service, they pointed the way to the jet age.[5]

These additional aircraft placed Allegheny in a favorable position to expand its operations. In October 1959, the company linked Pittsburgh and Philadelphia with reduced-fare, no-reservation flights using the new turboprop Convairs. The service, named the Penn Commuter, was an overnight sensation; it attracted nearly 61 thousand passengers and earned a million dollars in its first year. The innovation, which anticipated later low-fare, no-frills commuter flights by other airlines, placed Allegheny in direct competition with TWA and United. After determining that the one-way fare charged by Allegheny was below cost and therefore illegal, the CAB decreed that the airline had to cancel the service. Nevertheless, because of its bold strategy Allegheny became firmly established on a major route that it has largely dominated ever since. By the end of the decade, Allegheny was flying more than 670 thousand passengers per year over routes connecting many Northeastern cities.[6]

During the 1960s, Allegheny continued to be one of the more aggressive regional airlines. It soon found its operations and maintenance base at Washington's National Airport too crowded and determined in 1961 to move those facilities to Greater Pittsburgh Airport. When a new six-million-dollar center opened there in the fall of 1963, it occupied a dual-bay hangar and employed two hundred people. The establishment of a computerized reservations system in Pittsburgh in 1966 gave further testimony to the company's commitment to that city as its operations hub. Equally significant was Allegheny's gaining a foothold in Midwestern markets through the acquisition of Lake Central Airlines. Leslie Barnes had had his eye on Lake Central since 1954 and signed an agreement in October 1967 to take over the airline, which was based in Indianapolis. The CAB approved the merger in June 1968. Although they were crucial to Allegheny's long-term expansion, these changes in the 1960s brought distressing short-term financial losses.[7]

Allegheny entered the jet age in the 1960s. Barnes committed the airline to an all-jet fleet and began by disposing of the Martin 2-0-2s and older Convairs; these were replaced by Fairchild-Hiller F27Js and Convair 580 turboprops. In April 1965, Allegheny ordered four Douglas DC-9-31 short-range fanjets and in September 1966 placed the first of the DC-9s in service on the lucrative Pittsburgh to Philadelphia route. In 1969, Allegheny had twenty-three DC-9s in its fleet, and new ones were being delivered at a rate of one per month. As more Convair 580s were added to its inventory, the company disposed of the old F27Js. To handle the new jets and increased passenger loads, Allegheny added to its ground facilities at Pittsburgh, Philadelphia, and Boston.[8]

As sometimes occurs with airlines that are rapidly expanding, Allegheny endured a series of fatal accidents in 1968 and 1969. Two involved Allegheny Convair 580s at Bradford Regional Airport. Twenty died on Christmas Eve, 1968, when the plane struck the ground short of the runway. Eleven passengers were killed in a similar accident on January 7, 1969. In both cases, the weather was poor, and the airport lacked adequate navigation equipment. On September 9, 1969, an Allegheny DC-9 collided with a light plane near Indianapolis. All eighty-two aboard the Allegheny jet died. None of the subsequent investigations revealed any wrongdoing by the firm or its employees, but the three crashes were a sobering end to a decade of heady growth.[9]

By the early 1970s Allegheny was so large that *Business Week* suggested it was more a "regional trunk" airline than a "second level" or merely regional carrier. Its route map included Chicago, St. Louis, Detroit, Columbus, Cleveland, and Indianapolis in the Midwest, and New York, Philadelphia, Pittsburgh, Washington, Baltimore, and Boston in the East. Revenues were $155 million per year, and profits were more than $500 thousand in 1970, at a time when many airlines were deeply in the red. Allegheny also expanded its local commuter services, which had begun in 1967 with agreements integrating small air taxi and scheduled operators into its route network. The Allegheny Commuter system, as it came to be known, proved highly successful in feeding passengers into the airline's burgeoning Pittsburgh hub. Barnes's expansion program continued in April 1972, when the CAB approved Allegheny's takeover of Mohawk Airlines. Immediately, Allegheny became the nation's sixth-largest carrier, operating 116 aircraft, flying ten million passengers per year, and employing 7,100 people. Profits the next year climbed to $6 million.[10]

In July 1975, Barnes relinquished his position as president and chief executive officer of Allegheny. Edwin I. Colodny, formerly executive vice president for marketing and legal affairs, succeeded him. It was not a propitious time to assume control of the company. Under the pressure of drastically higher fuel costs and the cancellation of federal subsidization, Allegheny recorded losses of $9.9 million in 1975. The company was also deeply in debt and faced potentially serious cash flow interruptions. Colodny tackled these vexing problems and set Allegheny on a long-term course of cautious expansion. Following the example of such larger carriers as Delta, he resisted the urge to merge or hastily to penetrate new markets that many airlines fell victim to immediately after the onset of deregulation in 1978. And his caution brought results. The airline's profits returned, and it began planning to extend its nonstop routes from the Pittsburgh hub to the South and the West.[11]

In the atmosphere of competition engendered by deregulation, Allegheny prospered. It inaugurated nonstop connections in late 1978 and early 1979 from Pittsburgh and Philadelphia to Tampa, Orlando, and West Palm Beach. Flights to New Orleans, Houston, and Phoenix followed in the spring and summer. New equipment included Boeing 727-200s for the longer routes and DC-9-30s for shorter hops. To go along with its new national image, the company's shareholders approved a name change in May 1979. The following October 28, Allegheny became USAir. Advertising campaigns urged potential customers to "Fly the USA on USAir," while projecting a high-technology look. Some may have regretted the passing of the firm's regional orientation, but in a sense it was only a long-delayed fulfillment of Lytle Adams's and Richard du Pont's vision of an airline that would bring aviation to the people on a national scale.[12]

Colodny's measured steps to expand USAir paid off handsomely in the 1980s. Despite a potentially disastrous strike by air traffic controllers in the summer of 1981, USAir continued its pattern of development, completing a building program at Greater Pittsburgh International Airport in 1982 that included a new overhaul facility, an addition to the terminal building, and a new flight-training center. The improvements totaled about $70 million. USAir also began taking deliveries of Boeing 737-200 aircraft in November 1982 and in March 1981 ordered new 737-300s from Boeing. When they entered service in December 1982, the 737-300 jets had more efficient engines, computerized avionics systems, and flight deck displays. Another big order was placed by USAir in 1985, this time for twenty Fokker F-100 medium-range jets worth $350 million. The new planes allowed USAir to begin retiring its older DC-9s, 727s, and a number of BAC-111s acquired as a result of the Mohawk merger. New routes opened in the 1980s as well: USAir moved into the west coast market for the first time in March 1983, with flights from Pittsburgh to Los Angeles and San Francisco.[13]

New planes and new routes in the 1980s helped USAir set new passenger volume records and generate remarkable profits during a period when many airlines were struggling just to break even. As the operating subsidiary of a holding company, USAir Group, Inc., created on February 1, 1983, the airline flew 16.2 million passengers that year, an increase of almost 11 percent over 1982. In 1984, USAir enplaned more than seventeen million travelers. Earnings soared from $51 million in 1981 to $121.6 million in 1984. Moreover, a conservative corporate strategy kept USAir's costs down, reduced its indebtedness, and made its stock especially attractive to potential investors. Hub operations continued to grow, with more than 40 percent of flights originating or ending at Pittsburgh in 1984. USAir boarded more than 70 percent of the total number of passengers at Pittsburgh by the middle of the decade. The airline also established secondary and tertiary hubs at Philadelphia and Buffalo to enhance its movement of planes and passengers in the Northeast.[14]

In the turbulent era of deregulation, USAir faced a new competitive environment. Low-fare airlines presented a challenge in the early 1980s. Most have had an ephemeral corporate existence, usually succumbing to a combination of inadequate financing and overzealous expansion. People Express was a case in point. Its bottom-dollar, no-frills flights offered an attractive alternative to many air travelers, but as it added new routes at a furious pace and acquired financially ailing Frontier Airlines, People was soon awash in red ink. Teetering on the edge of bankruptcy in 1986, People was bought by Texas Air, itself an aggressive new competitor in the air transport market, and was merged with Continental Airlines, another Texas Air acquisition. USAir, in contrast, has adapted well to the changed economic world brought on by deregulation, taking a cautious approach while offering its own discount fares and retaining most of the services passengers have grown accustomed to. Colodny has emphasized the significance of niching, or concentrating on providing specified services and amenities in a given geographic area and using equipment tailored to those requirements.[15]

But even this strategy, as successful as it has been for USAir, may not be sufficient for the 1990s and beyond. A wave of mergers swept the industry in 1986 and 1987, among them the merger of Texas Air and Eastern, making the Texas Air group, with People Express and Continental, the largest carrier in the nation. Delta and Western Airlines also merged, as did Northwest and Republic Airlines. USAir, which had resisted the temptation to join with another carrier and to invite all the attendant uncertainties, finally had to make a decision or risk the erosion of its competitive position. On December 8, 1986,

USAir Group, the airline's parent company, announced the planned $400 million acquisition of Pacific Southwest Airlines. PSA was a San Diego based company with hubs in Los Angeles and San Francisco and a strong route structure on the west coast. Under the agreement, PSA became a wholly owned subsidiary of USAir Group; following a transition period, it would be fully integrated with USAir. Though some analysts thought the merger would unbalance USAir's route orientation, the company's executives were confident that it would open the west coast market, lead to more transcontinental operations, and secure the airline as the nation's sixth largest carrier.[16]

Following the USAir-PSA merger came another with possibly even more far-reaching consequences. On March 9, 1987, USAir culminated a month of negotiations with an agreement to buy Piedmont Aviation, Inc., for $1.59 billion. Piedmont was a profitable airline based in Winston-Salem, North Carolina, with a well-balanced route structure in the Southeast, and it had been considered for some time for a takeover by the Norfolk Southern Corporation, a transportation conglomerate seeking entry into the airline business. When the Norfolk Southern acquisition effort failed, USAir seized the opportunity to gain Piedmont and its important connections in the South. There were complications, however, chiefly caused by TWA, which for some time had been buying USAir stock. On the eve of the Piedmont merger, TWA stated its determination to acquire USAir. The company considered TWA's move a hostile one and successfully resisted the takeover attempt. By the end of March, TWA had sold its USAir stock and ended its acquisition bid. The full consequences of the spring 1987 drama are yet to be felt, but most in the industry viewed the USAir-Piedmont merger in a positive light, arguing that it confirmed the basic strength of USAir and assured that the company would remain for the forseeable future among the nation's major air carriers.[17]

Of some concern to observers in the region where USAir had its strongest traditional presence was the meaning of the mergers with PSA and Piedmont for the airline's hub operations at Pittsburgh. As Allegheny County began planning for a new $500 million midfield terminal at Greater Pittsburgh International Airport, it found USAir, upon which much of the financial burden would fall, reluctant to enter into new long-term leasing arrangements. Colodny at first insisted merely that the present terminal building was adequate for the airline's foreseeable needs, but an independent analysis in 1984 revealed that renovation and expansion costs would be excessive. Consequently, USAir and Allegheny County agreed to cooperate on the design for the new terminal and began serious lease negotiations in August 1986. These talks broke off in January 1987 when the two parties failed to agree on who should pay for the inevitable cost overruns incurred during construction. An end to the standoff came on March 17, 1987, when Allegheny County and the airline resumed discussions. They agreed to continuous negotiations, and reached an understanding that the county would hold airport contractors within strict budgetary limits, while USAir reaffirmed that Pittsburgh would remain its major hub.[18] This was encouraging for both parties. The airport, which the Federal Aviation Administration predicted would be the nation's fastest growing through the mid-1990s, needed the most up-to-date facilities to handle increased passenger traffic. USAir's mergers with PSA and Piedmont, promising as they did more flights, indicated that the Pittsburgh hub would take on even more significance as passengers sought more convenient alternatives to congested airports on the east coast and in the Midwest. The compromise was clearly in the best interests of both the airline and the county.

Because of its unique origins, USAir still retains a sense of perspective about its past. Its nearly fifteen thousand people cherish much of the camaraderie from the pickup years, even though almost all the old-timers have left the payroll. Newcomers to the company probably will not recognize the names Adams, du Pont, Rintoul, Yesulaites, or Wendt, but they have a feeling that they work for an organization with a unique history. The pickup was in part an experiment in democracy, and it gave rise to a prosperous competitor in an industry where many have fallen victim to managerial, technical, and financial pitfalls. Today, members of the 49'er Club, the group of pickup veterans who flew Route 49, gather yearly to reminisce and do some "hangar flying," reminding us of the rich heritage of All American Aviation and the many people whose sacrifice and hard work made the pickup a reality and the company a success.

Appendix

Notes

Bibliography

Index

Appendix
All American Aviation Pickup Aircraft

Registration	No.	Model	Engine	Remarks
NX 2311	75910	Stinson SR-10F	P&W Wasp	Exp. pickup plane; preserved in Garber facility, NASM
NC 18488	35817	Stinson SR-10C	Lycoming R680 D5	
NC 18489	35816	Stinson SR-10C	Lycoming R680 D5	
NC 18496	35829	Stinson SR-10C	Lycoming R680 D5	
NC 18499	35808	Stinson SR-10C	Lycoming R680 D5	
NX 21107	NA	Stinson SR-10C	Lycoming R680 D5	First aircraft owned by All American Aviation
NC 21109	35844	Stinson SR-10C	Lycoming R680 D5	
NC 21130	35855	Stinson SR-10C	Lycoming R680 D5	
NC 21131	35856	Stinson SR-10C	Lycoming R680 D5	
NC 21182	35908	Stinson SR-10C	Lycoming R680 D5	
NC 23757	5923	Stinson SR-10J	Lycoming R680 E3A	
NC 47303	5942	Stinson SR-10J	Lycoming R680 E3A	
N 44784	NA	Schweizer	glider	May have been used in commercial glider tests, 1945
N 44785	108	Schweizer TG3A	glider	
N 44786	109	Schweizer TG3A	glider	
NC 3317	NA	Noorduyn Norseman V	P&W Wasp	Unsuccessful SR-10 replacement, 1945-46
NC 80010	AA-2/A-70	Beechcraft D-18C	2 Continental R9A	
NX (NC) 80011	AA-3/A-71	Beechcraft D-18C	2 Continental R9A	Crashed Dec. 6, 1947
NC 80363	AA-17/A161	Beechcraft D-18C	2 Continental R9A	

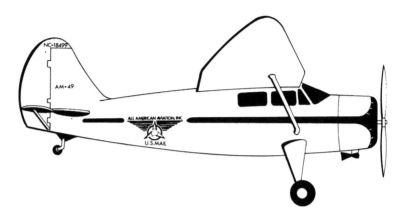

Stinson SR-10C

Manufacturer	Stinson Division, Aviation Manufacturing Corporation, Wayne, Michigan
Type	Strut-braced, high-wing monoplane, welded steel tube construction, fabric covered
Dimensions	Span: 41 feet, 10½ inches Length: 27 feet, 7½ inches Wing Area: 258.5 sq. feet Weights: empty—2,515 pounds; full load—3,875 pounds
Engine	One Lycoming R680-D5 9 cyl. air-cooled radial; 260 hp.
Performance	Cruising speed: 155 mph Range: 620 miles

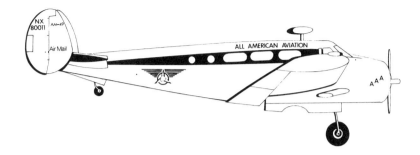

Beechcraft D-18C

Manufacturer	Beech Aircraft Corporation, Wichita, Kansas
Type	Low-wing cantilever monoplane, all metal construction, flush-riveted skin
Dimensions	Span: 47 feet, 7 inches Length: 34 feet, 3 inches Wing Area: 349 sq. feet Weights: empty—5,934 pounds; full load—9,000 pounds
Engines	Two Continental R9A 9 cyl. air-cooled radials; 525 hp.
Performance	Cruising speed: 240 mph Range: 1370 miles

Sources: Directory of Certified U.S. Civil Aircraft, through Gary L. Killion; Beechcraft, through Robert Parmeter.

Notes

Prologue

1. For varying perspectives, see Frederick, *Commercial Air Transportation*, rev. ed., pp. 195–222, and 5th ed., pp. 108–11, 202–06; Wilson and Bryan, *Air Transportation*, pp. 187–97; Davies, *Airlines of the United States Since 1914*, pp. 388–420; and Fradenburg, *United States Airlines*, pp. 255–385.

2. A clear explication of the invention-to-innovation model of technological change appears in Sahal, *Patterns of Technological Innovation*, esp. pp. 41–42, 57–62. For thoughtful modifications to this model, see Hughes, "Development Phase of Technological Change"; Bryant, "Development of the Diesel Engine"; and Hughes, *Networks of Power*, pp. 1–17.

3. Corn, *The Winged Gospel*.

4. Smith, *Military Enterprise and Technological Change*.

Chapter 1. The Apostle of Pickup

1. *National Cyclopedia of American Biography, Current Volume F, 1939–42*, p. 519.

2. Ibid.; ACP files, vol. 5, interview with Lytle S. Adams, Morgantown, W. Va., May 12, 1939, p. 2.

3. *National Cyclopedia of American Biography, Current Volume F, 1939–42*, p. 519.

4. ACP files, vol. 5, Adams interview.

5. Kouwenhoven, *Arts in Modern American Civilization*; Meier, "Technology and Democracy, 1800–1860."

6. *Hearings Before the President's Aircraft Board*, vol. 4, p. 1482; U.S. Patent Office, *Gazette*, vol. 270, p. 414, patent no. 1,328,560; ibid., vol. 318, p. 122, patent no. 1,479,222.

7. Stringer, *A Headline History of the Air Pick-up, 1939–1942*, p. 54, clipping from *Business Week*, August 31, 1940; U.S. Patent Office, *Gazette*, vol. 394, p. 534, patent no. 1,758,880; ibid., vol. 409, p. 530, patent no. 1,818,835; ibid., vol. 409, p. 554, patent no. 1,818,956; ibid., vol. 418, p. 527, patent no. 1,858,127.

8. U.S. Patent Office, *Gazette*, vol. 410, p. 1231, patent no. 1,825,329; ibid., vol. 436, p. 481, patent no. 1,935,283; "Air Mail Pick Up and Release."

9. ACP files, vol. 1, unidentified clipping, 1928; AAEC collection, box 27, Jennings Randolph, "The R.F.D. Grows Wings," reprint from *National Aeronautics*, May 1941; *Popular Mechanics*, December 1928, p. 886; ACP files, vol. 1, *Aviation Show News*, bulletin no. 11, February 10, 1929; Adams, "Dr. Lytle S. Adams and His Airmail Pick-Up System," June 1983, pp. 316–18.

10. *Who's Who in America, 1928–1929*, p. 1926; ACP files, vol. 1, Lawrance to Lindbergh, October 1, 1928. For more information on the Guggenheim Fund, see Hallion, *Legacy of Flight*.

11. ACP files, vol. 1, clipping, *New York Evening Journal*, March 13, 1929; ibid., vol. 1, unidentified clipping (probably July 1930).

12. Ibid., vol. 1, *Aviation Show News*, bulletin no. 11, February 10, 1929; ibid., vol. 1, George B. Bodenhoff to Gordon Smith, February 16, 1929.

13. *New York Times*, February 14, 1929; ACP files, vol. 1, Adams Air Express Corporation, Capital Stock Set-Up; ibid., vol. 1, memorandum, Adams Air Express, Inc., September 28, 1929.

14. ACP files, vol. 1, Adams Air Express, Inc., to Chamber of Commerce, Aurora, Ill., undated.

15. Ibid., vol. 1, telegram, Frank Mallen to Adams, March 24, 1929; ibid., vol. 2, Mallen to Adams, March 27, 1929; ibid., vol. 2, clipping, *Daily News Record*, March 30, 1929.

16. Ibid., vol. 2, clipping, *New York Journal*, June 12, 1929; ibid., vol. 2, clipping, *Newark Star-Eagle*, June 12, 1929.

17. Ibid., vol. 2, clippings, *New York Times*, June 13, 1929, *Philadelphia Record*, June 13, 1929.

18. *New York Times*, June 23, 24, July 23, 24, 1929. The Germans in 1933 began using airplanes to hasten transatlantic mail. Catapult-equipped depot ships along the air route to South America recovered flying boats, refueled them, and catapulted them back into the air to continue their flights, usually at extremely low altitudes. See Davies, *Airlines of Latin America Since 1919*, pp. 366–69.

19. Trimble, *High Frontier: A History of Aeronautics in Pennsylvania*, pp. 125–26, 127–30; Ball papers, report on Adams air mail pickup and delivery device, October 6, 1930, pp. 1–2.

20. ACP files, vol. 1, Ball to Adams, April 17, 1929; ibid., vol. 1, clipping, *Youngstown Vindicator*, August 9, 1929; Ball papers, report on Adams air mail pickup and delivery device, October 6, 1930, p. 2.

21. ACP files, vol. 1, clipping, *Youngstown Vindicator*, August 31, 1929; Ball papers, report on Adams air mail pickup and delivery device, October 6, 1930, pp. 3–4.

22. ACP files, vol. 1, clipping, *Pittsburgh Press*, March 16, 1930; Ball papers, report on Adams air mail pickup and delivery device, October 6, 1930, pp. 4–5.

23. ACP files, vol. 1, Glover to Adams, April 1, 1930; Ball papers, report on Adams air mail pickup and delivery device, October 6, 1930, p. 5; *Beaver Falls News-Tribune*, August 4, 1930.

24. Ball papers, report on Adams air mail pickup and delivery device, October 6, 1930, pp. 6–8; ibid., unidentified clipping, Dixon Markey scrapbook; *Beaver Falls News-Tribune*, August 5, 1930; *New Castle News*, August 5, 1930.

25. *New Castle News*, September 24, 1930; Ball papers, report on Adams air mail pickup and delivery device, October 6, 1930, pp. 4, 6, 8–10; Trimble, *High Frontier*, p. 159.

26. Komons, *Bonfires to Beacons*, pp. 202–10; *New Castle News*, September 24, 1930.

27. ACP files, vol. 3, report to the Aviation Committee, Chicago Association of Commerce, May 17, 1932; ibid., vol. 3, Irvin J. Ott, manager, Milwaukee Air Service Bureau, to J. E. Vesey, Chicago Association of Commerce, May 26, 1932.

28. Ibid., vol. 4, Alfred D. Olena to Adams, May 5, 1932.

29. Komons, *Bonfires to Beacons*, pp. 259–75; ACP files, vol. 3., Adams to T. E. Braniff, September 15, 1934; ibid., vol. 3, Paul R. Braniff to U.S. Post Office Dept., August 14, 1934; ibid., vol. 3, Adams to Paul R. Braniff, August 17, 1934.

30. ACP files, vol. 3, clippings, *Chicago Daily Tribune*, September 20, 1934, *Chicago Sunday Tribune*, October 4, 1934; ibid., vol. 3, T. E. Braniff to Adams, October 1, 1934; ibid., vol. 3, telegram, T. E. Braniff to Adams, October 6, 1934; ibid., vol. 3, telegram, T. E. Braniff to Adams, October 27, 1934.

31. Ibid., vol. 3, T. E. Braniff to Adams, October 27, 1934; ibid., vol. 3, Branch to James P. Haynes, Chicago Association of Commerce, December 7, 1934; ibid., vol. 3, Adams to T. E. Braniff, December 6, 1934; ibid., vol. 3, T. E. Braniff to Adams, December 10, 1934.

32. *New York Times*, March 26, 1934; Adams, "Dr. Lytle S. Adams and His Airmail Pick-Up System," September 1983, pp. 488–89; ACP files, vol. 5, Adams interview, May 12, 1939, pp. 2–3; ibid., vol. 4, photographs; U.S. Patent Office, *Gazette*, vol. 476, p. 1136, patent no. 2,075,690.

33. Macaulay, *Sandino Affair*, p. 68; ACP files, vol. 1, clipping, *Air Travel News*, March 1929; *New York Times*, June 2, 1929; *Aero Digest*, September 1930, p. 127.

34. ACP files, vol. 5, Adams to W. P. Wilson, May 31, 1939; interview with Jennings Randolph; Randolph, "Airmail for Punkin' Center."

35. Roosevelt collection, box 1364, Adams to Mrs. Franklin D. Roosevelt, December 31, 1935 (emphasis in document); ibid., box 1364, G. Hall Roosevelt to Eleanor Roosevelt, January 11, 1935[36]; ibid., box 1364, Malvina T. Scheider to Adams, January 15, 1936.

36. AAEC collection, box 7, Certificate of Incorporation of All American Aviation, Inc., March 5, 1937; ibid., box 5, minutes of the board of directors, All American Aviation, Inc., July 16, 1937. Davis was a self-taught inventor who went to work for the Brooklyn Edison Company at an early age and later went into business for himself, manufacturing submarine detection devices. Interview with Charles W. Wendt, August 21, 1980.

37. *Civil Aeronautics Board Reports*, vol. 2, p. 161; interview with Randolph; Payne, *Short-Haul Air Transportation for Mail and Property*, pp. 20–21, 31–32, 38.

38. Payne, *Short-Haul Air Transportation for Mail and Property*, pp. 10, 14–19, 22–23; U.S. Congress, *To Create a Civil Aeronautics Authority*, pp. 153–54, 157–58; *New York Times*, August 21, 1938.

39. *Washington Times*, June 3, 1937; *Congressional Record*, vol. 81, pt. 5, p. 4508; ibid., pt. 6, p. 8014; ibid., vol. 83, pt. 4, pp. 4453–55; ibid., vol. 83, pt. 5, pp. 4855–56, 5539.

40. *Statutes at Large of the United States of America, 1938*, vol. 53, pp. 218–20; interview with Jennings Randolph; *Congressional Record*, vol. 83, pt. 8, p. 8559.

41. Roosevelt collection, box 732, Raymond Kenny to Malvina T. Scheider, February 10, 1938; ibid., box 10, official file 2955-A, Adams to Franklin D. Roosevelt, March 10, 1938.

42. Ibid., box 3144, Eleanor Roosevelt, "My Day," June 28, 1938; ACP files, vol. 5, statement of E. R. Miller, June 6, 1939.

43. *Pittsburgh Sun-Telegraph*, June 28, 1938; *New York Times*, July 1, 1937.

Chapter 2. Takeoff in Delaware

1. *National Cyclopedia of American Biography*, vol. 32, p. 38; Writers' Program, *Who's Who in Aviation*, p. 123; obituary of du Pont, *New York Times*, September 13, 1943; Stringer, *Headline History of the Air Pick-up, 1939–42*, p. 81: Arthur Bartlett, "He Gave an Idea Wings."

2. Interview with Charles W. Wendt, August 29, 1985.

3. AAEC collection, box 1, agreement between Lytle S. Adams and Richard C. du Pont, September 12, 1938.

4. Ibid.

5. Ibid., box 5, minutes of the board of directors, All American Aviation, Inc., September 12, November 16, 1938.

6. Ibid., box 1, copy of "Contract for Experimental Air Mail Service," dated December 13, 1938, with signatures of company officials and witnesses dated December 17, 27, 1938.

7. Ibid., box 1, All American Aviation, Inc., Exhibit B, statement of assets and liabilities as of September 15, 1938, attached to above contract.

8. Shamburger, "All American Aviation," p. 199; Trimble, *High Frontier*, pp. 127, 137, 176, 203; interview with Charles W. Wendt, August 29, 1985; Writers' Program, *Who's Who in Aviation*, p. 348; Serling, *From the Captain to the Colonel*, pp. 11, 16; Stringer, *Headline History of the Air Pick-up, 1939–1942*, p. 103: undated clipping, "All American Names New Department Heads," in column headed "Dixie Air News," from unidentified journal.

9. Jackson et al., *Flying the Mail*, p. 169; Shamburger, "All American Aviation," p. 200; AAEC collection, Thomas E. McBride, "The First Hundred Years Are the Hardest," typescript history of All American Aviation dated 1963.

10. Stringer, *Headline History of the Air Pick-up, 1939–1942*, pp. 18–19: undated clipping from the *Gettysburg* (Pa.) *Times*; *Pick-Up*, June/July, 1944, p. 2; Writers' Program, *Who's Who in Aviation*, pp. 336–37, 444. The revolution in Cuba from which Kincheloe fled was connected with the fall from power of Gerado Machado and the rise of Fulgencio Batista; see Langley, *Cuban Policy of the United States*, pp. 153–69.

11. Johansen, "The Flights of the Liberty."

12. Stringer, *Headline History of the Air Pick-up, 1939–1942*, pp. 18–19: undated clipping from the *Gettysburg* (Pa.) *Times*. On the nature of the arrangement under which Yesulaites worked for All American in these early months, see ACP files, vol. 5, Adams to All American Aviation, Inc., attention of Henry A. Wise, Jr., August 14, 1939.

13. Underwood, *Stinsons*, pp. 55–64; Grey and Bridgman, *Jane's All the World's Aircraft, 1939*, pp. 89d, 279–81c. According to the latter source, eight models of the SR-10 had been produced by 1939, with different horsepower ratings and speed capabilities depending upon the power unit fitted. Although former All American employees have given varying estimates, we have accepted the figures given in *Jane's* for the SR-10C, the model first acquired by the company. According to Shamburger, "All American Aviation," p. 200, the fifth SR-10 acquired by the company had a Pratt and Whitney engine rated at 450 horsepower. For other material on the SR-10 Reliants, see Underwood, "Stinson Production Notes, 1920–1948," pp. 215–16. Thomas E. McBride, "The First Hundred Years Are the Hardest" (AAEC collection), states that All American's equipment as of October 1, 1938, included a Stinson Detroiter aircraft, but this cannot be corroborated from other sources; it may have belonged to Adams's Tri-State Aviation firm.

14. Interviews with Charles W. Wendt, September 9, 11, 1980; AAEC collection, box 5, minutes, regular meeting of board of directors and annual meeting of stockholders, All American Aviation, Inc., both held February 3, 1939. On du Pont's connections with the Kirkham Engineering and Manufacturing Company, see ibid., box 5, Exhibit A, attached to "Contract for Experimental Air Mail Service," December 1938.

15. Detailed documentation concerning the process of development and modification that took place at Granogue in early 1939 is missing; the account here given of the changes that were made has been pieced together from several sources: interviews with Charles W. Wendt, August 21, September 9, 11, 1980, and August 29, 1985; AAEC collection, "Description of Pick-Up and Delivery System," undated manuscript; the discussion in Shamburger, "All American Aviation," p. 199; and correspondence between Adams and du Pont to be cited later. Shamburger errs in placing these modifications after, rather than before, a demonstration of the pickup system conducted at the time of a postmasters' convention held in Washington, D.C., in October 1939, which is misdated to 1938. On the other hand, the technical details Shamburger gives are consistent with what can be gleaned from the other sources. The assistance of Professor Malcolm Crocker, head, Department of Mechanical Engineering, Auburn University, has been of great value in reviewing and assessing the engineering problems involved, both in the Granoque experiments and the modified pickup system that resulted from them.

16. ACP files, vol. 5, Lytle S. Adams to All American Aviation, Inc., attention of Richard C. du Pont, president, February 3, 1939.

17. Interviews with Charles W. Wendt, September 11, 1980, August 29, 1985.

18. Stringer, *Headline History of the Air Pick-up, 1939–1942*, pp. 4–5, 30–31; miscellaneous clippings from newspapers in Franklin, Natrona, Oil City, and other Pennsylvania communities; ibid., pp. 30–31, clipping from *Altoona Tribune*.

19. Ibid., p. 7, "Great Crowd Sees Airmail Pick-Up Test," clipping from *Coatesville* (Pa.) *Record*.

20. Ibid., pp. 12–13, miscellaneous clippings.

21. In addition to AAEC collection, "Description of Pick-Up and Delivery System," undated manuscript, circa 1939, and Shamburger, "All American Aviation," p. 199 (with illustration of the shock-absorbing apparatus involved), see the excellent information in Stringer, *Headline History of the Air Pick-up, 1939–1942*, pp. 55, 101: Alexander Klemin, "Airmail for Small Towns," from undated issue of *Scientific American*, "All American Improves Pickup Equipment," from undated issue of *Aero Digest*, and Charles Morrow Wilson, "R.F.D. Gets Wings," from undated issue of *Popular Science Monthly*. The last two articles deal in part with improvements made in 1940, but much of the description they provide is also appropriate to the system with which the firm began operations in 1939.

22. See particularly AAEC collection, "List of Towns to Receive Air-Mail Service from All American Aviation, Inc. Showing Dates On or Before Which Service Will Begin."

23. Stringer, *Headline History of the Air Pick-up, 1939–1942*, pp. 36–37, clippings from *Latrobe* (Pa.) *Bulletin* and *Pittsburgh Sun-Telegraph*.

24. Ibid., pp. 33–37, clippings from *Morgantown* (W. Va.) *Dominion-News* and *Washington Star*.

25. Ibid., pp. 37–49, clippings from *Philadelphia Public Ledger, Coatesville* (Pa.) *Record, Clearfield* (Pa.) *Progress*, and other newspapers.

Chapter 3. Visions and Vexations

1. Stringer, *Headline History of the Air Pick-up, 1939–1942*, pp. 77–78; report to Congress by Postmaster General James A. Farley, May 13, 1940; Shamburger, "All American Aviation," pp. 199–201.

2. *Pittsburgh Post-Gazette*, February 15, 16, 17, 19, 21, 1940; Stringer, *Headline History of the Air Pick-up, 1939–1942*, p. 80: "Airmail Pickup Is Big Help In Valley During April Flood"; "Pilot Unable to Land Drops Mail at Post Office"; and other clippings from unidentified newspapers.

3. ACP files, vol. 5, balance sheet for operations from May 12 through June 30 and correspondence pertaining thereto, particularly letters from Richard C. du Pont to Helen Demmer, August 22, 1939, and from W. P. Wilson to unidentified stockholder, August 29, 1939; AAEC collection, box 2, balance sheet, June 30, 1940, with profit and loss for year ending May 13, 1940.

4. ACP files, vol. 5, Richard C. du Pont to board of directors, All American Aviation, Inc., August 21, 1939.

5. Stringer, *Headline History of the Air Pick-up, 1939–1942*, pp. 58–59, "Air Feeder Program: A plan for the establishment of a comprehensive air feeder system throughout the United States, based on the use of the air pick-up principle, as submitted to the Civil Aeronautics Authority and the Post Office Department by Richard C. du Pont, President, All American Aviation, Inc., August 1939."

6. Ibid., pp. 61–62: "Fortnightly Review: American Aviation"; Bulkeley Griffin, "Washington," column in *Hartford* (Conn.) *Times*; "Speeding up the Mails," from *Boston Traveler*; "Aviation Looks Ahead," from *St. Paul* (Minn.) *Dispatch*; "Air

Service for Small Centers," from *St. Louis Star-Times;* "Air Line Feeder," from *Bridgeport* (Conn.) *Telegram;* Al Williams, "Cities Need 'Feeder Lines,' " syndicated column from unidentified newspaper; "Air-mail Feeders," editorial from *New York Times.*

7. Ibid., pp. 60–62: "More Air Mail," from *Kalamazoo* (Mich.) *Gazette;* "Mail Air Catchers," from *Springfield* (Mass.) *Evening Union;* "Feeder Lines for Air Service," from *Worcester* (Mass.) *Gazette & Post;* "Feeders for the Airpost," from *Rome* (New York) *Sentinel;* "Direct Air Service?" from *Ashland* (Ohio) *Times-Gazette;* "Feeder Airmail Lines," from *Hickory* (N.C.) *Record;* "Want Rockford Placed on Air Mail Network," from *Tyler* (Texas) *Courier-Times.*

8. Ibid., p. 63: "Flying Mailman Gives Exhibition"; "Officials Witness Airmail Pick-Up Demonstration"; "Air Mail Pick-up Exhibit on Display"; "Postmasters See Airplane Service"; and other clippings from *Washington Times* and other newspapers, mostly unidentified. See also Shamburger, "All American Aviation," pp. 198–99, with photograph showing the demonstration in progress. Shamburger, however, errs in stating that the demonstration took place in November 1938 rather than October 1939.

9. Stringer, *Headline History of the Air Pick-up, 1939–1942,* p. 64: "Night Mail Pick-Up Successful in Test at Bellanca Field"; "Night Pick-up of Mail is Started"; "Night Airmail Starts Nov. 15"; "First Night Mail Pickup Here Success"; and other clippings from various newspapers, mostly unidentified.

10. AAEC collection, box 6, text of du Pont's address, included in "Development of Aviation," remarks by Congressman Jennings Randolph, from the *Congressional Record.*

11. *Civil Aeronautics Board Reports,* vol. 2, Docket no. 363, pp. 134–44.

12. See the large number of clippings and maps reproduced in Stringer, *Headline History of the Air Pick-up, 1939–1942,* pp. 66–71.

13. Corn, *Winged Gospel,* particularly pp. 91–111.

14. For overviews of the background of the Civil Aeronautics Act of 1938 and the early years of the Civil Aeronautics Authority and Civil Aeronautics Board, see Komons, *Bonfires to Beacons,* pp. 347–79, and Wilson, *Turbulence Aloft,* pp. 9–61. On the crash in which Senator Cutting was killed, see Komons, *Cutting Air Crash.*

15. *Civil Aeronautics Board Reports,* vol. 2, pp. 147–55.

16. Ibid., pp. 145–46.

17. Ibid., pp. 146–47.

18. ACP files, vol. 5, du Pont to Adams, July 14, 1939. Du Pont's attitude toward the matter is best expressed in a July 13, 1939, letter (in ibid.) to West Virginia industrialist W. P. Wilson in which he took issue with the latter's characterization of the pickup system as "Dr. Adams's device." According to du Pont, "From the corporation's standpoint, better results would be obtained from publicity centered on the corporation and not the individual. In addition, it is through the corporation that Dr. Adams expects to receive his reward. Actually, the present system uses only a few of Dr. Adams's original principles, and the present workable method, which may or may not be patentable, was developed by the corporation since September of last year."

19. Ibid., vol. 5, Adams to du Pont, undated (probably late July 1939); ibid., vol. 5, Henry A. Wise, Jr., to Adams, August 5, 1939.

20. Ibid., vol. 5, Adams to All American Aviation, Inc., attention Henry A. Wise, Jr., August 14, 1939.

21. Ibid., vol. 5, du Pont to Adams, August 26, 1939.

22. Ibid., vol. 5, Adams to All American Aviation, Inc., attention Richard C. du Pont, September 11, 1939.

23. Ibid., vol. 5, copy of list of items for discussion or information at directors' meeting of All American Aviation, Inc., May 9, 1939; ibid., vol. 5, copy of minutes of

special meeting of directors of All American Aviation, Inc., May 9, 1939; interview with Charles W. Wendt, August 29, 1985.

24. ACP files, vol. 5: call for special meeting of board of directors of All American Aviation issued by Charles W. Wendt, Secretary, June 1, 1939; Adams to All American Aviation, Inc., attention Richard C. du Pont, June 2, 1939.

25. Ibid., vol. 5: W. P. Wilson to H. H. Howes, June 29, 1939; Adams to All American Aviation, Inc., attention Richard C. du Pont, July 3, 1939; du Pont to Wilson, July 13, 1939; du Pont to Adams, July 14, 1939; Wilson to du Pont, July 15, 1939; Howes to Wilson, July 15, 1939.

26. Ibid., vol. 5: Adams to du Pont, August 2, 1939; letter, correspondent identified only as "Ray," to du Pont, August 3, 1939. The correspondent may have been either the pilot Raymond Elder or the company vice president James Ray, Sr.

27. Adams's straitened finances in mid-1939 are indicated in letters in ACP files, vol. 5. A letter from Adams to W. P. Wilson dated May 31, 1939, discusses his need for a loan from a Wheeling bank and connects this matter directly to Adams's desire to retain "valuable franchise rights in the Tri State Aviation Corporation that is entirely controlled by me." A letter dated June 27, 1939, from Adams to Charles W. Wendt indicates that Adams was transferring 3,800 shares of his stock in All American Aviation at this time to a number of outside parties, chiefly persons in Wheeling. In the August 29, 1985, interview, Charles W. Wendt stated that these transfers were in connection with Adams's sales of All American stock to various persons in order to satisfy business obligations and that Adams was apparently in a difficult financial position at this time. Testimony presented at the CAA hearings of February–March 1940 involving permanent certification of All American and extension of its route structure indicated that by this time Adams, who was now listed as holding only 25 percent of All American's class A stock, actually had less than that because, as his own statements to the examiner revealed, "he has recently sold some of his shares in payment of debts." See Stringer, *Headline History of the Air Pick-up, 1939–1942*, p. 88, "All American Expansion Hearing Ends; Interveners State Positions," from *American Aviation*.

28. *Civil Aeronautics Board Reports*, vol. 2, docket 59-401-E-1, pp. 159–60.

29. Ibid., pp. 160–61; AAEC collection, box 6, Frank W. Boykin, U.S. Representative from the First Congressional District, Alabama, to George T. Weymouth, Laird and Company, Wilmington, Delaware, February 8, 1940.

30. Stringer, *Headline History of the Air Pick-up, 1939–1942*, p. 88: undated column, "Washingtonia," by Arnold Kruckman in unidentified publication; clipping, "All American Hearing Ends; Interveners State Positions," from *American Aviation*.

31. Ibid., p. 79; undated clippings from unidentified newspapers, "Year Long Test of Pickup Ends in Big Success" and "Airmail Hope Here Is Ended."

32. Ibid., pp. 77–78, report of May 13, 1940, to the Congress by Postmaster General James A. Farley.

33. *Valley Daily News*, May 17, 1940; Stringer, *Headline History of the Air Pick-up, 1939–1940*, pp. 79, 82, 85–87: headlines from unspecified newspaper; various clippings on pages headed "Fight Organized in Congress"; undated clippings from *Oil City* (Pa.) *Derrick*, *Weston* (W. Va.) *Democrat*, and other newspapers relating to pilot visits.

Chapter 4. "The Biggest Little Airline in the World"

1. *Valley Daily News*, May 17, 1940.

2. *Congressional Record*, vol. 86, pt. 6, pp. 6468, 6955; ibid., pt. 7, pp. 7075, 7255.

3. *Oil City Derrick*, May 28, 1940; Stringer, *Headline History of the Air Pick-up, 1939–1942*, pp. 84–86: clipping from *Parkersburg* (W.Va.) *News*, dated May 28, 1940; miscellaneous, unidentified, undated clippings.

4. *Warren Times-Mirror*, May 11, 1940; *Oil City Derrick*, May 14, 1940; *New York Times*, May 26, 1940.

5. *American Aviation*, June 1, 1940, p. 25; ibid., June 15, 1940, p. 4; Stringer, *Headline History of the Air Pick-up, 1939–1942*, p. 86: unidentified, undated clipping.

6. *American Aviation*, June 1, 1939, p. 7; *Pittsburgh Press*, May 19, 26, 1942; *Oil City Derrick*, May 28, 30, 1940; Stringer, *Headline History of the Air Pick-up, 1939–1942*, p. 87: miscellaneous, unidentified, undated clippings.

7. *Pittsburgh Press*, June 2, 1940.

8. Ibid.

9. U.S. Congress, *Air Mail: Extending Jurisdiction of Civil Aeronautics Authority Over Certain Air-Mail Services; Congressional Record*, vol. 86, pt. 8, p. 8416.

10. *Congressional Record*, vol. 86, pt. 8, pp. 8887, 9899, 9140, 9232; ibid., pp. 8809, 8965, 9095; *Statutes at Large of the United States of America, 1939–1941*, pp. 735–36.

11. Wilson, *Turbulence Aloft*, pp. 43–57.

12. *Civil Aeronautics Board Reports*, vol. 2, pp. 134–35, 138–40, 148–49, 153–55.

13. Ibid., pp. 149–52.

14. Ibid., pp. 157–58; AAEC collection, box 6, "All American Aviation, Inc.: The Story of an American Pioneer," prepared by Blyth & Co., Inc., pp. 13–14; ibid., box 3a–3e, press release, July 1940.

15. *Civil Aeronautics Board Reports*, vol. 2, pp. 145–47.

16. Ibid., pp. 159–74.

17. *Civil Aeronautics Board Reports*, vol. 4, pp. 100–03; *Business Week*, August 31, 1940, p. 22; interview with Charles W. Wendt, taped response to written questions; interview with Willis B. Adams, Lytle Adams's son, corroborated the cash payment story, although he said the amount was $60,000. The CAB *Reports* state that du Pont's interest in Tri-State was 50 percent.

18. Feist, "Bats Away!"; *Washington Northwest Frontier*, pp. 410–12; *Tucson Daily Citizen*, December 31, 1970.

19. *Civil Aeronautics Board Reports*, vol. 3, p. 91; *Congressional Record Appendix*, vol. 86, pt. 16, p. 4678; *Pittsburgh Press*, August 12, 1940; Petee, *Triple A Story*, p. 13; Stringer, *Headline History of the Air Pick-up, 1939–1942*, pp. 92–99: unidentified, undated clippings.

20. Herron, "Swoop, Snatch and Zoom"; *Williamsport Sun*, December 2, 1940; *Civil Aeronautics Board Reports*, vol. 3, p. 81.

21. Descriptions of the new pickup system appear in Stringer, *Headline History of the Air Pick-up, 1939–1942*, p. 109: "Air Pick-up System in the United States," clipping from *Modern Transport* (London), August 9, 1941; "Air Mail Put on a 'Local' Circuit"; "Air Mail Pick-up"; Thorp, "Airmail Goes RFD"; also Shamburger, "All American Aviation"; AAEC collection, box 6, Blyth & Co., "All American Aviation," pp. 4; *Pick-Up*, March 1944, p. 4.

22. All American Aviation, Inc., *Annual Report, 1941*, pp. 4, 8.

23. *Aero Digest*, December 1941, p. 108; *Congressional Record Appendix*, vol. 87, pt. 13, pp. A3865–66.

24. AAEC collection, box 6, Blyth & Co., "All American Aviation," pp. 31–33; All American Aviation, Inc., *Annual Report, 1941*, p. 4; *Civil Aeronautics Board Reports*, vol. 3, pp. 79–96, 320–22.

25. AAEC collection, box 5, Blyth & Co., "All American Aviation," p. 33; *Civil Aeronautics Board Reports*, vol. 3, p. 83; Stringer, *Headline History of the Air Pick-up, 1939–1942*, pp. 104–05: miscellaneous, unidentified, undated clippings.

26. *Civil Aeronautics Board Reports*, vol. 3, pp. 7–18.

27. *Aero Digest*, April 1941, p. 78.

28. Stringer, *Headline History of the Air Pick-up, 1939–1942*, pp. 91, 103.

29. *Congressional Record Appendix*, vol. 87, pt. 13, p. A3865; All American Aviation, Inc., *Annual Report, 1941*, pp. 4, 6; *New York Times*, October 12, 1941.

30. Interview with William M. Wiley, Jr.; AAEC collection, box 6, Blyth & Co., "All American Aviation," pp. 25-26.

31. *Pick-Up*, November 1945, p. 2; interview with Lloyd C. Santmyer; Shamburger, "All American Aviation," p. 203.

32. Interview with Lloyd C. Santmyer; Shamburger, "All American Aviation," pp. 202-03; *Pick-Up*, September 1944, p. 4.

33. Herron, "Swoop, Snatch and Zoom," pp. 17-18; Petee, *Triple A Story*, p. 17.

34. Smith and Harrington, *Aviation and Pennsylvania*, pp. 78-79; interview with Mildred Albertson, taped response to written questions.

35. Herron, "Swoop, Snatch and Zoom," p. 18; Stringer, *Headline History of the Air Pick-up, 1939-1942*, p. 110: miscellaneous, undated clippings.

36. All American Aviation, Inc., *Annual Report, 1941*, p. 4.

Chapter 5. The Pickup Goes to War

1. *American Aviation*, January 15, 1942, p. 38; AAEC collection, box 6, Blyth & Co., "All American Aviation," p. 26; All American Aviation, Inc., *Annual Report, 1945*, pp. 7, 13.

2. *American Aviation*, April 15, 1942, p. 34; ibid., December 15, 1941, p. 36; AAEC collection, box 5, minutes, special meetings of board of directors, August 31, 1942, January 5, 1943; Bramley, "Lines Hire Women at Record Rate"; *Pick-Up*, November 1945, p. 2; AAEC collection, box 6, Blyth & Co., "All American Aviation," p. 25; AAEC collection, box 5, minutes, regular meeting of board of directors, December 22, 1942; All American Aviation, Inc., *Annual Report, 1945*, p. 3.

3. Shamburger, "All American Aviation," p. 204; interview with Victor J. Gasbarro; *Congressional Record Appendix*, vol. 88, pt. 8, p. A798; *Pick-Up*, January 1945, p. 2.

4. All American Aviation, Inc., *Annual Report, 1943*, p. 4; ibid., *Annual Report, 1945*, p. 2; AAEC collection, box 6, Edward D. Musser, "All American Maintenance," in Charles W. Wendt scrapbook; interview with Walter Sartory; Thorp, "Maintenance System Mainsprings Pick-Up Line's Efficiency."

5. *American Aviation*, January 1, 1942, p. 32; *Civil Aeronautics Board Reports*, vol. 4, pp. 60-63, 389-91, 638-41; *Pick-Up*, October 1943, n.p.; AAEC, box 6, unidentified, undated clippings in Wendt scrapbook.

6. "Triple A Goes to Washington"; *Aviation News*, January 17, 1944, p. 40; ibid., August 7, 1944, pp. 51-52; All American Aviation, Inc., *Annual Report, 1945*, p. 2; *Pick-Up*, June 1945, p. 1.

7. *Pittsburgh Post-Gazette*, April 13, 1943; AAEC collection, box 6, miscellaneous, unidentified, undated clippings in Wendt scrapbook.

8. "One of Our Planes Was Missing"; interview with Victor J. Gasbarro; AAEC collection, box 6, miscellaneous, unidentified, undated clippings in Wendt scrapbook; Stringer, *Headline History of the Air Pick-up, 1942-1946*, p. 9, miscellaneous, unidentified, undated clippings.

9. *Pick-Up*, August 1944, p. 3; Stringer, *Headline History of the Air Pick-up, 1942-1946*, p. 79, "Mail Plane Crashes, Burns Near Yorkville," unidentified clipping.

10. AAEC collection, box 6, "Mail Pick-up Pilot Killed in Crash," undated clipping, *Wilmington News*, in Wendt scrapbook; *Pick-Up*, October 1944, pp. 1-2; *Aviation News*, October 9, 1944, p. 46; *Pick-Up*, January 1945, p. 2, erroneously dates the accident on January 5; *Greensburg Daily Tribune*, January 11, 12, 1945.

11. AAEC collection, box 5, minutes, special meeting of board of directors, August 31, 1942; ibid., box 5, minutes, regular meeting of board of directors, December 22,

1942; Petee, *Triple A Story*, p. 18; All American Aviation, Inc., *Annual Report, 1943*, p. 5; Wendt file, March 24, 1943, pp. 3–4.

12. All American Aviation, Inc., *Annual Report, 1944*, p. 3; Petee, *Triple A Story*, p. 18; AAEC collection, box 5, minutes, regular meeting of board of directors, pp. 2–3; ibid., box 5, minutes, meeting of administrative committee, January 19, 1943.

13. AAEC collection, box 5, minutes, special meeting of board of directors, August 31, 1942; ibid., box 5, minutes, meeting of administrative committee, February 16, 1943; Petee, *Triple A Story*, pp. 18–19; Wendt file, pp. 4–5.

14. Shamburger, "All American Aviation," p. 204; "Triple A 5 Years Old Friday May 12."

15. Shamburger, "All American Aviation" p. 203. Stringer, *Headline History of the Air Pick-up, 1939–1942*, pp. 117–29, and Stringer, *Headline History of the Air Pick-up, 1942–1946*, pp. 28–29, 31–33, contain numerous references to the military use of gliders and All American's experiments. A recent general account of the military development of the glider is Devlin, *Silent Wings*.

16. Stringer, *Headline History of the Air Pick-up, 1939–1942*, pp. 119–23; *American Aviation*, July 1, 1942, p. 4; *Aviation*, August 1942, p. 234.

17. AAEC collection, box 5, minutes, annual meeting of board of directors, October 13, 1942, pp. 3–4; ibid., box 5, minutes, special meeting of board of directors, January 5, 1943; Wendt file, p. 11; All American Aviation, Inc., *Annual Report, 1945*, p. 4; AAEC collection, box 6, Blyth & Co., "All American Aviation," pp. 26–27.

18. Interview with Lloyd C. Santmyer; All American Aviation, Inc., *Annual Report, 1945*, p. 4.

19. *Pick-Up*, October 1944, p. 1; "Glider Pick-Up Used in Invasion"; AAEC collection, box 6, "Air Pick-Up Apparatus," in Wendt scrapbook.

20. Link and Coleman, *Medical Support of the Army Air Forces in World War II*, pp. 886–89; *New York Times*, March 25, June 9, 30, July 10, 1945; AAEC collection, box 6, "Rescue from Shangri-La," undated clipping from *Yank*, in Wendt scrapbook.

21. AAEC collection, box 1, Richard C. du Pont, "Cargo Glider Pick-Up," paper delivered at the Aviation Session, Sixty-third Annual Meeting of the American Society of Mechanical Engineers, December 2, 1942; see also "Du Pont Sees Short-Haul Use for Gliders on Future Airlines."

22. AAEC collection, box 1, Du Pont, "Cargo Glider Pick-Up"; "Du Pont Sees Short-Haul Use for Gliders."

23. Stringer, *Headline History of the Air Pick-up, 1939–1942*, p. 115, undated press release, Post Office Department; ibid., pp. 123–24, 128, 132, miscellaneous, undated clippings; AAEC collection, box 6, Robert M. Hyatt, "Trains in the Sky," in Wendt scrapbook.

24. *Pick-Up*, October 1945, p. 1; AAEC collection, box 6, unidentified, undated articles in Wendt scrapbook.

25. Petee, *Triple A Story*, p. 17; Davis, "Hitchhiking to Heaven"; AAEC collection, box 6, undated clipping from *Aviation News* in Wendt scrapbook; Stringer, *Headline History of the Air Pick-up, 1942–1946*, pp. 34–35, Paul Gallico, "Human Pickup."

26. Davis, "Hitchhiking to Heaven"; AAEC collection, box 6, undated clipping from *Aviation News* in Wendt scrapbook; Stringer, *Headline History of the Air Pick-up, 1942–1946*, pp. 34–35, Paul Gallico, "Human Pickup."

27. AAEC collection, box 6, undated clipping from *Contact* in Wendt scrapbook; Shamburger, "All American Aviation," p. 205.

28. *Pick-Up*, October 1945, pp. 1, 3; Davis, "Clothesline Air Strip"; van Deurs, "Navy and the Brodie"; AAEC collection, box 7, "Model 20 (Brodie) Arresting Gear," June 30, July 1, 3, 5, 6, 1944.

29. AAEC collection, box 7, "Undrawn Nylon," August 10, 1944; ibid., box 7,

"Pick-up with undrawn nylon," February 2, 1945; ibid., box 7, "Trail Tests of a Gasoline Tank," August 11, 23, 24, September 11, 15, 1944.

30. AAEC collection, box 6, Blyth & Co., "All American Aviation," pp. 26–27, 30–31; All American Aviation, Inc., *Annual Report, 1943*, p. 5, *1945*, p. 4; AAEC collection, box 6, undated clipping, *Wilmington Journal–Every Evening*, in Wendt scrapbook; *American Aviation*, November 1, 1943, p. 64.

31. Petee, *Triple A Story*, p. 18; All American Aviation, Inc., *Annual Report, 1943*, p. 5, *1944*, p. 3; AAEC collection, box 5, minutes, regular meetings of board of directors, May 27, June 22, 1943; Henry Belin du Pont collection, box 6, miscellaneous correspondence.

32. AAEC collection, box 6, Blyth & Co., "All American Aviation," p. 31; ibid., box 5, minutes, special meeting of board of directors, August 31, 1942; ibid., box 5, minutes, annual meeting of stockholders, September 30, 1943; All American Aviation, Inc., *Annual Report, 1944*, p. 3; *Pick-Up*, June/July 1944, p. 4.

33. All American Aviation, Inc., *Annual Report, 1943*, p. 3; AAEC collection, box 5, minutes, special meeting of board of directors, March 13, 1943; ibid., box 5, minutes, regular meeting of board of directors, January 25, 1944; ibid., box 5, minutes, special meeting of board of directors, April 24, 1943.

34. *Wilmington Journal–Every Evening*, September 13, 1943; AAEC collection, box 6, miscellaneous clippings in Wendt scrapbook; All American Aviation, Inc., *Annual Report, 1943*, p. 4; *Pick-Up*, April/May 1944, p. 2; Stringer, *Headline History of the Air Pick-up, 1942–1946*, pp. 1, 5–8, miscellaneous clippings.

35. Writers' Program, *Who's Who in Aviation*, p. 30; AAEC collection, box 3A—3B, press release, February 24, 1949; interview with Victor J. Gasbarro; interview with Jennings Randolph.

36. AAEC collection, box 5: minutes, regular meeting of board of directors, December 22, 1942; minutes, special meeting of board of directors, January 5, 1943; minutes, regular meeting of board of directors, July 27, 1943; minutes, special meeting of board of directors, August 31, 1942; minutes, annual meeting of board of directors, October 13, 1942.

37. Ibid., box 5: minutes, annual meeting of board of directors, October 13, 1942; minutes, special meeting of board of directors, January 5, 1943; minutes, adjourned regular meeting of board of directors, February 1, 1943; minutes, special meeting of stockholders, March 17, 1943; ibid., box 6, Blyth & Co., "All American Aviation," p. 36; All American Aviation, Inc., *Annual Report, 1944*, p. 2.

38. AAEC collection, box 5, minutes, regular meeting of board of directors, December 22, 1942; *Civil Aeronautics Board Reports*, vol. 4, pp. 354–72.

39. All American Aviation, Inc., *Annual Report, 1943*, pp. 4–6; ibid., *Annual Report, 1944*, pp. 4, 6–7; ibid., *Annual Report, 1945*, pp. 1, 8, 10–11.

40. *American Aviation*, July 1, 1943, p. 15; AAEC collection, box 5: minutes, regular meeting of board of directors, May 27, 1943; minutes, regular meeting of board of directors, June 22, 1943; minutes, meeting of board of directors, July 7, 1943; All American Aviation, Inc., *Annual Report, 1943*, pp. 5, 11–12; Stringer, *Headline History of the Air Pick-up, 1939–1942*, pp. 115–16, article from *Flight* (London), August 1941.

41. *American Aviation*, September 15, 1943, p. 37; *Civil Aeronautics Board Reports*, vol. 6, pp. 9, 20–25; AAEC collection, box 6, unidentified, undated clipping in Wendt scrapbook.

42. *Civil Aeronautics Board Reports*, vol. 6, pp. 23, 57.

43. *Pick-Up*, March 1944, p. 2; Bramley, "Pickup Routes Doing a Big Job."

44. *Pick-Up*, January/February 1944, p. 2; ibid., April/May 1944, p. 2; All American Aviation, Inc., *Annual Report, 1944*, p. 3; AAEC collection, box 6, "Experts Draw Up

Plans for Ideal Feederliner at Parley in St. Louis," *Air Transportation*, undated, in Wendt scrapbook; Stringer, *Headline History of the Air Pick-up, 1942–1946*, p. 66; "Feeder Airlines Chart Program," undated clipping.

45. *Pick-Up*, January/February 1944, p. 4; ibid., December 1944, pp. 1, 4; ibid., June 1945, pp. 1–2, 4; All American Aviation, Inc., *Annual Report, 1945*, p. 3; Stringer, *Headline History of the Air Pick-up, 1942–1946*, p. 88, miscellaneous undated clippings.

46. *Congressional Record Appendix*, vol. 91, pt. 12, p. A3352.

47. *Pick-Up*, August 1944, p. 1; ibid., July 1945, pp. 2, 4; AAEC collection, box 6, miscellaneous articles from *Aviation News* and *American Aviation* in Wendt scrapbook; *Pick-Up*, December 1944, p. 1; ibid., March 1945, p. 1; ibid., July 1945, p. 1.

Chapter 6. Changing the Flight Plan

1. Shamburger, "All American Aviation," p. 205; *Pick-Up*, October 1945, pp. 1, 3; All American Aviation, Inc., *Annual Report, 1945*, pp. 1, 4–5; AAEC collection, box 5: minutes, regular meetings of board of directors, May 22, June 26, July 24, September 17, November 26, 1945; minutes, regular meeting of executive committee, July 24, 1945; minutes, annual meeting of stockholders, September 17, 1945.

2. All American Aviation, Inc., *Annual Report, 1945*, pp. 8, 13; ibid., *Annual Report, 1946*, p. 5.

3. Ibid., *Annual Report, 1945*, pp. 2–3, 5; Stringer, *Headline History of the Air Pick-up, 1942–1946*, p. 95; undated clipping from *Aviation News*.

4. Interviews with Charles W. Wendt, September 9 and 11, 1980.

5. Stringer, *Headline History of the Air Pick-up, 1942–1946*, p. 81; "Colonel Robert M. Love Made President of All American," *Pick-Up*, January 1946, pp. 1, 4; AAEC collection, box 6, clippings from *American Aviation, Aviation News*, and *Wilmington News*, in Wendt scrapbook; ibid., box 5, minutes, regular meetings of board of directors, November 26, December 18, 1945.

6. AAEC collection, box 5, minutes, regular meeting of board of directors, December 18, 1945; *Pick-Up*, February 1946, p. 3. The minutes of the special meeting of stockholders at which the election of Davis, du Pont, and Lunger took place are missing from the file in which the other minutes for this period are located.

7. Interview with Charles W. Wendt, September 11, 1980.

8. Ibid.; Shamburger, "All American Aviation," p. 205.

9. "All American Lines Expanded to Cincinnati"; All American Aviation, Inc., *Annual Report, 1946*, pp. 2, 8, 11, 12; AAEC collection, box 5, minutes, regular meetings of board of directors, February 26, April 23, 1946.

10. All American Aviation, Inc., *Annual Report, 1946*, pp. 5, 8.

11. AAEC collection, box 5: minutes, executive committee, October 17, 1945; minutes, regular meetings of board of directors, November 26, 1945, December 18, 1945, April 23, 1946, May 23, 1946.

12. Ibid., box 5, minutes, regular meetings of board of directors, October 30, 1945, May 23, 1946.

13. Ibid., box 5, minutes, regular meetings of board of directors, October 30, November 26, 1945, May 23, 1946.

14. *Jane's All the World's Aircraft, 1947*, p. 96c; Stringer, *Headline History of the Air Pick-up, 1942–1946*, p. 95, clippings from *Aviation News*; AAEC collection, box 6, clippings from *Aviation News* in Wendt scrapbook; *Pick-Up*, November 1945, pp. 1, 3; AAEC collection, box 5, minutes, regular meetings of board of directors, April 23, May 23, 1945. According to various sources including the *Pick-Up*, article cited above, the

Noorduyn Norseman V acquired by All American could carry only 750 pounds more than the company's Stinsons. Here, as always, the figures given by *Jane's* should be used with caution, particularly when one is dealing with a plane specially adapted for pickup operations.

15. All American Aviation, Inc., *Annual Report, 1946*, p. 4; AAEC collection, box 6, Wendt scrapbook and Stringer, *Headline History of the Air Pick-up, 1942–1946* both contain clippings of articles: "AAA Pick-up Passenger Tests will Start in June with D-18C" and "All American Asks CAB for Passengers Permit," from May and July 1946 issues of *Aviation News*; AAEC collection, box 5, minutes, regular meetings of board of directors, October 30, 1945, April 23, May 23, July 23, 1946.

16. All American Aviation, Inc., *Annual Report, 1946*, p. 4; Ingells, *L-1011 TriStar and the Lockheed Story*, pp. 105, 107–08; Francillon, *Lockheed Aircraft Since 1913*, pp. 279–81; Stringer, *Headline History of the Air Pick-up, 1942–1946*, pp. 98–100, 104, and AAEC collection, box 6, Wendt scrapbook, contain clippings from various newspapers and journals including *Philadelphia Inquirer, Pittsburgh Courier, Washington Post,* and *Aviation News* regarding All American's Saturn purchase.

17. For a full text of the decision, see *Civil Aeronautics Board Reports*, vol. 6, pp. 961–1039. The results of the case were discussed by All American's board of directors at its May 1946 meeting and figured prominently in the ensuing annual report. See AAEC collection, box 5, minutes, regular meeting of board of directors, May 23, 1946, and All American Aviation, Inc., *Annual Report, 1946*, p. 3.

18. For the full text of the decision see *Civil Aeronautics Board Reports*, vol. 7, pp. 27–82.

19. AAEC collection, box 5, minutes, regular meeting of board of directors, June 25, 1946; All American Aviation, Inc., *Annual Report, 1946*, pp. 2, 11. Stringer, *Headline History of the Air Pick-up, 1942–1946*, p. 101, and AAEC collection, box 6, Wendt scrapbook, contain the clipping, "Aviation Common Offered to Public," from New York *Journal of Commerce.* Another clipping from an unidentified newspaper, also in the Wendt scrapbook and in Stringer presents the following breakdown of the intended disposition of the proceeds from the stock sale: $160,000 to replace capital expended for the two Beechcrafts; $400,000 to complete purchase of five Lockheed Saturns; $140,000 for spare engines and parts; $65,000 for organizational expense, communications equipment, and initial operating losses in providing expanded services; and $75,000 to manufacture twenty-five new air pickup units. This adds up to only $840,000 of the $877,500 realized from the sale. In any case, the matter is of purely academic interest in view of the fact that All American never purchased the Saturns and never acquired the hoped-for routes.

20. All American Aviation, Inc., *Annual Report, 1947*, pp. 12, 15.

21. Ibid., *Annual Report, 1947*, p. 15.

22. Ibid., *Annual Report, 1946*, p. 2; ibid., *Annual Report, 1947*, pp. 9, 14; AAEC collection, box 5, minutes, regular meetings of board of directors, October 22, 1946, February 25, 1947.

23. All American Aviation, Inc., *Annual Report, 1947*, pp. 8, 12; AAEC collection, box 5, minutes, regular meetings of board of directors, December 17, 1946, January 29, July 22, 1947; AAEC collection, Thomas E. McBride, "The First Hundred Years are the Hardest," p. 11.

24. All American Aviation, Inc., *Annual Report, 1947*, p. 8; AAEC box 5, minutes, regular meeting of board of directors, October 22, 1946; All American Aviation, Inc., *Air Pick-Up Handbook*, particularly material on p. 9 describing "Mail and Cargo Pick-up: All American Aviation Model 4 in Beechcraft." See also, "Improved Air Pickup Installed by Beech," p. 29, describing the altered unit in the Beechcrafts as follows:

Basically the pickup unit is the same as that the carrier has used for over five years. A major change is the mounting in the Beechcraft, in which the winch mechanism is installed near the cabin ceiling over the hatch, instead of on the floor forward of it. Pivot for the pickup arm has been moved to an extreme forward position on the plane, making it more accessible. Delivery problems created by the higher speed of the new planes have resulted in improvements in methods of dropping mail or express cargo containers. Electrical and pneumatic controls have reduced to a minimum the physical effort required of pilot and pickup operator.

During the same year, in yet another late refinement of the pickup system, the United States Rubber Company developed a new and more rugged mailbag for All American. "Heavily reinforced to withstand severe punishment," it was capable of dropping cargo "ranging from eggs to hardware" from a delivery plane without damage. See undated clippings from *Modern Industry* and other sources in Stringer, *Headline History of the Air Pick-up, 1942–1946*, p. 102.

25. AAEC collection, box 5, minutes, regular meeting of board of directors, October 22, 1946; Francillon, *Lockheed Aircraft Since 1913*, pp. 80–81; All American Aviation, Inc., *Annual Report, 1947*, p. 5.

26. All American Aviation, Inc., *Annual Report, 1947*, p. 5; Hedrick, *Pageantry of Flight* p. 21–22; McDaniel, *History of Beech*, pp. 87–88.

27. "86 Ride First Air Pick-Up Passenger Flights," pp. 1–3. Earlier in the year, two CAB examiners, Charles J. Frederick and Joseph L. Fitzmaurice, had flown from Philadelphia to Harrisburg and back aboard an All American plane piloted by Norm Rintoul on one of the company's normal mail runs serving twelve destinations between the two cities. Upon their return to Philadelphia, Frederick stated that he was "greatly impressed by the smoothness of the operation," and that "there was not the least shock or other sensation during the pick-up, and that the descent to the pickup station was less marked than an ordinary bump in large airplane travel." See Stringer, *Headline History of the Air Pick-up, 1942–1946*, p. 95, clippings from *Philadelphia Bulletin* and *Air Transport*.

28. *Pick-Up*, December 1946, pp. 1, 2; All American Aviation, Inc., *Annual Report, 1947*, p. 7; AAEC collection, box 5, minutes, regular meeting of board of directors, March 25, 1947.

29. Interview with Charles W. Wendt, September 9, 1980.

30. Ibid., September 9, 11, 1980.

31. AAEC collection, box 5: minutes, regular meetings of board of directors, July 22, August 8, November 26, 1946; minutes, special meeting of board of directors, November 7, 1946; *Pick-Up*, December 1946, p. 2.

32. AAEC collection, box 5, minutes, regular meeting of board of directors, January 29, 1947; All American Aviation, Inc., *Annual Report, 1947*, p. 3, showing directors and officers of the firm; interview with Charles W. Wendt, September 11, 1980. On the backgrounds of Hale and Rheinstrom, see also Serling, *Eagle*, passim.

33. For the full text of the decision see *Civil Aeronautics Board Reports*, vol. 7, pp. 863–941.

34. For the full text of the decision see *Civil Aeronautics Board Reports*, vol. 8, pp. 360–456.

35. For the full text of the decision see ibid., pp. 805–23.

36. For the full text of the decision see ibid., pp. 241–43.

37. AAEC collection, box 5, minutes, regular meeting of board of directors, March 25, 1947.

38. Ibid., box 5, minutes, regular meeting of board of directors, May 27, 1947.

Chapter 7. The Transformation

1. AAEC collection, box 5, minutes, regular meeting of board of directors, June 24, 1947.

2. Ibid., box 5, minutes, regular meeting of board of directors, December 23, 1947; ibid., box 7, minutes, regular meetings of board of directors, January 27, March 2, 1948. There is a discrepancy between the March 2 minutes, which specify a net return on the auction of approximately $141,000, and the All American Aviation, Inc., *Annual Report, 1948*, p. 4, which gives a figure of approximately $131,000.

3. All American Aviation, Inc., *Annual Report, 1948*, p. 4.

4. Ibid., pp. 8–9, 12; AAEC collection, box 5, minutes, regular meetings of board of directors, November 25, December 23, 1947; ibid., box 7, memorandum to board of directors, March 18, 1948; statistics on mail volume and revenue in *Civil Aeronautics Board Reports*, vol. 10, p. 39.

5. AAEC collection, box 5, minutes, regular meeting of board of directors, November 25, 1947; *Civil Aeronautics Board Reports*, vol. 8, pp. 672–75; AAEC collection, box 5, minutes, annual meeting of stockholders, September 15, 1947; All American Aviation, Inc., *Annual Report, 1948*, p. 3, shows list of directors; interview with Charles W. Wendt, September 11, 1980.

6. AAEC collection, box 5, minutes, regular meeting of board of directors, December 23, 1947.

7. *Civil Aeronautics Board Reports*, vol. 9, pp. 171–78.

8. Ibid., p. 176.

9. Ibid., p. 196.

10. AAEC collection, box 7, minutes, regular meetings of board of directors, March 2, 30, 1948.

11. Ibid., box 7: minutes, regular meetings of board of directors, March 30, April 27, May 25, June 29, July 27, August 24, October 26, 1948, March 22 postponed to March 29, 1949; All American Aviation, Inc., *Annual Report, 1948*, p. 8.

12. Interview with Charles W. Wendt, September 11, 1980; interview with Ray Garcia; interview with Frank Petee.

13. AAEC collection, box 7: minutes, regular meeting of board of directors, July 27, 1948; minutes, annual meeting of stockholders, September 20, 1948; and miscellaneous documents pertaining to name change; All American Aviation, Inc., *Annual Report, 1948*, p. 9.

14. AAEC collection, box 7, minutes, regular meeting of board of directors, October 26, 1948; interview with Charles W. Wendt, September 11, 1980.

15. AAEC collection, box 7: minutes, regular meetings of board of directors, October 26, November 23, December 28, 1948; January 25 postponed to February 1, 1949; and September 19, 1949; interview with Charles W. Wendt, September 11, 1980.

16. AAEC collection, box 7, minutes, regular meeting of board of directors, May 25, 1948.

17. *Civil Aeronautics Board Reports*, vol. 10, pp. 24–40.

18. Ibid., pp. 41–48.

19. AAEC collection, box 7: minutes, regular meetings of board of directors, October 26, November 23, December 28, 1948; January 25 postponed to February 1, 1949; February 22 postponed to March 1, 1949; March 22 postponed to March 29, 1949; and April 26, 1949.

20. Ibid., box 7: minutes, regular meeting of board of directors, January 25 postponed to February 1, 1949; and schedule and route map of All American Airways, March 19, 1949.

21. Ibid., box 7, minutes, regular meeting of board of directors, April 26, July 26, 1949; interview with Frank Petee.

22. Interview with Lloyd C. Santmyer; interview with Frank Petee.

23. *Washington Post,* March 8, 1949; *Pittsburgh Press,* March 7, 1949.

24. *Washington Post,* March 8, 1949; *Pittsburgh Post-Gazette,* March 10, 1949.

25. *Pittsburgh Post-Gazette,* March 27, June 20, 1949; AAEC collection, box 7, minutes, regular meeting of board of directors, June 28, 1949; *New York Times,* June 26, July 25, 1949.

26. Petee, Speech before the Aero Club of Pittsburgh; *New York Times,* June 26, 1949.

27. AAEC collection, box 7, minutes, regular meetings of board of directors, March 29, May 24, 1949; *Aviation Week,* May 23, 1949, p. 48; interview with Frank Petee; Shamburger, "All American Aviation," p. 206.

28. *Pittsburgh Press,* July 1, 3, 1949; "AAA Seeks Route Revision"; *Aviation Week,* February 12, 1951, p. 44; ibid., July 16, 1951, p. 76; ibid., March 24, 1952, p. 85.

29. "AAA Seeks Route Revision"; AAEC collection, box 7: memorandum, Love to board of directors, February 23, 1950; minutes, regular meeting of board of directors, January 24, 1950; listing applications, New York Curb Exchange, September 27, 1951, p. 8.

30. AAEC collection, box 7, minutes, regular meetings of board of directors, May 23, October 24, 1950, May 22, August 28, 1951; *Aviation Week,* July 16, 1951, p. 76.

31. *Aviation Week,* December 13, 1948, p. 48; AAEC collection, box 7, minutes, regular meetings of board of directors, January 23, February 27, 1951.

32. AAEC collection, box 7, minutes, regular meeting of board of directors, April 24, 1951; *New York Times,* January 23, 1951.

33. AAEC collection, box 7, minutes, regular meeting of board of directors, April 26, 1949. For postwar developments in the ALPA, see Hopkins, *Airline Pilots,* pp. 192–93. AAEC collection, box 7, minutes, regular meeting of board of directors, November 22, 1949; "AAA Seeks Route Revision"; *New York Times,* December 2, 1951.

34. All American Aviation, Inc., *Annual Report, 1951,* p. 2; AAEC collection, box 7, closing papers, separation of All American Airways, Inc., and All American Engineering Co.

35. AAEC collection, box 7, minutes, regular meetings of board of directors, January 24, December 12, 1950.

36. Ibid., box 7: prospectus, All American Aviation, Inc., July 2, 1946, pp. 8–9; listing application, New York Curb Exchange, September 27, 1951, pp. 9–10; minutes, regular meeting of board of directors, February 27, 1951.

37. Ibid., box 7, certified copy of resolution, September 9, 1952; ibid., box 7, All American Airways, proxy statement, October 28, 1952.

Epilogue

1. Shamburger, "All American Aviation," p. 206; *Science,* August 26, 1960, p. 537; Wagner, *Lightning Bugs and Other Reconnaissance Drones,* pp. 108–09.

2. Shamburger, "All American Aviation," p. 206; *New York Times,* May 18, 1974.

3. *New York Times,* January 20, 1970, September 30, 1980, May 10, 1982.

4. *Aviation Week,* May 4, 1953, p. 7; *Erie Times,* June 9, 1953; *Aviation Week,* August 31, 1953, p. 57; ibid., December 21, 1953, p. 73; ibid., February 8, 1954, p. 96; ibid., October 11, 1954, p. 102.

5. *Aviation Week,* April 12, 1954, pp. 79–80; ibid., May 30, 1955, p. 94; ibid., April 6, 1959, p. 39; ibid., January 11, 1960, p. 47.

6. *Aviation Week and Space Technology* September 14, 1959, p. 48; *Wall Street Journal*, May 19, 1961.

7. Fry, "Riding an Upward Curve"; Foster, "Allegheny Airlines, 1939–1966"; *Aviation Week*, October 18, 1954, p. 40; *Civil Aeronautics Board Reports*, vol. 48, pp. 664–73.

8. *New York Times*, April 29, 1965; *Wall Street Journal*, September 7, 1966; *1970 Aerospace Year Book*, pp. 228–29.

9. *Pittsburgh Press*, December 26, 1968, January 7, 1969; *New York Times*, September 10, 1969.

10. "Sky's the Limit for Allegheny"; *Aviation Week and Space Technology*, April 17, 1972, p. 24; "Allegheny's Ascent."

11. *New York Times*, July 11, 1975; "I'm Allegheny—Fly Me"; Griffiths, "Allegheny Links Airbus Buy, West Coast Rights."

12. *USAir Annual Report, 1979*, pp. 1, 4, 6, 8.

13. *Pittsburgh Post-Gazette*, September 7, 1981; *USAir News*, November 5, 1982, p. 1; *Pittsburgh Post-Gazette*, February 24, 1982; *Aviation Week and Space Technology*, September 5, 1983, p. 30; *Pittsburgh Post-Gazette*, February 22, 1983, August 3, 1985.

14. Press releases, USAir Group, Inc., April 21, 1983, January 5, March 21, 1984; "USAir."

15. Colodny, "Survival of the Fittest."

16. Ott, "USAir Buy of PSA Would Create Sixth Largest U.S. Carrier"; *New York Times*, December 9, 1986.

17. Preble, "USAir-Piedmont Merger"; *Aviation Week and Space Technology*, March 30, 1987, p. 29; *Pittsburgh Post-Gazette*, March 5, 6, 18, 1987.

18. *Pittsburgh Post-Gazette*, April 27, 1984, March 19, 1986, February 5, March 18, 1987; *Pittsburgh Press*, June 13, December 15, 1986, February 1, 1987.

Bibliography

Manuscript and Archival Material

AAEC collection: All American Engineering Company. Collection. Hagley Museum and Library, Wilmington, Delaware.

ACP files: Aero Club of Pittsburgh. Files. Air Mail Pick-Up and Delivery System. 5 vols. OX-5 Aviation Pioneers, Pittsburgh Chapter Office.

Ball papers: Ball, Clifford. Papers. Archives, Historical Society of Western Pennsylvania, Pittsburgh.

Roosevelt collection: Roosevelt, Eleanor. Collection. Franklin D. Roosevelt Library, Hyde Park, New York.

Wendt file: Charles W. Wendt. "Summary of the History of All American Aviation, Inc.," file no. 146.01–19: United States Air Force Historical Research Center, Maxwell Air Force Base, Alabama.

Public Documents

U.S. Cong. House. *To Create a Civil Aeronautics Authority: Hearings Before the Committee on Interstate and Foreign Commerce.* 75th Cong., 3d sess. Washington, D.C.: GPO, 1938.

U.S. Cong. House. *Congressional Record.* 75th Cong., 1st sess. Vol. 81, pts. 5, 6.

———. *Congressional Record.* 75th Cong., 3d sess. Vol. 83, pts. 4, 5, 8.

———. *Congressional Record.* 76th Cong., 3d sess. Vol. 86, pts. 6, 7, 8.

———. Senate. *Congressional Record.* 75th Cong., 3d sess. Vol. 83, pt. 4.

———. *Congressional Record.* 76th Cong., 3d sess. Vol. 86, pt. 8.

———. *Congressional Record Appendix.* 76th Cong., 3d sess. Vol. 86, pt. 16.

———. *Congressional Record Appendix.* 77th Cong., 1st sess. Vol. 87, pt. 13.

———. *Congressional Record Appendix.* 77th Cong., 2d sess. Vol. 88, pt. 8.

———. *Congressional Record Appendix.* 79th Cong., 1st sess. Vol. 91, pt. 12.

U.S. Cong. *Air Mail. Extending Jurisdiction of Civil Aeronautics Authority Over Certain Air-Mail Services.* H. Rep. 2505. 76th Cong., 3d sess. June 11, 1940. Washington, D.C.: GPO, 1940.

———. S. Rep. 1869. 76th Cong., 3d sess. June 18, 1940. Washington, D.C.: GPO, 1940.

U.S. *Civil Aeronautics Board Reports.* Vol. 2. *Decisions of the Civil Aeronautics Board, July 1940 to August 1941.* Washington, D.C.: GPO, 1943.

———. Vol. 3. *Economic Decisions of the Civil Aeronautics Board, August 1941 to December 1942.* Washington, D.C.: GPO, 1945.

———. Vol. 4. *Economic Decisions of the Civil Aeronautics Board, December 1942 to June 1944.* Washington, D.C.: GPO, 1945.

———. Vol. 6. *Economic Decisions of the Civil Aeronautics Board, July 1944 to May 1946.* Washington, D.C.: GPO, 1947.

———. Vol. 7. *Economic Decisions of the Civil Aeronautics Board, June 1946 to March 1947.* Washington, D.C.: GPO, 1948.

———. Vol. 8. *Economic Decisions of the Civil Aeronautics Board, April to December 1947.* Washington, D.C.: GPO, 1949.

———. Vol. 9. *Economic Decisions of the Civil Aeronautics Board, January to December 1948.* Washington, D.C.: GPO, 1951.

———. Vol. 10. *Economic Decisions of the Civil Aeronautics Board, January to November 1949.* Washington, D.C.: GPO, 1952.

———. Vol. 48. *Economic Decisions of the Civil Aeronautics Board, January to July 1968.* Washington, D.C.: GPO, 1968.

U.S. *Hearings Before the President's Aircraft Board.* 4 vols. Washington, D.C.: GPO, 1925.

U.S. Patent Office. *Official Gazette of the United States Patent Office.* Vols. 270 (January 20, 1920), 318 (January 1, 1924), 394 (May 13, 1930), 409 (August 11, 1931), 410 (September 29, 1931), 418 (May 10, 1932), 436 (November 14, 1933), 476 (March 1937).

U.S. *The Statutes at Large of the United States of America, 1938.* Vol. 52. Washington, D.C.: GPO, 1938.

———. *The Statutes at Large of the United States of America, 1939–1941.* Vol. 54, pt. 1. Washington, D.C.: GPO, 1941.

Books and Pamphlets

All American Aviation, Inc. *Air Pick-Up Handbook.* Wilmington, Del.: All American Aviation, 1947.

———. *Annual Report, 1941, 1943, 1944, 1945, 1946, 1947, 1948, 1951.*

Corn, Joseph J. *The Winged Gospel: America's Romance with Aviation, 1900–1950.* New York: Oxford University Press, 1983.

Davies, R.E.G. *Airlines of Latin America since 1919.* Washington, D.C.: Smithsonian Institution Press, 1984.

———. *Airlines of the United States since 1914.* London: Putnam, 1972.

Devlin, Gerard M. *Silent Wings: The Saga of the U.S. Army and Marine Combat Glider Pilots During World War II.* New York: St. Martin's, 1985.

Fradenburg, Leo G. *United States Airlines: Trunk and Regional Carriers, Their Operation and Management.* Dubuque, Iowa: Kendall-Hunt, 1980.

Francillon, Rene J. *Lockheed Aircraft Since 1913.* London: Putnam, 1982.

Frederick, John H. *Commercial Air Transportation.* Rev. ed., Chicago: Irwin, 1947. 5th ed., Homewood, Ill.: Irwin, 1955.

Grey, C. G., and Bridgman, Leonard, eds. *Jane's All the World's Aircraft, 1939.* London: Sampson, Low, Marston, 1939.

Hallion, Richard P. *Legacy of Flight: The Guggenheim Contribution to American Aviation.* Seattle: University of Washington Press, 1977.

Hedrick, Frank E. *Pageantry of Flight: The Story of Beech Aircraft Corporation.* New York: Newcomen Society of North America, 1967.

Hopkins, George E. *The Airline Pilots: A Study in Elite Unionization.* Cambridge, Mass.: Harvard University Press, 1971.

Hughes, Thomas P. *Networks of Power: Electrification in Western Society, 1880–1930.* Baltimore and London: Johns Hopkins University Press, 1983.

Ingells, Douglas J. *L-1011 TriStar and the Lockheed Story.* Fallbrook, Calif.: Aero Publishers, 1973.

Jackson, Donald Dale, and the Editors of Time-Life Books. *Flying the Mail.* Alexandria, Va.: Time-Life Books, 1982.

Jane's All the World's Aircraft, 1947. New York: Macmillan, 1947.

Komons, Nick A. *Bonfires to Beacons: Federal Civil Aviation Policy under the Air*

Commerce Act, 1926–1938. Washington, D.C.: Department of Transportation, Federal Aviation Administration, 1978.

———. *The Cutting Air Crash.* Washington, D.C.: Department of Transportation, Federal Aviation Administration, 1973.

Kouwenhoven, John A. *The Arts in Modern American Civilization.* New York: Norton, 1967.

Langley, Lester D. *The Cuban Policy of the United States.* New York: Wiley, 1968.

Link, Mae Mills, and Coleman, Hubert A. *Medical Support of the Army Air Forces in World War II.* Washington, D.C.: Office of the Surgeon General, USAF, 1955.

Macaulay, Neil. *The Sandino Affair.* Durham, N.C.: Duke University Press, 1985.

McDaniel, William H. *The History of Beech.* Wichita, Kans.: McCormick-Armstrong, 1982.

National Cyclopedia of American Biography. Current Volume F, 1939–42. New York: James T. White, 1942.

———. Vol. 32. New York: James T. White, 1945.

The 1970 Aerospace Year Book. Washington, D.C.: Aerospace Industries of America, 1970.

Payne, John Howard. *Short-Haul Air Transportation for Mail and Property: A Report Based on the Operating Experience of the Tri-State Aviation Corporation . . . for the Year 1938.* Irwin, Pa.: Tri-State Aviation, 1939.

Petee, Frank. *The Triple A Story, 1938–1946.* Pittsburgh: Allegheny Airlines, 1964.

Sahal, Devendra. *Patterns of Technological Innovation.* Reading, Mass.: Addison-Wesley, 1981.

Serling, Robert J. *Eagle: The Story of American Airlines.* New York: St. Martin's, 1985.

———. *From the Captain to the Colonel: An Informal History of Eastern Airlines.* New York: Dial, 1980.

Smith, Frank Kingston, and Harrington, James P. *Aviation and Pennsylvania.* Philadelphia: Franklin Institute Press, 1981.

Smith, Merritt Roe, ed. *Military Enterprise and Technological Change: Perspectives on the American Experience.* Cambridge, Mass.: MIT Press, 1985.

Stringer, Harry R., ed. *A Headline History of the Air Pick-up, 1939–1942, As Told in Selected Press and Magazine Articles and Photographs, Newspaper Captions and Public Documents.* Wilmington, Del., and Pittsburgh, Pa.: All American Aviation, n.d.

———. *A Headline History of the Air Pick-up, 1942–1946, As Told in Selected Press and Magazine Articles and Photographs, Newspaper Captions and Public Documents.* Wilmington, Del., and Pittsburgh, Pa.: All American Aviation, n.d.

Trimble, William F. *High Frontier: A History of Aeronautics in Pennsylvania.* Pittsburgh, Pa.: University of Pittsburgh Press, 1982.

Underwood, John W. *The Stinsons.* Glendale, Calif.: Heritage, 1969.

USAir Annual Report, 1979.

Wagner, William. *Lightning Bugs and Other Reconnaissance Drones: The Can-Do Story of Ryan's Unmanned "Spy Planes."* Fallbrook, Calif.: Aero Publishers, 1982.

Washington Northwest Frontier: Family and Personal History. New York: Lewis Historical Publishing, 1957.

Who's Who in America, 1928–1929. Chicago: Marquis, 1928.

Wilson, G. Lloyd, and Bryan, Leslie A. *Air Transportation.* New York: Prentice-Hall, 1949.

Wilson, John R. M. *Turbulence Aloft: The Civil Aeronautics Administration Amid Wars and Rumors of Wars, 1938–1953.* Washington, D.C.: Department of Transportation, Federal Aviation Administration, 1979.

Writers' Program. Works Progress Administration, State of Illinois. *Who's Who in*

Aviation: A Directory of Living Men and Women Who Have Contributed to the Growth of Aviation in the United States, 1942–1943. Chicago and New York: Ziff-Davis, 1942.

Articles

"AAA Seeks Route Revision." *Aviation Week* 51 (December 26, 1949): 36–37.

Adams, Willis B. "Dr. Lytle S. Adams and His Airmail Pick-Up System." *Airpost Journal* 54 (June 1983): 316–18; (July 1983): 384–88; (August 1983): pp. 460–64; (September 1983): 486–89; 55 (October 1983): 4–9.

"Air Mail Pick-Up." *Aviation* 39 (November 1940): 46, 126.

"Air Mail Pick Up and Release." *Scientific American* 140 (March 1929): 226–27.

"Air Mail Put on a 'Local' Circuit." *Business Week* (August 31, 1940): 22–23.

"All American Lines Expanded to Cincinnati." *Pick-Up* 6 (April 1946): 1.

"Allegheny's Ascent." *Time*, March 5, 1973.

Bramley, Eric. "Lines Hire Women at Record Rate." *American Aviation* 5 (February 1, 1942): 33.

———. "Pickup Routes Doing a Big Job, Writer Observes After AAA Trip." *American Aviation* 8 (June 1, 1944): 46–48.

Bryant, Lynwood. "The Development of the Diesel Engine." *Technology and Culture* 17 (July 1976): 432–46.

"Colonel Robert M. Love Made President of All American." *Pick-Up* 6 (January 1946): 1, 4.

Davis, Ken. "Clothesline Air Strip." *Flying* 37 (December 1945): 63–64, 119.

———. "Hitchhiking to Heaven." *Flying* 36 (February 1945): 46–47, 86.

"Du Pont Sees Short-Haul Use for Gliders on Future Airlines." *American Aviation* 6 (January 1, 1943): 36–37.

"86 Ride First Pick-up-Passenger Flights." *Pick-Up* 6 (October 1946): 1–3.

Feist, Joe Michael. "Bats Away." *American Heritage* 33 (April/May 1982): 93–95.

Foster, Helen. "Allegheny Airlines, 1939–1966." *Greater Pittsburgh* 48 (October 1966): 84, 86.

Fry, Nelson B. "Riding an Upward Curve." *Greater Pittsburgh* 46 (May 1964): 16–17.

"Glider Pick-Up Used in Invasion." *Pick-Up* 4 (June-July 1944): 1–2.

Griffiths, David R. "Allegheny Links Airbus Buy, West Coast Rights." *Aviation Week and Space Technology* 108 (February 6, 1978): 31, 33.

Herron, James T., Jr. "Swoop, Snatch and Zoom." *Jefferson College Times* 14 (May 1981): 14–17.

Hughes, Thomas P. "The Development Phase of Technological Change." *Technology and Culture* 17 (July 1976): 423–31.

"I'm Allegheny—Fly Me." *Forbes* 119 (March 1, 1977): 63.

Johansen, Jens P. "The Flights of the Liberty." *American Aviation Historical Society Journal* 24 (Summer 1979): 111–21.

"Improved Air Pickup Installed by Beech." *Aviation News* 6 (November 11, 1946): 29.

Meier, Hugo A. "Technology and Democracy, 1800–1860." *Mississippi Valley Historical Review* 43 (March 1957): 618–40.

"One of Our Planes Was Missing." *Pick-Up* 3 (November–December 1943): 5.

Ott, James. "USAir Buy of PSA Would Create Sixth Largest U.S. Carrier." *Aviation Week and Space Technology* 125 (December 15, 1986): 29–31.

Preble, Cecilia. "USAir-Piedmont Merger Pending Government, Shareholder Approval." *Aviation Week and Space Technology* 126 (March 16, 1987): 34–36.

Randolph, Jennings. "Airmail for Punkin' Center." *Popular Aviation* (January 1940): 24.

―――. "The R.F.D. Grows Wings." *National Aeronautics* (May 1941).

Shamburger, Page. "All American Aviation." *American Aviation Historical Society Journal* 9 (Fall 1964): 198–206.

"The Sky's the Limit for Allegheny." *Business Week* (April 17, 1971): 118–19.

Thorp, Edward E. "Airmail Goes RFD." *Aviation* 43 (November 1944): 170–72, 177.

―――. "Maintenance System Mainsprings Pick-Up Line's Efficiency." *Aviation* 44 (December 1945): 128–30.

"Triple A 5 Years Old Friday May 12." *Pick-Up* 3 (April–May 1944): 1.

"Triple A Goes to Washington." *Pick-Up* 3 (January–February 1944): 1.

Underwood, John W. "Stinson Production Notes, 1920–1948." *American Aviation Historical Society Journal* 19 (Fall 1974): 215–16.

"USAir." *Pittsburgh Business Times*, February 4–10, 1985.

Van Deurs, R. Adm. George. "The Navy and the Brodie." *United States Naval Institute Proceedings* 102 (October 1976): 88–90.

Periodicals

Aero Digest
Airpost Journal
Air Travel News
American Aviation
American Aviation Historial Society Journal
Aviation
Aviation News
Aviation Week and Space Technology
Business Week
Flying
Forbes
Greater Pittsburgh
Jefferson College Times
Mississippi Valley Historical Review
National Aeronautics
Pick-Up
Popular Aviation
Popular Mechanics
Science
Scientific American
Technology and Culture
Time
United States Naval Institute Proceedings
USAir News

Newspapers

Altoona Tribune
Beaver Falls (Pa.) *News-Tribune*
Clearfield Progress
Coatesville (Pa.) *Record*
Greensburg (Pa.) *Daily Tribune*
New Castle (Pa.) *News*
New York Times
Oil City (Pa.) *Derrick*
Pittsburgh Business Times
Pittsburgh Post-Gazette
Pittsburgh Press
Pittsburgh Sun-Telegraph
Tucson Daily Citizen
Valley Daily News (Tarentum, Pa.)
Wall Street Journal
Warren (Pa.) *Times-Mirror*
Washington Post
Washington Times
Williamsport (Pa.) *Sun*
Wilmington Journal–Every Evening

Interviews

Mildred Albertson, taped response to written questions from William F. Trimble, April 15, 1986, West Chester, Pa.

Ray Garcia, by William F. Trimble, September 5, 1985, Pittsburgh, Pa.

Victor J. Gasbarro, by William F. Trimble, April 30, 1985, Connellsville, Pa.

Frank Petee, by William F. Trimble, June 11, 1986, Pittsburgh, Pa.

Jennings Randolph, by William F. Trimble, June 24, 1982, Washington, D.C.

Lloyd C. Santmyer, by William F. Trimble, June 18, 1985, Greensburg, Pa.

Walter Sartory, by William F. Trimble, June 13, 1986, Pittsburgh, Pa.

Charles W. Wendt, by W. David Lewis, August 21, September 9, 11, 1980, August 29, 1985, Wilmington, Del.
Charles W. Wendt, taped response to written questions from W. David Lewis, June 11, 1985, Sarasota, Fla.
William M. Wiley, Jr., by William F. Trimble, June 11, 1986, Coraopolis, Pa.

Miscellaneous

Colodny, Edwin I. "Survival of the Fittest." Speech before the National Association of Accountants, Pittsburgh Chapter, March 21, 1984.
McBride, Thomas E. "The First Hundred Years are the Hardest." 1963. All American Engineering Company Collection.
Petee, Frank. Speech before the Aero Club of Pittsburgh, August 19, 1982.

Index